Books Come Alive

Books Come Alive

Reading Aloud and Reading Along with Young Children

WILLIAM H. TEALE,
MIRIAM G. MARTINEZ, AND JUNKO YOKOTA

Copublished with

INTERNATIONAL
LITERACY
ASSOCIATION

ROWMAN & LITTLEFIELD
Lanham • Boulder • New York • London

Published by Rowman & Littlefield
An imprint of The Rowman & Littlefield Publishing Group, Inc.
4501 Forbes Boulevard, Suite 200, Lanham, Maryland 20706
www.rowman.com

6 Tinworth Street, London SE11 5AL, United Kingdom

British Library Cataloguing in Publication Information Available

Library of Congress Cataloging-in-Publication Data

Names: Teale, William H., author. | Martinez, Miriam G., 1948– author. |
   Yokota, Junko, author. | International Literacy Association.
Title: Books come alive : reading aloud and reading along with young
   children / William Teale, Miriam G. Martinez, and Junko Yokota with the
   International Literacy Association.
Description: Lanham, Maryland : Rowman & Littlefield, 2021. | Includes
   bibliographical references. | Summary: "This book provides
   research-based information about the many ways in which teachers can use
   read alouds to foster children's literacy development"—Provided by
   publisher.
Identifiers: LCCN 2021005607 (print) | LCCN 2021005608 (ebook) | ISBN
   9781475859935 (cloth) | ISBN 9781475859942 (paperback) | ISBN
   9781475859959 (epub)
Subjects: LCSH: Reading (Early childhood) | Oral reading. | Children—Books
   and reading. | Storytelling in education.
Classification: LCC LB1139.5.R43 T44 2021 (print) | LCC LB1139.5.R43
   (ebook) | DDC 372.4—dc23
LC record available at https://lccn.loc.gov/2021005607
LC ebook record available at https://lccn.loc.gov/2021005608

For Alyssa, Elia, Annabelle, Emma, and Sky, who
know a good story when they hear one!
Miriam G. Martinez

For the International Youth Library and the
Stippis, from whom I have learned much!
Junko Yokota

Contents

Preface

This new book on reading aloud to and with young children has been written as a companion to our earlier book, *Thinking and Learning through Children's Literature* (Martinez et al., 2017), also published by Rowman & Littlefield. In the preface of that book, we write about how literature can move us in many ways and how books can reflect our lives or offer us insights into other lives: "Books reveal new worlds and ideas and can inspire us to take action. And, of course, books can simply offer good reads that make us laugh or pull us deep into worlds of mystery or suspense." Our first book, *Thinking and Learning through Children's Literature*, is intended to serve as a guide for teachers as they support children reading independently. The first chapters look at how reading works and how to analyze literature, both text and illustration, to fully understand the opportunities for learning through literature. We conclude with literary and content units to organize teaching through literature.

In writing *Books Come Alive: Reading Aloud and Reading Along with Young Children*, we focus on the experiences of reading aloud with the teacher serving as a *mediator* to bring literary experiences to children. The books we select, how we enact the reading-aloud experience, and the ways in which we scaffold children's thinking, learning, and extending beyond the reading aloud—these are all aspects of how our role as teacher is central to the read-aloud experience. Reading aloud is powerful in how literature is shared with children. When teachers are doing the reading, children can focus on listening and learning without any struggle or need to work on the act of reading independently. The conceptual information and vocabulary used may be at a higher level than children can read on their own. But most of all, teachers can influence the kinds of books children will be exposed to and give the entire class a shared group experience on which to base conversations and extended experiences. Also, teachers who enact "thinking aloud" can give students a peek into how the teacher is thinking while reading the book, offering insights into ways of responding to the literature.

Our hope is that this book will support teachers in maximizing their time with students in meaningful literary experiences through reading aloud.

Acknowledgments

The authors gratefully acknowledge the generosity of publishers who have given permission to use illustrations from their books. We are thankful for the book communities to which we belong, the committees we serve, and the professional friends with whom we have many intense conversations about books—for this is how we learn, how we refine our own thinking, and how we prepared to write this book.

Introduction

Sometimes, when something is part of our everyday experience, we stop paying close attention to it, even if that something holds the potential to enrich our lives. We simply begin to take it for granted.

In the context of early childhood classrooms, read alouds may sometimes become such a taken-for-granted activity. We know they are important; we are committed to reading to our students, and yet in the flurry of daily teaching demands, we may take read alouds for granted. It is our hope that *Books Come Alive: Reading Aloud and Reading Along with Young Children* will disrupt that inattention and help you carefully consider the ways in which read alouds can contribute to young children's development and how these experiences might be implemented to maximize their potential. That is what *Books Come Alive* is about—using read alouds to ensure not only that books have maximum instructional value but also that they spark children's lifelong love of literature.

It is widely acknowledged that early childhood is a particularly significant period in children's literacy development. Literacy-rich experiences can provide the foundation that children need for later success in school, and the read aloud is a particularly potent tool for fostering many facets of young children's literacy development—including the ability to think deeply about literature; however, read alouds are not a magic potion that automatically results in early literacy success for children. Their potential is realized when they are conducted by knowledgeable and skillful teachers. What children get out of being read to on a regular basis in the classroom depends on 1) how teachers conduct their read alouds, 2) what is being read aloud, and 3) the follow-up experiences children have that are linked to those read alouds.

Books Come Alive offers teachers of young children research-based information about the many ways in which they can use read alouds to foster children's literacy development, guidelines for selecting and evaluating picturebooks for read alouds, suggestions for preparing for and conducting read alouds, and ideas for extending children's experiences with read-aloud books.

Books Come Alive also offers a vetted and extensive compendium of high-quality books for read alouds, accompanied by a framework for teaching with those books. Each annotation in the compendium includes a short summary of the book, suggested content and skill connections, customized tips for sharing that particular book, illustration features that can be included as part of the read-aloud discussion, and suggestions for one to four related books appropriate for young children. We believe these annotations will be a useful resource as you plan for daily reads, and, more importantly, the annotations can serve as models for analyzing picturebooks to make thoughtful instructional decisions for other books you may want to bring into the classroom.

We do not intend to present our ideas about these topics as rules—there is no one set of books that are best to read aloud or one method of reading aloud that is best practice for all young children or all teachers. Instead, we offer the information in this book as a resource for you to draw on.

The following is an overview of what you will find in each of the chapters.

Chapter 1

- Research-based reasons why teachers of young children should read aloud
- Information about the specific knowledge and skills children develop as a result of teachers reading aloud to them
- The perspective of this book on reading aloud in the early grades

Chapter 2

- Research-based reasons why teachers of young children should read aloud
- Information about the specific knowledge and skills children develop as a result of teachers reading aloud to them
- The perspective of this book on reading aloud in the early grades

Chapter 3

- Information about the ways authors and illustrators craft picturebooks
- Ways to determine if a book would be a good read aloud for young children
- Descriptions of the different types of books that make good read alouds
- Sample titles and descriptions of good read alouds

Chapter 4

- Ideas for scheduling read-aloud times in your classroom
- Ways to prepare for a read aloud
- Ideas for conducting engaging, effective read alouds

Chapter 5

- Research-based reasons for doing repeated readings of books
- Ideas for structuring the classroom book center to extend children's experiences with stories
- Suggestions for inviting children to respond to literature through talk, art, and drama
- Suggestions for extending story experiences by building connections to the family

Ultimately, the actual why, what, when, and how of reading aloud are enacted in the context of your particular classroom by you and the group of children you are teaching; however, we believe the resources provided in the chapters that follow—research-based reasons for read alouds, criteria to use in selecting books, methods for how to read aloud and discuss books with children, and suggestions for follow-up activities—will prove useful to you as you make the decisions about teaching, learning, and literacy that are most appropriate in your situation. We provide the guidance; you provide the implementation.

CHAPTER 1

Read Alouds

First Considerations

As adults who have chosen to read this book, it is clear that you value the act of reading, and you prioritize books as vehicles through which we teach children to read—these are assumptions we make about those of us who have gone into the field of educating young children. While this book addresses how read alouds help children develop the skills and strategies they need to become proficient readers, the focus is broader. We are concerned with the act of reading *and* with being able to think in response to what is read. We believe the two must be viewed as inseparable and intertwined.

We begin this book by thinking about *what* we choose to read aloud and *why*. We call attention to how the read-aloud choices we make affect the ways in which we offer children vicarious experiences through literature, experiences that they might never personally have yet important experiences that affect the bigger world to which they belong. More importantly, we look for ways in which we can expand the discussions that follow these read alouds, giving children a shared experience they can refer to as they learn to articulate their ideas, consider various perspectives, and formulate further understandings.

▪ EXPANDING EMOTIONAL RANGE THROUGH BOOKS

Reading aloud can evoke a range of responses, from joyful and amused to serious and thoughtful. Some books are simply fun. Others provide the opportunity to learn about the physical or social world. Still others offer joyful experiences and thereby provide a respite from the worries of the world. As such, they may present ideas for how to purposefully go about finding the small delights of each day. Books can help children gain insight into how to deal with some of the problems they may face—fear of the dark, making friends, helping others, dealing with personal losses.

There are also books that challenge our emotions in ways we might find uncomfortable. Being truthful about the range of emotions children may experience as they come to deeply know the world requires a full array of books. Such books move us beyond our cocoons to see experiences that are part of the wider world in which we live. These are books that can help extend understandings and build empathy. As adults who are selecting what we bring to read-aloud experiences in both book and related activity, being purposeful about widening children's life experiences and thereby nurturing empathy for our world should guide what we choose.

Illustrations are one pathway through which empathy is nurtured. When children see images that express emotions through realistic portrayals, they are offered the opportunity to examine the facial expressions, body language, and actions of characters and even engage in role-play that allows them to replicate the physical response of characters in various emotional situations. Also, when children are offered books with visual poetics and metaphors—not literal images of what is happening but rather interpretive images—they may have the basis for understanding how art expresses emotion in expressionistic or abstract ways. For example, in Leo Lionni's (1967) *Frederick*, the mice are preparing for winter by gathering food, and it seems that Frederick is not working alongside them. Yet, when the cold days of winter arrive, Frederick is able to share what he *has* gathered: colors, sunrays, and words. He instructs the mice to close their eyes as he describes what he has observed, and the thought bubbles of the mice show swatches of color that fill their souls with feelings of warmth. The color swatches are not representational of the actual flowers and plants Frederick describes but instead show colors that also warm the souls of viewers, much as what happened with the mice.

While picturebooks offer rich opportunities to learn about being a better human, we are not advocating for books that tell children how to think and behave or that moralize in didactic ways. There is a fine line in selecting intentional content for thoughtful consideration that does not cross over to being patronizing or judgmental. To thoughtfully select, one must look beyond titles and covers to carefully consider the content and presentation of themes. Our goal is to suggest books that expand children's emotional understandings and offer opportunities to consider the perspective of others across a range of emotions, from joy and happiness to fear and sorrow (Yokota, 2020).

Selecting books that invite discussion—in fact, some books even demand discussion—can also serve as a way for students to engage in topics that don't point out individual student situations but rather center discussion on characters and situations within a book. Of course, such discussions may be extrapolated into the events of daily lives, but using books of this nature offers a safety net to help students in your class not feel singled out. Uncomfortable topics may range from situations close to children's daily experiences, such as difficulties in peer friendships, to bigger world issues like socioeconomic diversity, poverty, and related insecurities like housing, family dynamics, the death of loved ones, and more. But rather than sensationalizing or making a topic a troubling one, or even considering it a difficult discussion, it is best to take such discussions in stride and therefore normalize those topics as everyday subjects for all students.

▪ DEVELOPING EMPATHY IN OUR COMPLICATED WORLD

There are some important considerations to call to mind in considering how to frame what's important in the world around us and how we learn through experiences. Certainly direct, concrete experiences are crucial for children's learning, but those everyday experiences are based on the lives they live and can be limiting when considering the world beyond. This is where the power of literature can help. Literature has the capacity to extend the experiential knowledge children already have, and it may extend their capacity to more broadly understand the experiences of others who live lives very different from their own. After all, literature offers readers experiences to extend beyond what is known to what can be learned. What we choose for read alouds can expand children's perspectives and offer new points of view. A *New York Times* article (Lahey, 2014) reports on a Harvard University study in which children were found to value what they perceive as being valued by the adults in their lives. The article emphasizes how book experiences can teach children empathy through the reading of stories that show emotions. This phenomenon has been reported by others as well, including The Reading Agency (2015) in the United Kingdom, which notes that reading for pleasure improves well-being and empathy.

Adults have a tendency to want to protect the innocence of children and keep them from knowing about complicated and difficult issues, but children are often quite aware of what the adults in their world are worried about and the topics the media raises to public attention; therefore, it is important to consider how and to what degree such issues can be shared with children. When adults talk honestly about the complexity of their world, it allows children to feel free to ask questions and develop their thinking about the world under adult guidance. Picturebooks can open the door to these discussions.

The complexity of our world means adults and children face many large and complicated issues. The range of those issues can be extreme even within one family, one neighborhood, or one community, from wealth and privilege to poverty leading to food and housing insecurity. Although children first face what is in their daily surroundings, the larger world affects their immediate lives as well. Larger issues may emerge from what initially seems to be a single issue. The question "How does global warming on the world scale affect my own daily life?" might well lead to consideration of a related question: "How does global warming affect a national and regional crisis of refugees in search of a place to live?" The fact is that issues are often so heavily intertwined that it is difficult to talk about one without it suddenly taking on octopus-like tentacles that reveal how the one issue actually affects the world in many ways. And surprising as it may seem, what first appears to be an issue that even national and international leaders cannot agree on can actually be made accessible to children in the context of a well-crafted picturebook. In *The Water Princess* (Verde, 2016), set in Burkina Faso, Gie Gie must wake before the sun rises and walk many miles with her mother to a well to retrieve their daily water—water that will be carried home by balancing filled jugs on their heads. Once home, the water must be boiled and made ready for drinking, cooking, bathing, and washing. This lack of access to clean water has made it impossible for many girls in Burkina Faso to go to school and get an education.

Discussions of complex issues around picturebooks require that teachers be able to scaffold the conversations, but to do so, teachers need an understanding of the issue. One example of such a topic is systemic racism, to which recent events in the United States have drawn so much attention. Picturebooks like Jacqueline Woodson's *The Other Side* (2001) that address racism can be important instructional tools, but only if teachers' own understanding of the issue has prepared them to thoughtfully talk with children. As an example of how teachers might build their understanding of this particular issue, we include further information in the boxed insert.

While there are many world issues we could discuss as examples of issues about which teachers may want to build their own background, because of time and space constraints we have chosen to focus on systemic racism. This is an issue that has received extensive attention of late and calls for action. Protests on racial injustice and discriminatory practices have drawn public attention to systemic racism. To be better able to talk with children about this issue, we might need to widen our own understandings of the topic. One way of doing this is by selecting books about the topic for our own reading. Only by widening our own understanding and questioning our own attitudes and perspectives can we be ready to do that with children. While learned experiences are not as vivid as lived experience, reading is, nonetheless, a way for us to consider points of view that we may not have known even as adults, to internalize empathy toward others, and to grow in compassion through that understanding. We can read books at all levels, from books for children to books for teens and adults. We can watch movies and listen to podcasts; we can seek multiple forms of media and engage in discussions with those who inform and even challenge our thinking. When we reflect on our own understandings, we can prepare to support and guide the discussions with children about books we read aloud with them.

The work of Ibram X. Kendi has sparked many publications, lectures, and discussions about antiracism and brought this issue to public awareness in a way that has been needed for decades. His book *How to Be an Antiracist* (2019) is an academic book for adults that offers depth of thinking for readers to consider. While his National Book Award–winning *Stamped from the Beginning: The Definitive History of Racist Ideas in America* (2017) is also for adults, Jason Reynolds created a version for young adults entitled Stamped: Racism, Antiracism, and You (2020), and Jason's narration in audiobook format is compelling and convincingly conveyed. For many, the reality addressed in these books has awakened an understanding of what it means to be Black in America. The books also provide insight into how systemic racism has privileged some and oppressed others and offer an eye-opening reckoning for many readers. In the New York Times article "The Heartbeat of Racism Is Denial" (January 13, 2018), Kendi states that those who hold the notion of "I'm not racist" allow systemic racism to continue. He goes on to argue that denial is a form of defending superiority by not examining one's own beliefs and attitudes.

The Black Lives Matter movement is founded and grounded in the history and culture of the United States, but it has had worldwide repercussions. From France to Japan to Australia, Black people have called to attention the oppressive systemic racism they face. Fueled by anger at the merciless killing of George Floyd, communities have risen to the cause to make their voices heard. This movement has been so powerful that even larger corporations that have not been moved to make changes in the past when made aware of their racist images and behaviors have finally been moved to action—advertisements and logos have been changed and sports teams have committed to changing their names. While changes such as these are welcomed, there is still so much more to address.

continues

Literature can be a way to address inequities, and literature can provide experiences one might not have had in person. Systemic racism has created generations of oppression, and those oppressions have negatively affected children who grow up in poverty or have families devastated by violence. This, in turn, affects how well the children are prepared for school experiences. How do these and other traumatic experiences affect the emotional well-being of the child? As adults, we have the power to thoughtfully consider issues of privilege and oppression, and how these issues affect the young children to whom we will be reading aloud. This issue is crucial, and we must continuously seek to stay informed and deepen our own understanding to scaffold children's understanding of this issue and the many others our society faces.

■ EMPOWERING THE LISTENER

In choosing the books for our read alouds, especially in selecting those that we hope foster empathy among our listeners, we must carefully consider the experiences of our listeners. Important considerations include the prior read-aloud and literacy experiences of the children in our classes. We know, for example, that different cultures structure stories in different ways. So teachers need to consider the text structures with which children may (or may not) be familiar. Likewise, while illustration styles can be quite varied within one country, they are even more varied when looking at books from other countries. So it is also important to consider the illustration styles with which children may be comfortable.

Perhaps the most important type of experience to take into account is the lived experiences of the children in our classrooms. Only then are we able to gauge the potential impact of a given book and the range of conversations that may be possible. Are the children's lived experiences reflected in the book? Do the situations and characters in the book mirror the home lives and lived experiences of the students? Or are those situations likely to be unfamiliar to children in the class? A book about refugees is likely to evoke very different responses depending on the experiences children bring to the book. Some may be able to relate to an aspect of being a migrant, an immigrant, or a refugee because of what they have lived themselves or have heard family or community members explain as their own stories. Others may only know about moving from place to place as something one does for a parent's work, a situation that does not have implications of political threat or the urgency of survival. Still others may know about moving as what happens when the rent goes unpaid for months and eviction is a result. The age range at which children are ready to hear about experiences that are life-changing and traumatic varies. What about the protagonist of a book who is herself a young child? How can we develop compassion without feeling "I'm glad I'm not one of them," thereby setting up the "othering" of people's experiences?

Rudine Sims Bishop (1990), a noted authority on literature and its power, coined the metaphor of "mirrors, windows, and sliding glass doors," which is helpful in thinking more deeply about the relationship between a child's experiences and the experiences represented in books. According to Bishop, books can serve as *mirrors* to the experiences we live, *windows* to the world beyond our own lives, and *sliding glass doors* to allow us to move in and out of our own worlds and those beyond. Books that serve as mirrors can be self-affirming because children see their lives valued through the books. Mirror books can even offer insights for children into how to live their own lives and deal with their own problems. When children see characters dealing with similar problems, they can learn from them.

Window books are also important because they move children beyond their own immediate experiences and help them see, understand, and explore the complexities of the world beyond themselves. Sometimes those books are intriguing and allow them to imagine a world they want to know more about and engage in; sometimes those books ask readers to stop and consider the troublesome complexities of the world. As a society we are also increasingly coming to recognize numerous issues that have far-reaching effects: global warming, social and racial inequities in our society and in our world that too many of us have not dealt with before. (Yet, it is also important to remember that books dealing with those inequities might be mirrors for some children.) Some adults think they need to protect children from these complexities, but children are aware of them at some level and need and want to understand these complex issues at a level appropriate for them. Books and the ensuing thinking and discussions around them can help children understand—and develop empathy.

We also want to bring into the classroom books that go beyond serving as mirrors or windows. Children also need books that offer the opportunity to move through *sliding glass doors*. This is most likely to happen when the adult who conducts the read aloud scaffolds children's literary experiences. Read-aloud, read-along, and read-and-respond experiences are all influenced by the adult who selects, reads, and guides thinking. One strategy that adults can use to help children move through sliding glass doors during a read aloud is the "think aloud," whereby the teacher can model for children how thinking develops through reading. Again, this is dependent on adults continuously broadening their own insights into issues to scaffold children's understanding and guide them through the sliding glass door rather than only looking through the window. Under these circumstances, children may then be able to move through those sliding glass doors and develop compassion and even agency to do something to change the world. That is, instead of only knowing about the lives of others or worlds beyond their own, they can be empowered to see themselves as agents of change who can actively engage in making a difference in the larger world.

One way of empowering listeners is by sharing books in which the character takes action. In *Maybe Something Beautiful: How Art Transformed a Neighborhood* (Campoy & Howell, 2016), the title and subtitle lead us into a book in which a little girl takes personal initiative to draw and share pictures that depict the colorful joy she feels in her own room at home—in contrast to the gray and physically uninviting community in which she lives. When she shares one of her drawings with a muralist, he invites her to join him in transforming a wall. Soon other members of the community join their effort, transforming the neighborhood in which they all live. This book is based on a true story that happened in East Village, a neighborhood near downtown San Diego, California. A community transformed their neighborhood by creating murals, painting benches, and writing poetry on sidewalks, all by working together to not only beautify their surroundings but also engage in philanthropic activity by auctioning some of their work to raise money for classrooms and scholarships. Sharing a book like this may provide teachers with the opportunity to think with children how they might take action in their own communities in ways that are specific to their communities' needs.

▪ WHAT YOU WILL FIND IN THIS BOOK

This book offers concrete ideas for using read alouds to help children learn to read and think deeply in response to read alouds. The book is organized into two sections. The first focuses on selecting books for read alouds and engaging children in them. The second consists of annotations of each picturebook we reference.

In the first section, you will find four chapters (beyond this first chapter). Chapter 2 focuses on facets of literacy development that can be affected through read alouds—facets including language, knowledge of text structures, phonemic awareness, and much more. Chapter 3 focuses on selecting high-quality books to use in read alouds, and chapter 4 explores how to effectively prepare for and conduct read alouds. Chapter 5 describes a range of ways to extend children's experiences with books—through repeated readings, discussion, drama, and art.

The second section of the book contains annotations for the picturebooks we've mentioned. While the annotations share common features, such as a book summary and content and skill connections, the annotations do not follow a cookie-cutter formula. Rather, each annotation takes into account the unique potential of the book to promote children's language and literacy development. To accomplish this, we have looked closely at the potential of each book and share with the reader what is distinctive about that book (e.g., the role illustrations play in developing the story, the inclusion of endnotes that extend information in the book, a related video on YouTube). We then offer suggestions for engaging children in the book and scaffolding their experiences. Finally, we share related titles of picturebooks that can enable teachers to engage their students more deeply in the experiences highlighted in the book.

▪ REFERENCES

Bishop, R. S. (1990). Mirrors, Windows, and Sliding Glass Doors. *Perspectives, 6*(3), ix–xi.

Lahey, J. (September 4, 2014). Teaching Children Empathy. *New York Times.* https://parenting.blogs.nytimes.com/2014/09/04/teaching-children-empathy/.

Reading Agency. (2015). Reading for Pleasure Builds Empathy and Improves Well-Being, Research from the Reading Agency Finds. *ReadingAgency.org.* https://readingagency.org.uk/news/media/reading-for-pleasure-builds-empathy-and-improves-wellbeing-research-from-the-reading-agency-finds.html.

Yokota, Junko. (2020). *What You Read Matters: Food for Young Minds and Souls* [conference presentation]. La Pietra, Italy.

▪ RECOMMENDED CHILDREN'S BOOKS

Campoy, Isabel, & Howell, Theresa. *Maybe Something Beautiful.* Illustrated by Rafael López. Boston: Houghton Mifflin Harcourt, 2016.

Lionni, Leo. *Frederick.* New York: Pantheon, 1967.

Reynolds, Jason, & Kendi, Ibram X. *Stamped! Racism, Antiracism, and You.* New York: Little, Brown, 2020.

Verde, Susan. *The Water Princess.* Illustrated by Peter H. Reynolds. New York: Putnam, 2016.

Woodson, Jacqueline. *The Other Side.* New York: Putnam, 2001.

CHAPTER 2

Why Read Alouds?

After reading the title of *Don't Let the Pigeon Drive the Bus!* to her kindergartners, Ms. Lopez opens the cover of the book to reveal a pigeon and his thought bubble, which shows various scenes of a pigeon driving a bus.

> Ms. Lopez: What does this pigeon want to do?
>
> Elena: He wants to go on the bus.
>
> Arturo: No, he wants to drive the bus. Look (pointing to the thought bubble), he's dreaming about it.
>
> Ms. Lopez: Let's read and see.
>
> Ms. Lopez (reading): Hi! I'm the bus driver. Listen, I've got to leave for a little while, so can you watch things for me until I get back? Thanks. Oh, and remember: Don't let the pigeon drive the bus!
>
> Ms. Lopez: Why wouldn't you want the pigeon to drive the bus?
>
> Anna (a child familiar with the pigeon's antics in other Mo Willems pigeon books): Because he is crazy!

As the read aloud of Mo Willems's beloved book continues, the children become engaged in animated discussions about the appropriateness of the pigeon's goal of driving a bus—as well as the appropriateness of his behavior as he pleads, beseeches, implores, and ultimately throws an all-out tantrum in an attempt to get his way. The discussion centering around Mo Willems's picturebook provided a perfect opportunity for rich discussion and nurturing children's social and emotional development.

Spend a day in a preschool, kindergarten, first-grade, or second-grade classroom, and you will almost certainly see teachers like Ms. Lopez reading books aloud to the children and engaging them in lively discussion. For some time now, teachers of young children have embraced reading aloud as part of their daily activities, and professionals and policy makers have extolled the benefits of reading aloud, saying things like this:

Two powerful instructional practices—teacher-led read alouds and in-school independent reading—have the power and promise to set students on a path of lifelong reading.—"The

Power and Promise of Read-Alouds and Independent Reading," a position statement of the International Literacy Association

The single most important activity for building . . . understandings and skills essential for reading success appears to be reading aloud to children.—"Learning to Read and Write: Developmentally Appropriate Practices for Young Children," a joint position statement of the International Reading Association and the National Association for the Education of Young Children

Read to children whenever the opportunity arises.—authors of the HighScope Preschool Curriculum

Reading aloud with children is the best way to inspire a love for reading and promote language and literacy skills.—Creative Curriculum for Preschool

Research backs these beliefs: Studies showing positive relations between being read to and subsequent reading achievement have been published in journals and scholarly books for the past seventy years.[1] More than a quarter-century ago, the National Academy of Education Commission on Reading, the National Institute of Education, and the Center for the Study of Reading issued a landmark report that stated, "The single most important activity for building the knowledge required for eventual success in reading is reading aloud to children."[2] This conclusion is still widely accepted and features prominently in position statements of such professional organizations as the National Council of Teachers of English,[3] in popular read-aloud books like Jim Trelease and Cyndi Giorgis's *The Read Aloud Handbook* (2019) and Mem Fox's *Reading Magic: Why Reading Aloud to Our Children Will Change Their Lives Forever* (2008), and in such school-oriented early childhood initiatives as Early Reading First and the Children's Literacy Initiative,[4] as well as, of course, scientific research on early literacy.[5]

In the past decade, teachers have felt increasing pressure to address standards and prepare students for mandated assessment, and finding time for read alouds can be challenging. Nonetheless, the many values of this practice cannot be denied, so teachers need to be prepared to argue for the importance of daily read alouds. With that goal in mind, we begin with a review of the ways in which reading aloud can contribute to children's literacy and learning development.

■ RESPONDING AND THINKING ABOUT LITERATURE

Perhaps the most important way in which read alouds can contribute to children's literacy development is by supporting their comprehension and engaging them in thinking deeply about stories. In a series of studies, Lawrence Sipe (2008) collected the talk of children ages five to eight during read alouds and found that they engaged in complex thinking about story elements. Character and plot are the most basic elements of stories, and Sipe found that during read alouds children worked to understand character feelings, thoughts, and motivations and to understand plots and causal relationships. They also shared their thinking about the themes of stories, especially when the teacher invited them to think about the "messages" of stories.

Another kind of thinking that the children did in response to stories was one that Sipe called intertextual responses. In this type of response, the children worked to connect the read-aloud story to other stories. Such connections helped them make predictions about what would happen in the story the teacher was reading and to interpret characters' feelings and motivations. Making connections across stories also helped the children draw conclusions about sets of stories (e.g., the common use of three in fairy tales).

Sipe also found that during read alouds children often shared personal experiences related to stories, a type of response that is particularly important as children work to understand stories. For example, they connected characters and events to their own lives, they questioned stories based on their own experiences, and, most importantly, they made text-to-life connections as they attempted to use stories to better understand the world beyond the story world. It is important for teachers to make room for children to share their personal responses and value those responses, especially in light of the increasing diversity in classrooms today. When children bring their personal experiences to stories, it enables them to draw on their funds of knowledge (Martinez-Roldán, 2003).

Equally important (and maybe surprising to some), young children can even assume a critical stance in response to stories. For example, researchers looked at how six- and seven-year-old children responded to read alouds of books dealing with issues of race and power (Copenhaver-Johnson et al., 2007). They found that, throughout time, these children moved away from entrenched cultural notions and began to pose questions about White privilege. So, when teachers thoughtfully select the books to read aloud and are open to children sharing their responses to stories, books can become portals for thinking thoughtfully and critically about the world beyond the book.

■ YOUNG CHILDREN'S LITERACY KNOWLEDGE, STRATEGIES, AND DISPOSITIONS

Read alouds are particularly important because they provide children with the opportunity to think about literature, but they can also develop a wide range of important skills, strategies, and dispositions. We will explore these benefits in this section.

Background Knowledge

We cannot overstate how important what a child knows is to his or her eventual reading ability. Especially as children get into upper elementary and beyond, background knowledge is closely related to reading level on both standardized tests and more comprehensive assessments of reading (Langer, 1984; Recht & Leslie, 1988). Being read to is one of the main ways young children learn about the world beyond their own communities. Books for young children cover a range of topics, from getting along in various social situations to information about places and animals to the moral and personal lessons of various cultures. By vicariously experiencing the situations, people, and details found in books, children can indeed learn much about the world.

Language Development

Reading aloud to children also fosters various facets of oral language development: listening comprehension (understanding what you hear), vocabulary (learning the meanings of individual words), and syntax (understanding how to organize words in sentences). Altogether, these oral language skills in young children are highly related to children's later reading achievement.[6] Reading aloud to children can give them experience with a wide variety of oral language structures, purposes, and uses, thus setting the stage for language and literacy development throughout their lives.

Vocabulary

The more words you know and the more you know about words, the more likely you are to be a strong reader. Research has shown that vocabulary knowledge is the single biggest factor in children's reading comprehension ability in upper elementary school and beyond. In particular, reading to children puts them in touch with the vocabulary of written language. What do we mean by the vocabulary of written language? The language of books, newspapers, magazines, online sources, and other texts contains a wider variety of words than the spoken language we use every day. Written language also uses infrequently occurring words much more often than typical conversation does. Where else except in *Where the Wild Things Are* (Sendak, 1963) is a child likely to hear the word *gnash*?

So, when children are read to, they encounter many words that they would not normally have a chance to hear and learn about in everyday activities. Being read to can definitely expand young children's vocabulary knowledge, and this can be particularly beneficial for English language learners.

Familiarity with Text Structures

Part of what enables children to comprehend what they read is their ability to follow the structure of the text being read—that is, how the ideas of the text are put together. Think of the variety of text structures as being a continuum (as shown in figure 2.1), with narrative on one end and informational text (also called nonfiction) on the other. Narratives tell stories, and most often stories focus on a central problem that a character is trying to solve through a series of events, as in books like *Knuffle Bunny: A Cautionary Tale* (Willems, 2004). If children are familiar with this problem/solution structure, then it is likely that when a problem arises in a story, they will anticipate that the character will try and solve the problem. In fact, during a read aloud, they might well begin to make predictions about *how* the character might try to solve the problem. Being able to make such predictions is an example of how knowledge of text structure supports children's story comprehension.

Informational texts, on the other hand, are organized differently. They have main ideas and details organized into patterns like listing, cause-effect, problem-solution, and other patterns shown in figure 2.1. Every text lies somewhere on the narrative-informational continuum, with most being rather clearly either narrative or informational, but some have features of both. For example, a book like *Shh! Bears Sleeping* (Martin, 2016) has some elements characteristic of informational books (e.g., the activities of bears throughout the seasons of the year) and also elements characteristic of stories. Hearing different types of text structures being read and having opportunities to discuss them helps young children understand the different genres they hear or read. Being able to use knowledge of text structures is especially important as children move into the later grades, where they have to read many different types of texts in a wide variety of subject areas.

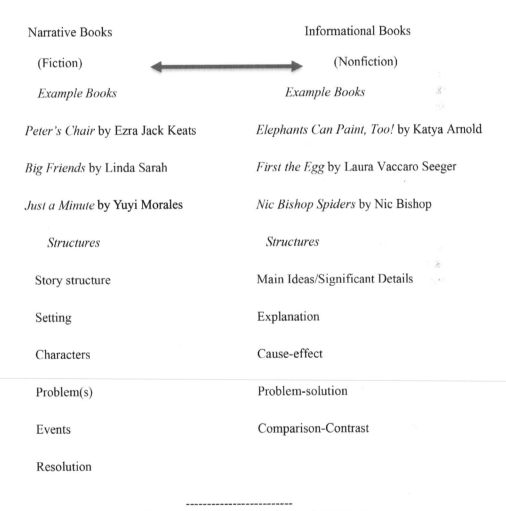

Narrative Books	Informational Books
(Fiction)	(Nonfiction)
Example Books	*Example Books*
Peter's Chair by Ezra Jack Keats	*Elephants Can Paint, Too!* by Katya Arnold
Big Friends by Linda Sarah	*First the Egg* by Laura Vaccaro Seeger
Just a Minute by Yuyi Morales	*Nic Bishop Spiders* by Nic Bishop
Structures	*Structures*
Story structure	Main Ideas/Significant Details
Setting	Explanation
Characters	Cause-effect
Problem(s)	Problem-solution
Events	Comparison-Contrast
Resolution	

Figure 2.1.   Written Language Continuum

Distinctive Nature of Written Language

We have discussed two ways in which written language is different from oral language: vocabulary and text organization. There is a third way that is also important for young children to recognize: what written language sounds like. If you play a tape recording with samples of people talking in everyday conversation and samples of people reading, it is easy for literate adults and even children who have learned to read to figure out which ones are which. Written language just sounds different. Becoming familiar with such patterns is a foundational insight for children when it comes to learning to read. Think of it as one of the first understandings on which their subsequent literacy concepts and strategies are built. Such understanding grows directly out of being read to. Remember all the young children you have seen throughout the years who, long before they can really read the print, sit down with a book someone has read to them and sound just like they are reading aloud as they look at the pictures. Using the intonation and language patterns of written language is something that children pick up by being read to.

How Illustrations Work

Picturebooks are typically used in read alouds with young children, and the contemporary picturebook is distinctive because of its reliance on both illustrations and words to tell the story. In fact, in some picturebooks crucial information is conveyed *only* through the illustrations. For example, in *Rosie's Walk* (Hutchins, 1971), the text tells readers about Rosie the hen; however, children only find out there is a second character (the fox) by looking at the illustrations. Furthermore, it is only through the illustrations that readers learn what the fox is up to as he repeatedly tries to capture the hen.

Illustrators also rely on various visual tools, such as color, line, and even the placement of objects and characters on the page, to communicate meaning. For example, sometimes illustrators manipulate color to give viewers insights into character emotions. This is the case in *When Sophie Gets Angry—Really, Really Angry . . .* (Bang, 1999). Readers recognize the change in Sophie's emotions when the outline of her body changes from yellow to red, signaling the rage she feels when her toy is taken away. In addition, illustrators often use every page of the picturebook in telling their stories, including the book's endpapers, title page, and sometimes even the dedication and copyright page. So children need to learn to "read" illustrations just as they learn to read the text. Learning to read illustrations in picturebooks also prepares them to read the many other types of texts they will encounter in our increasingly visual world.

Concepts about Print

Read alouds also contribute to young children's literacy development by helping them learn how *print* works. (In fact, very young children need to learn that adults read the print in books—not the illustrations.) In an alphabetic language like English or Spanish, there are rules about how one reads: print is read left to right and top to bottom (directionality). Also, a book is opened to its front with the binding on the left side. For students whose families have books at home written in languages like Chinese, Arabic, or Japanese, concepts of print like this work differently. As younger children participate in read alouds—especially if the teacher uses big books—they can see concepts like directionality and using the words (not just the pictures) to read being demonstrated and talked about and thus can pick up on book-handling skills and basic concepts about print.

Phonemic Awareness

You have probably heard about phonemic awareness. It is a very important part of the early literacy development of children. Basically, phonemic awareness refers to a child's ability to hear the individual sounds (phonemes) in words. Figure 2.2 shows the individual sounds of several different words. As you look at the words in the chart, notice that the number of letters in a word does not necessarily correspond to the number of sounds in the word. For example, the word *tree* in English has four letters but only three sounds, while the equivalent word *arbor* in Spanish has five letters and five sounds. The word *street* in English has six letters but only five sounds, while in Spanish, the word *calle* has five letters and four sounds.

As adults, we have little reason to focus on the individual sounds in words; however, children have to realize that words are made up of individual sounds and to hear those sounds before they can really learn about phonics or letter-sound relationships.

	English	Spanish
sun	3: /s/ /ʌ/ /n/ (sun)	3: /s/ /o/ /l/ (sol)
cat	3: /k/ /æ/ /t/ (cat)	4: /g/ /a/ /t/ /o/ (gato)
dog	3: /d/ /a:/ /g/ (dog)	4: /p/ /e/ / r̃ / /o/ (perro)
tree	3: /t/ /r/ /i/ (tree)	5: /a/ /r/ /b/ /o/ /r/ (arbor)
street	5: /s/ /t/ /r/ /i:/ /t/ (street)	4: /k/ /a/ /j/ /e/ (calle)
cheese	3: /tʃ/ /i/ /z/ (cheese)	4: /k/ /ey/ /s/ /o/ (queso
bone	3: /b/ /o/ /n/ (bone)	3: /u/ /m/ /o/ (humo)
thimble	5: /θ/ / ɪ/ /m/ /b/ /l/ (thimble)	5: /d/ /ey/ /d/ /a/ /l/ (dedal)

Figure 2.2. Sounds (Phonemes) That Make Up Different Words

Young children typically do not become able to hear the individual phonemes of words merely by being read to, but a wide variety of children's books focus on the sounds of language and thereby help children develop phonemic awareness. For example, there are many rhyming books and numerous versions of Mother Goose rhymes, such as *Diez Deditos and Other Play Rhymes and Action Songs from Latin America* (Orozco, 1997), that serve as good read alouds and promote awareness of word parts in spoken words. There are also books such as *A, My Name Is Alice* (Bayer, 1984) that play with words through alliteration. Opportunities to hear and re-create such elements of language play a role in moving children toward the development of phonemic awareness, which they will need in kindergarten and first grade to become good at decoding and word recognition in reading.

Letter Knowledge

Learning the letters of the alphabet supports the development of a number of other skills important in learning to read. Alphabet books, of which there are always scores in print at any time, are used by parents and teachers alike to build children's recognition of letters. Reading such books can positively influence children's learning about letters, as is evident in a number of studies conducted in home and classroom settings (e.g., Yaden et al., 1993; for a more comprehensive discussion of alphabet knowledge and classroom instruction, see McKay & Teale, 2015). We'll have more to say about alphabet books in chapter 3.

Letter-Sound and Sight Word Knowledge

Although being read to is not a major source of phonics skill or sight word development for children, young children do pick up some knowledge about phonics and perhaps a few sight words (*no, stop, mom,* etc.) as a result of frequent rereadings of the same book by parents or teachers. During read alouds, children naturally focus on the story or the content information of the book presented more than they do on letter-sound relationships. This is especially true on the first reading of a picturebook. But it is also true, especially with alphabet books and predictable books, that some children will focus on specific letters or words during the read-aloud activity. Teachers can encourage children to focus on the print when reading picturebooks like *Brown Bear, Brown Bear, What Do You See?* (B. Martin, 1967) in which basic sight words are repeated.

Support for Independent Reading

Read alouds can also support independent reading. For young children who are not yet reading words, independent reading is actually an emergent reading or "pretend reading." That is, the child picks up a book that has been read aloud to them, and, relying on memory of the words and the illustrations in the book, the child "reads" the story, often sounding very much like a fluent reader. This is a valuable activity for young children.

For beginning readers (who are starting to read print), read alouds also support their independent reading. These children often choose for their independent reading familiar books that have been read aloud to them. The read aloud provides them with knowledge of story content. This, in turn, can free them to devote attention to identifying challenging words they may encounter in the story rather than having to simultaneously work to understand the story and identify/decode words in the text.

The Joy of Reading

In conducting a study of teacher read-aloud style, Martinez and Teale (1993) asked a number of kindergarten teachers why they read aloud to their students. Without exception, the first reason each teacher mentioned was that she felt the experience helps children to develop a love of reading. All you have to do is read what Mem Fox (2008), Jim Trelease and Cyndi Giorgis (2019), or Lester Laminack (2019) have to say in their books about reading aloud to realize how powerful an influence reading aloud can have on children. When adults read to young children, a bond is created between people and books, a bond that helps promote lifelong reading habits.

▪ BEYOND FOUNDATIONAL LITERACY SKILLS

Early childhood educators have likely heard about different ways of conducting read alouds, such as shared reading or dialogical reading (e.g., Holdaway, 1979; Mol et al., 2009; Zevenbergen & Whitehurst, 2003). Such approaches typically employ specific procedures for reading aloud that tend to promote particular kinds of learning by children. For example, shared reading as typically used by kindergarten or first-grade teachers (Holdaway, 1979; Parkes, 2000) is a structured way of sharing a book with children in which the teacher uses a big book (very often a predictable book, with repetitive language and a repetitive structure) and follows steps like these:

- Introduce the book and talk about the title, author/illustrator, and cover illustration.
- Read the story in an engaging manner, tracking each word/line of print with a pointer.
- Reread the book, encouraging everyone to join in "reading" certain words or phrases as they are able.

This approach to reading aloud especially helps children focus on print awareness—understanding that the print in books carries a message; that when reading, one goes left to right, top to bottom; that words in print are separated by white spaces—and sight word recognition.

Dialogic reading has received considerable attention in recent years because several studies have shown that it results in positive effects on young children's oral language development.[7] Dialogic reading is also an interactive way of sharing a book with children. During a typical dialogic reading session, the teacher (or parent) and the child switch roles, with the teacher assisting the child to become the storyteller. While reading the story aloud, the teacher should do the following:

- Prompt the child to say something about the book (using one of five different kinds of specified prompts: completion prompts, recall prompts, open-ended prompts, wh-prompts, and distancing prompts).
- Evaluate the child's response.
- Expand the child's response by rephrasing and adding information to it.
- Repeat the prompt to make sure the child has learned from the expansion.

This strategy can be particularly supportive for English language learner students as the teacher invites children to talk and then expand on their responses. Of all the teacher responses during the exchange, of particular importance is the corrective feedback the teacher provides when the child gives a wrong or unclear statement. Beyond affirmation or simply avoiding being negative by noting the error, being corrective or framing a different direction for thinking can add to children's knowledge base and ways of thinking.

In reading the book *How Are You Peeling?* (Freyman, 2004), for example, the exchange might go something like this:

> Teacher (pointing to a picture): What is this? (prompt)
>
> Child: A vegetable.
>
> Teacher: That's right (evaluation or clarification if child's response is not correct); it's a green pepper, and it looks kind of grumpy (expansion). Let's say the name of the vegetable again: green pepper. (repetition)

Shared reading and dialogic reading are designed to affect children's foundational literacy skills but do not address the development of rich background knowledge, critical thinking, a deep understanding of literature, insights into how narratives and informational texts work, or the formation of positive dispositions toward reading and books that will continue to develop throughout a lifetime. So the approach we have taken in this book is more broad-based than either shared reading or dialogic reading. In the pages that follow, we talk a great deal about issues like what books to choose to read to your children, how to foster children's thinking about and responses to books so that they develop a deep appreciation of authors' and illustrators' craft, ways young children's deep background and vocabulary knowledge can be enhanced, and read-aloud techniques that can put children on the road to developing positive life-long reading habits. In other words, our purpose is to offer suggestions about reading aloud to teachers who are interested in fostering young children's early literacy skills, children's ability to think deeply about books and their crafting, children's knowledge about the world, and children's delight in books to nurture their positive dispositions to reading rather than focusing only on important foundational literacy skills.

What Reading Aloud Does for Children—and for Teachers

We suspect that we didn't need to convince you that reading aloud was a good thing to do, but we hope we have helped you develop a fuller understanding of the benefits that good classroom read-aloud practices provide for children. We believe that reading aloud is *the* major means by which young children can develop much of what they need in the way of early literacy knowledge and strategies—if they are read to regularly. Thus, there is great potential for what children can learn from being read to.

What we didn't talk about very much in the preceding discussion—but we feel is every bit as important—is what reading aloud can do for you as a teacher. We are fortunate to live in a society with a rich tradition of children's books. There are so many interesting, engaging, well-crafted books available for young children that even the three authors of this book have trouble keeping up with all of them. This means that you'll have no shortage of materials that children will both enjoy and learn from. This treasure trove of books helps make teaching fun and interesting. And that is no small thing.

When you spend anywhere from four to twelve hours each day with children, you want the time to be interesting for you as well as for them. Reading children's books is one activity that makes that time engaging and even fascinating. Reading and talking with children about books like *Mice and Beans* (Ryan, 2005), *Niño Wrestles the World* (Morales, 2013), *The Lion and the Mouse* (Pinkney, 2009), or *Gravity* (Chin, 2014) is something that is rewarding for both four-year-olds and forty-four-year-olds.

Implications for You and Your Classroom

The most obvious implication for you as a teacher is to make reading aloud a valued and significant part of the everyday instructional plan of the classroom—and it should not stop as children begin to gain proficiency as readers. First and second graders—and beyond—need to participate in read alouds as much as younger children do. Reading aloud has many potential benefits for children, but we have also learned that there are a number of important things for teachers to think about and do to realize those potential benefits. That is what the remainder of this book is about—how you and your children can get the most out of the experience of reading aloud, discussing, and responding to the wide range of literature available for young children.

To provide further support, in the final section of this book we offer a compendium of resources—annotations for more than one hundred picturebooks. These annotations offer recommendations for engaging students in the read alouds to maximize student learning. We have not kept each annotation with parallel structure as a fill-in-the-blank format but have instead individualized annotations for each book based on its potential for literacy learning. Of course, you will be able to extend those frameworks to other books, and in each annotation we have included a few book recommendations for you to do so. Beyond the publication of this book, when newer books are published, and to make the best use of the books available to you at your schools and in your communities, we recommend that you rely on the knowledge and training of school and public librarians to point out similar books that are accessible to you.

◼ REFERENCES

Copenhaver-Johnson, J., Bowman, J., & Johnson, A. (2007). Santa Stories: Children's Inquiry about Race during Picture-Book Read-Alouds. *Language Arts, 84*(3): 234–44.

Fox, Mem. (2008). *Reading Magic: Why Reading Aloud to Our Children Will Change Their Lives Forever* (updated ed.). San Diego, CA: Harcourt.

Holdaway, D. (1979). *Foundations of Reading.* Portsmouth, NH: Heinemann.

Laminack, L. L. (2019). *The Ultimate Read-Aloud Resource* (2nd ed.). New York: Scholastic.

Langer, J. (1984). Examining Background Knowledge and Text Comprehension. *Reading Research Quarterly, 19*(4), 468–81.

Martinez, M., & Teale, W. H. (1993). Teacher Storybook Reading Style: A Comparison of Six Teachers. *Research in the Teaching of English, 27*, 175–99.

Martinez-Roldán, C. (2003). Building Worlds and Identities: A Case Study of the Role of Narratives in Bilingual Literature Discussion. *Research in the Teaching of English, 37*(4): 494–526.

McKay, R., & Teale, W. H. (2015). *Not This but That: No More Teaching a Letter a Week.* Portsmouth, NH: Heinemann.

Mol, S. E., Bus, A. G., & de Jong, M. T. (2009). Interactive Book Reading in Early Education: A Tool to Stimulate Print Knowledge as Well as Oral Language. *Review of Educational Research, 79*(2), 979–1,007.

Parkes, B. (2000). *Read It Again! Revisiting Shared Reading.* Portsmouth, NH: Stenhouse.

Recht, D. R., & Leslie, L. (1988). Effect of Prior Knowledge on Good and Poor Readers' Memory of Text. *Journal of Educational Psychology, 80*(1), 16–20.

Sipe, L. R. (2008). *Storytime: Young Children's Literary Understanding in the Classroom.* New York: Teachers College Press.

Trelease, J., & Giorgis, C. (2019). *The Read Aloud Handbook* (8th ed.). London: Penguin.

Yaden, D., Smolkin, L., & MacGillvray, L. (1993). A Psychogenetic Perspective on Children's Understanding about Letter Associations during Alphabet Book Readings. *Journal of Literacy Research, 25*(1), 43–68.

Zevenbergen, A. A., & Whitehurst, G. J. (2003). Dialogic Reading: A Shared Picturebook Reading Intervention for Preschoolers. In A. Van Kleech, S. A. Stahl, & E. B. Bauer (Eds.), *On Reading Books to Children: Parents and Teachers* (pp. 170–80). New York: Routledge.

◼ RECOMMENDED CHILDREN'S BOOKS

Arnold, Katya. *Elephants Can Paint, Too!* New York: Atheneum, 2005.

Bang, Molly. *When Sophie Gets Angry—Really, Really Angry . . .* New York: Scholastic, 1999.

Bayer, Jane E. *A, My Name Is Alice.* Illustrated by Steven Kellogg. New York: Dial, 1984.

Bishop, Nic. *Nic Bishop Spiders.* New York: Scholastic Nonfiction, 2007.

Chin, Jason. *Gravity.* New York: Roaring Brook, 2014.

Freyman, Saxton. *How Are You Peeling?* Illustrated by Joost Elffers. New York: Scholastic, 2004.

Hutchins, Pat. *Rosie's Walk.* New York: Aladdin, 1971.

Keats, Ezra Jack. *Peter's Chair.* New York: Picture Puffins, 1998.

Martin, Bill, Jr. *Brown Bear, Brown Bear, What Do You See?* Illustrated by Eric Carle. New York: Henry Holt, 1967.

Martin, David. *Shh! Bears Sleeping.* Illustrated by Steve Johnson and Lou Fancher. New York: Viking, 2016.

Morales, Yuyi. *Just a Minute: A Trickster Tale and Counting Book*. New York: Chronicle, 2003.

Morales, Yuyi. *Niño Wrestles the World*. New York: Roaring Brook, 2013.

Orozco, José Luis. *Diez Deditos and Other Play Rhymes and Action Songs from Latin America*. Illustrated by Elisa Kleven. New York: Dutton, 1997.

Pinkney, Jerry. *The Lion and the Mouse*. New York: Dial, 2009.

Ryan, Pam Muñoz. *Mice and Beans*. Illustrated by Joe Cepeda. New York: Scholastic, 2005.

Sarah, Linda. *Big Friends*. Illustrated by Benji Davies. New York: Henry Holt, 2016.

Seeger, Laura Vaccaro. *First the Egg*. New York: Roaring Brook, 2007.

Sendak, Maurice. *Where the Wild Things Are*. New York: Harper and Row, 1963.

Willems, Mo. *Don't Let the Pigeon Drive the Bus!* New York: Hyperion, 2003.

Willems, Mo. *Knuffle Bunny: A Cautionary Tale*. New York: Hyperion, 2004.

▪ NOTES

1. The book *On Reading to Children* (edited by A. van Kleeck, S. A. Stahl, and E. Bauer, Mahwah, NJ: Lawrence Erlbaum, 2003) includes research chapters on the effects and limitations of book sharing as well as chapters about promising read-aloud programs. See also Mol, S. E., Bus, A. G., De Jong, M. T., & Smeets, D. J. H. (2008). Added Value of Dialogic Parent–Child Book Readings: A Meta-analysis. *Early Education and Development, 19,* 7–26, and Sénéchal, M., Pagan, S., & Lever, R. (2008). Relations among the Frequency of Shared Reading and Four-Year-Old Children's Vocabulary, Morphological and Syntax Comprehension, and Narrative Skills. *Early Education and Development, 19*(1), 27–44.

2. The report entitled *Becoming a Nation of Readers* was edited by R. Anderson, E. H. Hiebert, J. Scott, and I. Wilkinson, and published by the National Academy of Education in 1985.

3. This position statement can be found at https://ncte.org/statement/readtogether/.

4. Many local, state, and national projects focus on the issue of reading aloud by either parents or teachers. Numerous state library systems, local public libraries, and nonprofit organizations have programs for parents focused on the importance of reading aloud to infants and preschoolers. The Children's Literacy Initiative (http://cliontheweb.org/) focuses its work on Head Start classrooms and early primary grades. The federally funded program Early Reading First, run by the U.S. Department of Education from 2002 to 2013, supported the development of preschool centers of early literacy excellence in states throughout the country.

5. See the following chapters from the various editions of the *Handbook of Early Literacy Research*: volume 1, chapter 13; volume 2, chapter 21; volume 3, chapter 13 (volume 1: S. B. Neuman & D. K. Dickinson, Eds., 2001; volume 2: D. K. Dickinson & S. B. Neuman, Eds., 2005; volume 3: S. B. Neuman & D. K. Dickinson, Eds., 2009, all published by Guilford, New York).

6. See *Developing Early Literacy: Report of the National Early Literacy Panel* (Washington, DC: National Institute for Literacy, 2008) for a comprehensive review of research on preschool oral language development and children's later literacy development. Also see NICHD Early Child Care Research Network (2005). Pathways to reading: The role of oral language in the transition to reading. *Developmental Psychology, 41*(2), 428–42.

7. See U.S. Department of Education, "What Works Clearinghouse Intervention Report: Dialogic Reading," *Institute of Education Studies*, https://ies.ed.gov/ncee/wwc/Docs/InterventionReports/WWC_Dialogic_Reading_020807.pdf.

CHAPTER 3

Choosing Well-Crafted Books to Read

Approximately five thousand books for children are published each year in the United States. Wow! With numbers like that, how in the world do you choose the very best picturebooks for your classroom? It is an important question, and here is how we answer it: when choosing picturebooks for young children, look for well-crafted books. What makes different kinds of books—narratives (stories), informational books, poetry—qualify as well-crafted, high-quality books is the focus of this chapter.

NARRATIVES

Most books published for young children are narratives—that is, stories. Stories have features that set them apart from other types of books, features called literary elements. These include setting, structure (or plot), character, theme, language, and mood. The creators of picturebooks use both text and illustrations to craft these literary elements.

Understanding how literary elements work helps us think about what quality literature is. Defining quality literature is not easy, but we like to think a good book is one in which one (or more) of its literary elements "sparkle." That is, at least one of the book's elements is distinctive and memorable. When authors employ literary elements in imaginative ways, the resulting book comes alive. Such books engage children and invite them to linger under the book's spell. So when you evaluate stories, take an especially careful look at their literary elements.

Setting

Setting refers to the time and place in which a story takes place. Vivid settings can contribute to a powerful literary experience by making children feel like they can enter and live in the story world. Some books have settings that reflect the child's own world, and children can readily connect with a familiar world. In other books, the author or the illustrator—or both—create a distinctive time and place for the story that may be far removed from the child's own world. Such settings can intrigue children and even extend their experiences.

Lengthier books for older children may take place during long periods of time; however, in picturebooks, smaller units of time are more likely to be central to the book's development. For example, nighttime (and fear of the dark) figures prominently in the bedtime book *Llama, Llama, Red Pajama* (Dewdney, 2005). In this book, the words describe the child's fear of the dark, but it is the visual darkness and the little llama's fear as seen in illustrations that seal children's understanding of the setting. In other books, the season of the year is the setting feature that is integral to the action. For example, *Snow* (Shulevitz, 1998) centers around a little boy's delight in an unexpected snowfall.

Some books sparkle primarily *because of* their settings and thus deserve a place in the classroom. *My Papi Has a Motorcycle* (Quintero, 2019) is such a book. In this story a little girl waits for the end of the workday when her *papi* will come home and take her on a motorcycle ride through their community. Along the way they pass a host of special places—Abuelita's church, the *tortillería*, and murals showing the town's history of citrus groves and the immigrants who worked in them. Both words and illustrations bring this community to life. As special as the town is, so too is the warm relationship between the child and her loving family.

Uptown (Collier, 2000) brings to life the neighborhood of Harlem. Each double-page spread features a scene in Harlem as well as a descriptor beginning with "Uptown is . . . " ("chicken and waffles served around the clock" or "a row of brownstones"). A sentence then follows the descriptor and provides further elaboration. The creative layout of the text font adds to the vibrancy of place that Collier conveys through text and illustration.

Bill Martin Jr.'s *A Beasty Story* (Martin, 1999) is another story in which setting matters. The story begins with these textual details: "In a dark, dark wood there is a dark, dark house." But Steven Kellogg's accompanying illustration is what really creates the sense of place integral to this story: Surrounding four little mice are tall, gnarled trees, and in the background looms a desolate, dark old house. The only light comes from four small candles that cast long shadows of the mice onto the tall, dark trees. The setting also plays an integral role in *A Dark, Dark Cave* (Hoffman, 2016). In this story tension builds as two siblings enter a "dark, dark cave" filled with stalactites and stalagmites, where they encounter lizards, bats, shining eyes, and giant paws—until their father turns on the light to reveal the children's room, where the reader sees various toys (such as toy bats) and pets (such as a real cat with shining eyes).

Setting is central to the development of *Maybe Something Beautiful* (Campoy, 2016). A little girl living in "the heart of a gray city" begins to share her paintings with neighbors. This makes the community "less gray—but not much." Then an artist joins the little girl, and together they begin to create murals. Soon members of the community join in, and the neighborhood is transformed—a transformation reflected in the colors that fill the pages of this upbeat and optimistic picturebook based on a true story.

The settings in these five books also sparkle:

- *And Then It's Spring* (Fogliano, 2012): Following a snowy winter, a little boy plants his garden and waits patiently for the browns of winter to recede and the greens of spring to transform the world.
- *The Hello, Goodbye Window* (Juster, 2005): A brick path, an inviting back porch, a hello/goodbye window, a big kitchen, luscious flowerbeds, and a host of other features make Nanna and Poppy's big home a special place to visit.
- *King Bidgood's in the Bathtub* (Wood, 1985): This book takes place largely inside a bathtub, but what a tub it is as the tub shifts from naval battleground to gourmet banquet to fishing pond! Children love to pore over the setting details shown in these illustrations.
- *The Snowy Day* (Keats, 1962): After snow blankets the landscape, Peter goes out to spend a joyous day playing in the snow.
- *Home in the Woods* (Wheeler, 2019): In the Great Depression, a family loses their home and moves into a shack in the woods. What initially seems like an uninviting place slowly becomes a warm and bright home filled with love.

Character

All kinds of characters populate the pages of books written for young children. Stories like *Knuffle Bunny: A Cautionary Tale* (Willems, 2004) and *Don't Throw It to Mo!* (Adler, 2015) feature human characters doing everyday activities. Toys and inanimate objects are the characters in books like *Bulldozer's Big Day* (C. Fleming, 2015). Fantasy creatures also appear in stories for young children. In *Where the Wild Things Are* (Sendak, 1963), Max meets the Wild Things that "roared their terrible roars and gnashed their terrible teeth and rolled their terrible eyes and showed their terrible claws."

In addition to this array of character types, many stories for young children feature only animals as characters. Some act (more or less) like real animals, as does the spider in *The Very Busy Spider* (Carle, 1984). Others are large and even fierce, like the lion in *The Lion and the Mouse* (Pinkney, 2009). But predominantly, the animals in books for young children are small, furry, and fuzzy—ducks, bears, kittens, mice, and rabbits—much like children's stuffed animal companions. These animals are created to act just like humans. Max and Ruby, the bunnies that populate the pages of the popular series written by Rosemary Wells, behave like brother-sister siblings in human families. Gossie and Gertie, characters in the series written by Olivier Dunrea, may be goslings, but children will recognize them as special friends learning to share. And the list goes on—Elephant and Piggie, Frog and Toad. These characters wear clothes, say things, and behave in ways that human children do.

Stories for children sometimes feature stock characters, by which we mean characters that play very predictable roles. When you find a chicken in a story for children, there is a good chance that the creature will not be very smart. And when a fox enters the scene, you can make a pretty good prediction that he will be sly and cunning (and frequently out to get a chicken!).

Some books are of particular note because they are character-rich books—ones in which you come away feeling you have *really* gotten to know the character—their traits, their actions, their feelings, and ways in which those feelings change. How do creators of picturebooks bring their characters to life?

Character Traits

One set of traits is physical traits. Children want to know how characters look and may need to have this information to understand the story. Picturebooks typically present this information through the illustrations. Julia Donaldson entitled one of her books *The Gruffalo* (Donaldson, 1999). What is a gruffalo? Axel Scheffler's illustrations reveal the answer: a huge, furry beast with terrible tusks, terrible claws, and terrible teeth. In Rosemary Wells's books about Max and Ruby, readers need to know which of the two bunny siblings is older; this information is revealed through the size difference apparent in the illustrations.

Traits also include inner qualities that make the character a unique person (or animal). Sometimes the narrator of the story simply tells the reader what the character is like. In the first line of *Wemberly Worried* (Henkes, 2000), we learn that the little mouse is a worrier: "Wemberly worried about everything." Characters' thoughts also give us insights. Henkes helps us get to know Wemberly by drawing her sitting in a chair beside a crack in the wall and worrying, "What if it gets bigger and something comes out of it?" In still other instances, an author may reveal something about a character through what others have to say. For example, Wemberly's mother announces, "You worry too much."

But in picturebooks—as in real life—we get to know characters best by what they do. Sometimes the author *tells* us what a character does, and in other instances the author or illustrator *shows* us. Such is the case in *My Name Is Sangoel* (Williams & Mohammed, 2009), in which readers discover how clever the young protagonist is by the way in which he addresses a problem. Sangoel, a young refugee from Sudan, finds no one can pronounce his name, so he feels he has now lost everything from his past—even his name. Yet, Sangoel devises a creative solution to this problem that also builds a bridge to his new classmates.

In *Bear Has a Story to Tell* (Stead, 2012), readers come to know the main character through his actions. Bear longs to tell his friends a special story, but they are all too busy preparing for winter to stop and listen. So, instead, Bear helps his friends with their preparations—he looks for seeds for Mouse and digs a hole for Frog to burrow in for the winter. The author does not need to tell readers that Bear is kind and gentle—he shows them.

In Jeremy Tankard's *Grumpy Bird* (Tankard, 2007), the illustrations play a central role in revealing character. Grumpy Bird's feelings of being grumpy take a turn when the other animals imitate his behavior in playful friendship. Whereas the text describes that he stops/the others stop, he stands on one foot/the others stand on one foot, he jumps/they jump, what is important to notice in the illustrations is that the bird's grumpy face softens throughout these pages. So when the text finally says, "Hey, this is fun!," we as the readers are not surprised.

Character Emotions

In many stories emotions are central to characterization, as is the case in *When Sophie Gets Angry—Really, Really Angry . . .* (Bang, 1999). When Sophie's mother insists that she give the toy she's playing with to her sister, Sophie's anger explodes. Only by going on a walk by the lake does Sophie become sufficiently calm to rejoin the family. Bang masterfully manipulates color shifts to convey Sophie's changing emotions throughout the story.

The emotional changes of the young boy in *Drawn Together* (Lê, 2018) are important to the story's development. When the boy is dropped off at his grandfather's house, he is none too happy, and it soon becomes clear why this is. The boy and his grandfather do not speak the same language. Then, when the boy pulls out his art supplies and begins to draw, the grandfather brings out his sketchbook. Soon the two are collaborating in the creation of a wonderful wordless adventure. Readers see a very happy boy saying goodbye to his grandfather at the end of the day.

In *Leonardo the Terrible Monster* (Willems, 2005), readers must infer how characters feel from clues found in both text and illustrations. When the little monster, Leonardo, finally succeeds in scaring someone, both text and illustration on one double-page spread suggest how Leonardo and his victim Sam are feeling. On the left side, the author tells us "the little boy cried," and the accompanying illustration shows a limp-looking Sam seated on the ground, his back turned away from his tormentor, with a single tear falling from his eye. It is in the details of the facial expression that we fully realize how Sam feels. On the facing page is Leonardo, and there can be no doubt but that Leonardo feels pleased by what he has succeeded in doing. This is what he says: "'Yes!' cheered Leonardo. 'I did it! I've finally scared the tuna salad out of someone!'" The body language of a confident Leonardo clearly reflects a "yes, I did it!" stance.

Distinctive Characterization

Books with vivid characterization are particularly memorable. Children relish meeting interesting characters. Mo Willems's much-beloved Elephant and Piggie are two such characters. Piggie is ever enthusiastic and optimistic, while Gerald the Elephant is best characterized as cautious, perhaps even apprehensive. For example, in *Today I Will Fly!* (Willems, 2007), Piggie is convinced that she *will* fly—no matter that she is a pig. But in increasingly larger and bolder speech bubbles, Gerald announces the impossibility of Piggie's goal: "You will not fly today." "YOU WILL NEVER FLY!" To which Piggie replies, "I will try."

Children are also drawn to characters with whom they can empathize. Many children know what it is like to feel different—perhaps because of the language they speak or the color of their skin. In *The Day You Begin* (Woodson, 2018), readers meet a girl who also feels different, but when she takes the courageous step of sharing her own stories, she discovers unexpected connections with her classmates.

Character Growth

People in real life grow because of the experiences they have. The same can happen to characters in books. Books in which a character grows often evoke children's most insightful thinking. In *Last Stop on Market Street* (de la Peña, 2015), CJ grumbles about having to take the city bus across town every Sunday with his grandmother. Each of CJ's complaints is countered by Nana, who helps him discover beauty in unexpected places and realize that helping out at the local soup kitchen each Sunday is just what he wants to do.

Yet another character who grows is Peter in *Peter's Chair* (Keats, 1967). Peter is not happy that he must be quiet when his new baby sister, Susie, is sleeping. Nor is he pleased that his father is painting his old crib pink for Susie. So Peter runs away with his baby chair—to ensure that it too is not taken away from him. But when Peter tries sitting in his old chair, he discovers that he has outgrown it! The story concludes with Peter choosing to sit in a grown-up chair and offering to help his father paint the baby furniture for Susie. Like Peter, many young children feel conflicted about new siblings, and discussion of Peter's new insights may well help children who are dealing with this same issue.

The characters in these five books are ones no child should miss:

- *After the Fall* (Santat, 2017): After his fall, Humpty Dumpty learns to conquer his fear and get back up on the wall.
- *Carmela Full of Wishes* (de la Peña, 2018): It is Carmela's birthday, and she is finally old enough to go on Saturday errands with her brother. But her relationship with her brother makes this adventure more complicated that Carmela anticipated.
- *Clever Jack Takes the Cake* (C. Fleming, 2010): Jack resourcefully gathers ingredients to make the princess a birthday cake only to have the cake dismantled as he travels to the castle. Yet, Jack finds a clever way to deal with his dilemma when he reaches the castle.
- *A Sick Day for Amos McGee* (Stead, 2010): When Amos McGee—a gentle zookeeper—gets sick, his animal friends prove they are equally kind as they visit Amos at his home.
- *Officer Buckle and Gloria* (Rathmann, 1995): On school visits to share safety tips, Officer Buckle puts everyone to sleep—until Gloria the dog becomes his partner.

Structure

Structure refers to the way story events are organized. Two common ways of organizing stories for young children are main character structures and problem-centered structures.

Main Character Structure

Books with main character structures introduce readers to a memorable character through a series of vignettes. More likely than not, the title of this kind of book is the name of the character—as we see with *Olivia* (Falconer, 2000). This popular book, with a main character structure, features an energetic little pig. As readers turn the pages of the book, they learn such things as who is in Olivia's family, things

Olivia is good at (e.g., wearing people out), her daily routine (which includes brushing her teeth, moving the cat), and her favorite activities. Olivia's personality can be understood through illustrations and words. For example, on one double-page spread, the text describes how good Olivia is at wearing people out—even herself—and the illustrations show thirteen images of Olivia engaging in a myriad of activities, from hammering to standing on her head to jumping rope to cooking. The illustrations confirm for us, "yes, Olivia wears ME out, too." Many children will feel they have met a kindred soul in Olivia.

Problem-Centered Structure

Many stories appropriate for children center around a problem. Once the problem emerges in these stories, the character makes one or more attempts to solve the predicament. Not all the attempts work out, but in books for children, the final attempt almost always results in a satisfactory solution to the problem and so ends the story. *Looking for Bongo* (Velasquez, 2016) features a problem and solution that resonate with many children. A little boy looks everywhere for his favorite stuffed animal, but even when he finds it, a mystery still exists: How did Bongo get there? Children delight in the clever trick the boy devises to solve the mystery. In *Thank You, Omu!* (Mora, 2018), Omu's generous spirit leads to the problem. As the delectable smell of Omu's thick red stew wafts out the window, her neighbors drop by, one by one, to try the stew. When Omu finally sits down for her evening meal, the pot is empty! Soon though, grateful neighbors show up with gifts to thank Omu for her generosity.

Other Appealing Features of Plot Structures

Suspenseful plots centering around interesting problems are a surefire way to engage young listeners. They want to know how the problem will be solved, and along the way they are likely to become caught up in making predictions about how the character will try to deal with the problem. Moreover, when story lines make unexpected twists and turns along the way, children become even more engaged. *Oh, No!* (C. Fleming, 2012) has this kind of plot. Tension is introduced on the book cover, which features Tiger leering up into the trees at timid-looking Loris. Tiger appears again on the title page—this time in pursuit of fleeing Frog, which, on the subsequent page, falls into a "deep, deep hole." As Tiger continues to stalk animal after animal—each of which joins Frog in the deep, deep hole—readers wait expectantly to see the fate of the trapped animals. Listeners will not only appreciate the unexpected twist at the end of the story; they will also likely be introduced to some new animals along the way, including the loris and sun bear.

Stories with humorous plots also have great appeal. Children listening to the classic story *Petunia* (Duvoisin, 1950) delight in the antics of the silly goose who finds a book in the meadow. But the illustrations showing her finding the book clearly indicate that she is not sure what the book is or what to do with it; the text explains that she sniffs it from all sides and decides it does not smell like food for a goose. But she does remember having overheard humans say that one who owns books and loves them is wise; so Petunia becomes convinced that her discovery has made her wise as well. With her newfound "wisdom," Petunia creates chaos in the barnyard as she offers advice to all her friends.

The plots of these five books will make children want to find out what happens next:

- *Sam and Dave Dig a Hole* (Barnett, 2014): Sam and Dave are on a mission—to dig a hole and keep digging until they find something spectacular. Readers must decide if their mission succeeds.
- *Doctor de Soto* (Steig, 1982): Doctor de Soto proves himself a clever mouse dentist as he outsmarts the fox that plots to eat him and his wife.
- *The Wolf's Chicken Stew* (Kasza, 1987): Wolf's attempt to fatten up a chicken before making her into a meal has unexpected consequences.
- *Don't Let the Pigeon Drive the Bus!* (Willems, 2003): Pigeon is determined to convince us (the readers) to let him drive the bus. He begs and pleads and finally resorts to an all-out temper tantrum that unfolds through the illustrations.
- *Mice and Beans* (Ryan, 2001): As Rosa María makes preparations for a birthday party, items she needs for the party begin to mysteriously disappear.

Theme

Theme refers to the idea or insight about life that an author expresses in a book. Books that explore important issues, or themes, are often the ones that engage children in the richest discussions. *The Other Side* (Woodson, 2001) is a book that offers children an opportunity to talk about racial injustice from a historical perspective. In this story, two girls—one Black and one White—live on different sides of a fence. Their mamas have warned them to stay on their own side of the fence. But no one has said anything about sitting on top of the fence, and so one summer a friendship begins on top of that fence. This book can spark conversations about how the characters in the book brought about change and how, as an extension, children today might also bring about needed changes.

Books by Leo Lionni also offer a great deal to ponder: Is Frederick really contributing in an important way to his mouse community by gathering words rather than nuts, or is he just a lazy good-for-nothing (*Frederick*, Lionni, 1967)? Did Alexander make the right decision by choosing to remain a real mouse rather than being turned into a toy mouse (*Alexander and the Wind-Up Mouse*, Lionni, 1969)?

Sometimes important themes emerge from books that at first glance seem more action-packed or even humorous. For example, the animals in *Bear Came Along* (Morris, 2019) live solitary lives, but when they are accidentally thrust together in a great adventure on the river, they discover the joy of community. Books like these that give children opportunities to talk about issues that really matter build a solid foundation for their subsequent literacy development.

These five books offer rich opportunities for children to talk about important issues:

- *Mr. Tiger Goes Wild* (P. Brown, 2013): Mr. Tiger decides to live his life as he wishes—whether the townspeople approve or not.

- *We Found a Hat* (Klassen, 2016): Two turtle friends find a hat, and each one wants it. This is a dilemma that children will understand—and will likely have much to say about the way the turtles should handle the problem.
- *A Good Day* (Henkes, 2007): Though all the characters in this book seem to be having a bad day, each one finds a way to turn a bad day into a good one. This book offers the intended audience of very young children an important idea to talk about.
- *The Squiggle* (Schaefer, 1996): Relying on her imagination, a little girl turns a squiggly rope into wonderful pictures—a big scaly dragon, a great long wall, popping fireworks, and much more.
- *Dear Juno* (Pak, 2001): Children know that staying in touch with the ones you love is important. Juno discovers how to communicate with his grandmother in faraway Korea—even though he doesn't yet know how to write a conventional letter.

Language

Learning language is an important job of young children, and stories that include rich language support this work. Children benefit from books that include literary language and rich vocabulary as well as fun rhythms and language patterns. Traditional tales offer one type of language that children need to acquire. They are filled with literary language—phrases like "once upon a time," "in the deep dark woods," and "they lived happily ever after."

The language of *Hip-Hop Lollipop* (Montanari, 2018) is infused with a very different kind of language. Not only does it feature a distinctive use of rhythm and rhyme (and can thereby contribute to the development of children's phonemic awareness), but for many children it is filled with the rhythms of a familiar and beloved style of music—hip-hop. In this bedtime story, a little girl named Lollipop is dancing hip-hop and just can't stop moving, even as she makes her way to bed: "Hands tutting. Knees jutting. Arms cranking. Body swanking. Hip gyration. Exultation!" The swirling lines that fill Brian Pinkney's illustrations reflect Lollipop's movement as she heads to bed. *The Day You Begin* (Woodson, 2018) fosters still another kind of language awareness. The book is filled with flowing, lyrical sentences and expressive repetition ("There will be times . . ."). Books like this one attune listeners to the poetry of language.

There are also contemporary writers who fill their stories with rich vocabulary. *Carry Me! Animal Babies on the Move* (Stockdale, 2005) features diverse ways animals carry their young, using rich verbs to describe different methods of transport: "clinging to their bellies [baboons] . . . propped on their shoulders [golden lion tamarinds] . . . perched on their feet [penguins]." William Steig is an author who never speaks down to children. In *Doctor de Soto* (Steig, 1982), Steig uses words like *shabby, outfoxed, morsel,* and *quiver*—all words that children will enjoy learning and using.

Children will delight in the language in these five books:

- *A Greyhound a Groundhog* (Jenkins, 2017): Filled with alliteration and flowing rhyme, a greyhound and groundhog frolic together—around and around!

- *Orange Pear Apple Bear* (Gravett, 2007): Only five words (of which four appear in the title) make up this humorous story about a bear and his fruit.
- *When Spring Comes* (Henkes, 2016): With repetitive, poetic language, the author describes the changes that spring brings to the world.
- *I Ain't Gonna Paint No More* (Beaumont, 2005): A child promises not to paint any more—but just can't help it. Rhythm, rhyme, and repetition make this book special: "Now I ain't gonna paint no more. Guess there ain't no harm if I paint my . . . ARM!"
- *Chicken Soup with Rice* (Sendak, 1962): Every month of the year is just right for eating chicken soup: "Sipping once/sipping twice/sipping chicken soup/ with rice."

Mood

Mood is established when the author and illustrator evoke emotions through the book. The mood of *The Uncorker of Ocean Bottles* (Cuevas, 2016) is a gentle one. The "Uncorker" (who is never named) has an important job—delivering messages found in ocean bottles. He does his job faithfully but is lonely and wishes for his own message. When an invitation to a party arrives—without any indication of who it is for—the Uncorker decides to go to the party. And for the first time, he is surrounded by friends. The soft colors and quirky details of Erin Stead's illustrations are the perfect accompaniment to this tender story about loneliness and community.

The mood of *Niño Wrestles the World* (Morales, 2013) stands in contrast to the previously described book. Niño envisions himself as a *luchador* (a world champion wrestler). In his play he takes on a host of opponents, including La Momia (the Mummy) of Guanajuato, La Llorona, Cabeza Olmeca (Olmec Head), and even an extraterrestrial. But ultimately he faces the greatest opponents of all—*las hermanitas* (little sisters)! Lively colors and bold fonts work together to establish an energetic and vibrant mood in this book.

While a single mood can permeate a book in its entirety, mood can also shift within a book. In *Snow* (Shulevitz, 1998), author/illustrator Uri Shulevitz uses words and illustrations to establish how gray the initial setting of the story is. The adults use words like *only*, *nothing*, and *melt* as they look down and trudge along. But from the very beginning (in fact, from the page before where the story starts), the little boy is depicted with his arms and legs outstretched, his body language showing joyful anticipation of the snow. The mood then shifts to one of magical realism as the boy is joined by Mother Goose characters who come down from a bookstore sign to dance with him in celebration of the snow.

The mood of each of these five books is of particular note:

- *Bear Has a Story to Tell* (Stead, 2012): A gentle mood permeates this story of a bear who befriends others.
- *Hello, Hello!* (Cordell, 2012): Pages filled with bright colors establish a joyous mood as a little girl goes outside to explore the world.

- *Silly Sally* (Wood, 1992): The author uses energetic descriptions of Sally, who is "walking/dancing/leaping backwards, upside down" while visually showing a bright-eyed girl sticking her tongue out of her mouth, curly hair bouncing, and lacy petticoat sticking out of a dress. The bright colors, the rhyming text, and the facial expressions combine to create a mood of sheer silliness.
- *A Good Day* (Henkes, 2007): A shift from a glum mood to an upbeat one is signaled through the inclusion in the middle of the book of a page featuring colorful stripes.
- *Goodnight Moon* (M. Brown, 1947): In this classic bedtime story, words and illustrations work together to establish a soothing mood.

Literary Elements Developed through Illustrations

Throughout this chapter we have made reference to stories that unfold through the interplay of words and illustrations. In picturebooks, illustrations often play a crucial role in developing three literary elements in particular: setting, character, and plot. Picturebooks are typically only thirty-two pages in length, so authors rarely devote many (if any) words to describing a story's setting or characters. Rather, illustrations likely give the reader important information about these literary elements. For example, in *Lilly's Purple Plastic Purse* (Henkes, 1996), illustrations show readers that Lilly feels embarrassed about the nasty note she gave her teacher. Henkes does this by using four side-by-side frames to show Lilly growing increasingly smaller.

Plot events are also sometimes revealed only through illustrations. In *My Friend Rabbit* (Rohmann, 2002), readers learn of Rabbit's attempts to solve the problem—retrieving Mouse's airplane from the tree—*only* through the illustrations. In *Sam and Dave Dig a Hole* (Barnett, 2014), two boys set out to dig a hole, determined to keep digging until they find something spectacular. As the boys repeatedly change the direction in which they are digging, the reader learns—through the illustrations—just how spectacular a find the boys keep missing. The ending of the story contains an unexpected twist as the boys seemingly fall from the sky. Only perceptive readers who have attended to the visual clues at the beginning and end of the story will understand what might actually be happening.

The development of plot in *Rosie's Walk* (Hutchins, 1971) is even more dependent on illustrations. When Rosie the hen goes for a walk, she has a problem—though she appears to be completely unaware of it. Rosie is being stalked by a fox! As the story progresses, the narrator states that Rosie walked "around the pond." The illustration accompanying this text shows Rosie making her way around the pond and being followed by the fox that is about to pounce on her. Turn the page and the double-page spread (which contains no words at all) reveals the fox having fallen into the middle of the pond with Rosie never even looking back as she continues on her way. This pattern is repeated across the story, and at no point does the author mention a fox. The sophisticated cognitive demand on the child is to go beyond only the words to also integrate the information presented through the visuals to fully appreciate the humor of what is happening.

In each of these five books, illustrations contribute important story information:

- *The Odd Egg* (Gravett, 2008): All the other birds lay eggs, but Duck *finds* an egg—an odd egg. Only the illustrations reveal just how odd the egg is—as well as the surprise that eventually emerges from the egg.
- *Bully* (Seeger, 2013): A little bull is transformed into a bully when a big bull tells him to go away. The extent of the transformation—and its impact on the other farm animals—is revealed largely through the illustrations.
- *Don't Let the Pigeon Drive the Bus!* (Willems, 2003): Pigeon tries to convince the reader/viewer that he should get to drive the bus, and at the height of his desperate, out-of-control demanding, the words are pictured in ways that incorporate them as part of the art, ensuring that the "yelling" occurs visually as much as through text.
- *Look!* (Mack, 2015): A vivacious gorilla wants to play, so he repeatedly tries to entice a little boy glued to the television to join him. An unexpected turn of events occurs when the gorilla and boy peek into a book.
- *In the Small, Small Pond* (D. Fleming, 1993): Poetic text describes life in a pond, and the words take on the shape of the actions described—wriggle, lunge, splatter, swirl, swoop, dip—as they visually integrate into the art.

Wordless Books

In wordless books, *all* literary elements are developed through illustrations. This format has proliferated in the twenty-first century, perhaps because our society has become so visual in nature. As the name suggests, stories in wordless books are told totally through illustrations (though some wordless books contain signs or symbols such as numerals integrated into illustrations). It is tempting to assume that wordless books will be easy for children to read; however, the visual complexity of many wordless books often requires careful attention to details embedded in the illustrations. So the role of the teacher may be crucial in scaffolding children's experiences with many wordless books. Teachers need to move slowly through wordless books, giving students time to look closely at each page—and to talk about what they see.

Little Fox in the Forest (Graegin, 2017) is a relatively simple wordless book. In the early pages of the book (all done in grayscale), readers meet a little girl who has taken her beloved stuffed fox to school. The first bit of color is introduced in an illustration when an actual fox steals the stuffed fox from the school playground. As the little girl and a friend follow the fox into the woods, they are soon immersed in a colorful fantasy world of the animals where their hunt continues, eventually reaching a satisfying ending. Graegin, the creator of the book, skillfully manipulates color in telling the story, as do many creators of wordless books.

Flashlight (Boyd, 2014) is a wordless exploration of nature. In this gentle story, a boy who is camping out at night uses his flashlight to highlight the wonders of nature that surround him—bats, skunks, night blossoms, and much more. Illustrations are done almost exclusively in black and gray. Only when the boy shines his flashlight on an animal or plant does it appear in color. Peek holes (or die cuts) also serve to focus the reader's attention on small but lovely details in these night scenes.

Christian Robinson's *Another* (Robinson, 2019) is both visually complex and very imaginative. A little girl is sleeping with her cat when a portal opens in her bedroom wall. When a seemingly identical cat (differentiated only by the color of its collar) enters and steals the cat's stuffed mouse, the cat and girl follow the thief and find themselves in another world (or is it another dimension?). Reading this wordless book requires attention to the color of the smallest details.

Children will be engaged by each of these wordless books:

- *Journey* (Becker, 2013): A bored girl enters another world, where she is swept up in a dramatic struggle of good versus evil.
- *Du Iz Tak?* (Ellis, 2016): This wordless book isn't wordless at all, but the words are in an unknown language that is spoken by the insect characters in this imaginative story. The story is launched when two insects encounter a tiny shoot that has just sprouted—a sprout that launches a dramatic backyard tale as it continues to grow.
- *Wolf in the Snow* (Cordell, 2017): Walking home in a snowstorm, a little girl encounters a wolf pup that has been separated from the pack. Determined to help the pup, the girl is soon in need of help herself.
- *Tuesday* (Wiesner, 1991): As the sun sets, lily pads lift off, and soon frogs are engaged in nocturnal adventures as they fly through town and countryside.
- *The Farmer and the Clown* (Frazee, 2014): When a little clown falls off the circus train, he finds a friend who at first appears to be a grumpy old farmer.

International Picturebooks

The bulk of the books available to us as read alouds are books written, illustrated, and published in the United States; however, there are many reasons why we would seek books from outside the United States. One is that many of the best of the world's books are available through import from other English-speaking nations and translated from other-language-speaking nations as well. Thus, international books are those that originate from outside the United States and are translated into English if the original edition is in another language. Some books, particularly those from other English-language countries, have long been available within the mainstream of children's book publishing. Authors such as Mem Fox from Australia and illustrators such as Martin Waddell from Ireland feel as familiar to us as U.S. authors like Kevin Henkes or Christian Robinson. Their books feel familiar. But when books come from countries where illustration styles are very different from ones in the United States, or story line development varies from story structures we know, the books feel less familiar.

Big Friends by Linda Sarah and illustrated by Benji Davies (Sarah, 2016) was first published in the United Kingdom. Although technically an imported book, there is nothing in this book that suggests its origins are outside the United States; therefore, the book enters the U.S. readership with ease. On the other hand, a book like *Feather*, written by Cao Wenxuan from China and illustrated by Roger Mello from Brazil (Wenxuan, 2017), has a distinct flavor that identifies it as being from outside the United States. Yet, the story line feels like others we know, and that makes the theme relatable. Even as adults, it takes curiosity, desire to know, and patience in understanding what seems unfamiliar at first—whether book, movie, food, or other experience. All in all, stretching children's experiences through read alouds of international books is one way to encourage our students to be curious about the world and to take time to understand what may initially feel unfamiliar.

Picturebooks with Extended Text

The picturebook has evolved across the decades, and there is one change that we believe is important to talk about. In many recently published picturebooks for young children, illustrations often play a far more central role in developing story elements than does the verbal text; however, the opposite was true in most picturebooks published in earlier decades. For example, in *Bedtime for Frances* (Hoban, 1960/1995) there is extensive text, and illustrations do not serve to develop the plot. Rather they largely serve to reveal the emotions of the little badger who is the main character in the book.

Many teachers choose not to read books like this with their more extensive text, and we believe this is a lost opportunity to develop what we call *sustained listening.* Sustained listening requires listeners to attend closely to the author's words and create visual images in their minds as they listen to the words of the story. Learning to visualize is an important cognitive skill that will be crucial as children begin to read (and listen to) chapter books. So introducing these more text-intensive picturebooks is a good way to prepare children for the books they will be reading in just a few years. So with this in mind, remember to include for read alouds classic picturebooks like *Bedtime for Frances* (Hoban, 1960), *Frederick* (Lionni, 1967), or *Petunia* (Duvoisin, 1950). And of course there are more recent books, such as *Mice and Beans* (Ryan, 2001), that also have extensive text.

Read Alouds Using Related Stories

We have talked about a range of different types of books for read alouds. We now want to offer one more important consideration for selecting books. Sometimes you will want to choose related books. The reason for this is that children often do their best thinking when you share books that are connected in some way. For example, if you share a different Mo Willems Elephant and Piggie book each day of the week, it is likely that children will begin to pay particular attention to characterization, noticing that the two characters have distinctly different personalities—Piggie is positive and upbeat, while Elephant is very much the worrier.

Books can be related in different ways. In our Elephant and Piggie example, the books are written and illustrated by the same person. You can also pull together books that address the same theme, books from the same genre, or books with the same structure. There are many possibilities. What is important to remember is that related sets of books offer special learning opportunities for children. Children learn in different ways, so related books can provide different entry points for children. Related books can also deepen and widen children's learning. For example, you might pair *My Friend Rabbit* (Rohmann, 2002) and *Bear Has a Story to Tell* (Stead, 2012). Both books are about friendship, and you can guide children to think about how the friends in the books are alike—they help one another. Yet, *My Friend Rabbit* adds another dimension; one of the friends "messes up" by repeatedly getting Mouse's airplane stuck in a tree. This is just like real life—friends sometimes make mistakes. Nonetheless, in *My Friend Rabbit*, children can also discover that friends *forgive* mistakes. *Big Friends* (Sarah, 2016) is yet another book on friendship that can widen the lens even further. In this book, Birt and Etho are best friends; they do everything together. But when Shu joins the friends, Birt feels left out and stops playing with the boys—until they bring him a special surprise. Like Birt, children are likely to discover a new dimension of friendship through this book—friendship can include more than two.

We hope you are convinced that sharing related books with children offers opportunities to think deeply. For that reason, each of the annotations in the second half of this book includes a list of books related to the featured book.

▪ NONFICTION

Another important part of children's education is learning about the world; it's a job that children love. In this section, we discuss two types of nonfiction books designed to help children learn about their world: concept books and informational books. Although there are fine examples of both types appropriate for young children, you should be aware that there are far fewer concept and informational books available for them than there are stories. But the good news is that, increasingly, publishers are recognizing the need for high-quality books of these types that support young children's learning.

Concept Books

Concept books convey knowledge, answering the question, "What's that?" You can find concept books that address all kinds of topics. For example, *Green Is a Chile Pepper* (Thong, 2014) introduces colors in the context of Latino culture—the pink of piñatas and the orange of marigolds for Day of the Dead. Color words are introduced in English and Spanish. *Freight Train* (D. Crews, 1978), a Caldecott Honor book, features all kinds of cars pulled by freight trains, and each type of car is a different color. So this concept book accomplishes two things: introducing information about the names of different types of train cars while simultaneously reinforcing color concepts. Concept books are especially important to use with young children because they stimulate vocabulary growth and help children enlarge their understanding of the world around them. You will also find that concept books can encourage discussions about the larger world, and these conversations build a foundation for the eventual reading of more complex informational books that will be central to learning about the world both in and out of school. Think of concept books as a stepping-stone into longer and more fully developed informational books.

Alphabet and counting books are types of concept books that play especially important roles in the preschool and kindergarten classrooms. There are many alphabet and counting books available, and more are published each year, but it is challenging to find the right books to use, both for your classroom in general and for read alouds in particular. A major reason to bring alphabet books into the classroom for read alouds is to help children learn to identify letters and learn sounds associated with those letters. For this purpose you will want to use alphabet books that are simple in design, ones that on a given page prominently display the featured letter and one object (or perhaps two) beginning with that letter. Many recently published books do not present the alphabet in such a simple, straightforward way. Rather, these books are more likely to integrate the alphabet into a story line, present it in a very visually elaborate fashion, or use highly unusual words. This means that the alphabet is not as central to the book. To introduce basic alphabet concepts, teachers will want to carefully select books appropriate for helping children learn letter names and/or sounds. One such book is *Eric Carle's ABC* (Carle, 2007).

When selecting counting books, similar considerations are important. That is, simpler counting books like *Count!* (D. Fleming, 1992), which present the featured number and items corresponding to that number on a single page, are the ones you will want to use to teach younger children to identify numbers and understand simple one-to-one correspondence. Another particularly inventive counting book that meets these criteria is Juana Medina's *1 Big Salad: A Delicious Counting Book* (Medina, 2016). One-to-one correspondence is established with the presentation of various salad ingredients (e.g., one avocado, two radishes, three peppers). And whimsy is introduced with line drawings that surround each salad ingredient. The one avocado is turned into an "avocado deer," the two radishes are transformed into "radish mice," and the three peppers become "pepper monkeys."

Informational Books

The main purpose of an informational book is to inform readers about a subject or idea. So informational books have been called the literature of fact. To ensure that the informational books shared in read alouds and placed in your classroom collection are of the highest quality, consider four especially important facets: accuracy, clarity, interpretation, and visual presentation; however, also keep in mind that many informational books for young children are works of narrative nonfiction (i.e., information presented through the format of a story); therefore, you will find that the elements of narrative nonfiction overlap somewhat with the literary elements of stories that were discussed earlier in this chapter.

Accuracy, Clarity, and Interpretation of Information

Once you begin searching for informational books to share with children, it soon becomes apparent that many informational books written for children are not appropriate for younger ones. They contain too much text or present concepts that are too complex for three-to-five-year-olds. Authors who write informational books appropriate for a young audience present information in a way that is easy to understand, provide strong visual support for the text, and do not overwhelm the reader with too much information. One book that meets these criteria is the award-winning book *First the Egg* (Seeger, 2007). Seeger uses a simple structure to explore the development of things in the natural world: first the _____, then the _____ (e.g., first the tadpole, then the frog). She relies on simple text, strategically placed page turns, and cleverly positioned die cuts to move the book forward.

In *Gravity* (Chin, 2014), Jason Chin relies largely on illustrations to explore a challenging concept. Chin first states what would happen without gravity: things would float away. Then a series of illustrations demonstrates this outcome. For example, in one double-page spread, the illustrator establishes an outer-space scene through the inclusion of a rocket and astronaut hovering above the earth. Also included in the illustration are a variety of typically earthbound objects that are also floating in space: shovel, banana, paper cup, lemon, thimble, and even a hotdog. More detailed textual information about gravity is included in a final double-page spread.

Visual Presentation of Information

Illustrations often play a crucial role in informational books. For example, while the text of *Honeybee* (C. Fleming, 2020) is relatively lengthy and filled with important factual information covering the life span of the honeybee, the accompanying illustrations do something that would be difficult for words to achieve. Rohmann's remarkable close-ups take us inside the hive to show us a brand-new honeybee emerging from her solitary cell, cleaning the hive's nursery, feeding "the grub-like larvae," and attending to numerous other chores as the honeybee waits to grow strong enough to emerge from the hive to seek nectar in the outside world.

Two kinds of visuals fill the pages of *It's Our Garden: From Seeds to Harvest in a School Garden* (Ancona, 2013). George Ancona's photographs accompany the text and detail the work of students and teachers (and even families) as they create, care for, and harvest produce from their school garden in New Mexico. Pages of the book also contain artwork created by the children.

Literary Elements Like Character, Setting, Language, and Theme in Informational Books

Because some informational books contain some of the same literary elements found in stories, certain criteria applied to stories can also be appropriate for evaluating these informational books. Authors of informational books should certainly use rich language, just as Robin Page does in *Move!* (Page, 2006). Page not only introduces readers to a variety of different animals; she also uses wonderful words to describe the movement of the animals: a snake *slithers* and *climbs*, while a penguin *slides* and *waddles*.

Authors of informational books can also use interesting structures. In *Elephants Can Paint Too!* (Arnold, 2005), Katya Arnold hooks young children by comparing and contrasting her human students with her elephant students. Readers learn, for example, that one difference between the two groups is that Arnold's human students have hands, while her elephant students have trunks, but both elephant students and human students like to be with their friends.

There are also books, intended primarily to convey information about a topic, that embed the information in a story format; so both literary and informational text criteria must be applied to these books. In *Zinnia's Flower Garden* (Wellington, 2007), children learn about plant growth as a little girl named Zinnia plants and tends her garden from spring, through summer, and into autumn. It is necessary to apply literary criteria to evaluate the quality of the story while using expository text criteria to consider the information.

These five informational books are ones that are likely to intrigue children:

- *Giant Squid* (C. Fleming, 2016): With poetic text and intriguing illustrations, this informational book explores the mysterious giant squid that lives deep in the ocean.
- *Actual Size* (Jenkins, 2004): This oversized book features both animal body parts (such as the head of an Alaska brown bear and the eye of the giant squid) and entire animals (such as the pygmy shrew and the goby fish). All body parts—or bodies—are depicted at their actual size.
- *If You Decide to Go to the Moon* (McNulty, 2005): This book introduces children to space travel and offers information about the moon.
- *Boats* (Barton, 1986): This simple informational book introduces children to different types of boats and the work they do.
- *Color Zoo* (Ehlert, 1989): This book features zoo animals made out of different shapes and colors.

▪ NURSERY RHYMES, POETRY, AND WORDPLAY

In many ways, traditional rhymes like Mother Goose are the mainstay of poetic literature for young children, but there are also contemporary poets who write poetry for very young children. In addition, there are writers who create books for young children that are built around wordplay. These books use devices like rhythm, rhyme, repetition, alliteration, and onomatopoeia. Because young children love to play with words and sounds, they especially enjoy books containing these features. (It is fortunate that children naturally delight in wordplay books because these books nurture phonological awareness—the ability to hear the individual sounds that make up words that we discussed in chapter 2.)

Mother Goose

Nursery rhymes are built around wordplay. Some favorite ones include "Hickory, dickory, dock/The mouse ran up the clock," "Hey diddle, diddle, the cat and the fiddle," and "Mary had a little lamb." Once introduced to lively rhymes like these, children soon begin chanting them along with the teacher. These experiences foster language development and also prepare children to enjoy a lifetime of allusions to nursery rhymes.

There are many fine collections of nursery rhymes for use in read alouds. *My Very First Mother Goose* (Opie, 1996), with large, vibrant illustrations by Rosemary Wells, is especially appealing. *The Neighborhood Mother Goose* (N. Crews, 2004) is an unusual collection that features traditional rhymes accompanied by photographs of contemporary children from diverse cultural groups in familiar home and neighborhood settings, including urban settings. We would also encourage you to include traditional rhymes from diverse cultures in your read-aloud program. A collection appropriate for young children is *Diez Deditos: Ten Little Fingers and Other Play Rhymes and Action Songs from Latin America* (Orozco, 1997).

Poetry

Poetry contains many of the same sound features as nursery rhymes (e.g., rhythm, rhyme, repetition, alliteration). A collection of poetry that children enjoy listening to is *Days Like This: A Collection of Small Poems* (James, 1999). Jump rope and street rhymes also appeal to young children. *Anna Banana: 101 Jump Rope Rhymes* (Cole, 1989) is an engaging collection of such rhymes compiled by Joanna Cole. *Let's Clap, Jump, Sing and Shout; Dance, Spin and Turn It Out!: Games, Songs, and Stories from an African American Childhood* (McKissack, 2017) is a compendium containing jump rope rhymes and much more, including hand claps, circle games, spirituals, and superstitions.

Wordplay Books

It isn't just nursery rhymes and poetry that stimulate young children's language growth. Many stories for young children feature wordplay. *Chugga-Chugga Choo-Choo* (Lewis, 1999), a story that describes a day in the life of a freight train, is told in rhyme and features a rhythmic pattern that mimics the wheels of the train. And children can't help tapping their toes and clapping along as they listen to rhythmic books like *The Lady with the Alligator Purse* (Westcott, 1988): "Miss Lucy had a baby,/His name was Tiny Tim,/She put him in the bathtub/To see if he could swim."

Alliteration is another facet of language that delights children. In *A, My Name Is Alice* (Bayer, 1984), for each letter of the alphabet a different character is described using alliterative words. A special type of wordplay is featured in books with repetitive structures. These books contain words, phrases, questions, sentences, or verses that are used repeatedly throughout the book. They are also called predictable books. There are many books of this nature geared toward the early childhood audience, and children often enjoy read alouds of predictable books because they can join in on refrains. In addition, children will often choose these books for independent use because it is relatively easy to engage in emergent reading (or pretend reading) of a book with a repetitive structure. Beginning readers also find books like this to be accessible. Denise Fleming uses a repetitive structure in *Mama Cat Has Three Kittens* (D. Fleming, 2002). As the story unfolds, we follow the activities of Mama Cat. As Mama Cat washes her paws, Fluffy and Skinny do the same, but "Boris naps." As each of Mama's new activities is presented, Fluffy and Skinny continue to do the same, and the narrator repeats the sentence "Boris naps"—until the story's ending offers an unexpected twist. Visually, it is easy to see that Boris is different from the rest; Mama Cat is black and white, Fluffy and Skinny are black/white or black/brown/white, but Boris is orange.

Some of the best-known and most popular books for young children contain repetitive structures, books such as *Brown Bear, Brown Bear, What Do You See?* (Martin, 1967) and *The Very Busy Spider* (Carle, 1984). In each of those books, the visual repetition is an important component supporting children's understanding of the repetitive structure. For example, in *Brown Bear, Brown Bear, What Do You See?* each page shows one animal portrayed in only one color. This allows the child to see the color and name the animal and then chime in chanting the rhythmic text. Songs for young children in book format, such as *Wheels on the Bus* (Zelinsky, 1990), frequently have repetitive structures as well.

The following five books feature poetic language or engaging wordplay:

- *Orange Pear Apple Bear* (Gravett, 2006): This book contains only five words, but through a creative interplay of illustrations and words, the book conveys a story that will charm readers young and old.
- *Clap Your Hands* (Cauley, 1992): Filled with engaging rhymes, this book invites children to join in the actions of the zany animal characters.
- *Confetti: Poems for Children* (Mora, 1999): A collection of poetry about the everyday world that surrounds children. It is also available in Spanish.
- *Look!* (Mack, 2015): This book contains only two words—*look* and *out*. Children will enjoy the challenge of using illustration clues to read the word(s) with the appropriate expression.
- *There Was an Old Lady Who Swallowed a Fly* (Taback, 1997): This cumulative tale demands that listeners join in on the repetitive lines.

▪ AWARD-WINNING BOOKS

There is one final word to share regarding the selection of well-crafted books for read alouds. As we noted earlier in this chapter, many books for children are published each year, with some estimates ranging up to five thousand new children's books published annually. So how does one choose from this assortment? As one way of keeping up with high-quality new books, we encourage you to become familiar with some of the awards given each year for children's books. These awards are presented for attention to quality as well as other criteria. In appendix A, we include a list of some of these awards as well as brief explanations about the basis of each award and websites where you can find lists of books that have won the awards. Some of the awards are given to chapter books as well as picturebooks, and not all the picturebooks will be age-appropriate for the children in your classroom. Nonetheless, we believe these websites will give you some good leads for finding high-quality books to use in read alouds.

▪ RECOMMENDED CHILDREN'S BOOKS

Adler, David. *Don't Throw It to Mo!* New York: Penguin, 2015.

Ancona, George. *It's Our Garden: From Seeds to Harvest in a School Garden.* Somerville, MA: Candlewick, 2013.

Arnold, Katya. *Elephants Can Paint, Too!* New York: Atheneum, 2005.

Bang, Molly. *When Sophie Gets Angry—Really, Really Angry . . . .* New York: Scholastic, 1999.

Barnett, Mac. *Sam and Dave Dig a Hole.* Illustrated by Jon Klassen. Somerville, MA: Candlewick, 2014.

Barton, Byron. *Boats.* New York: HarperCollins, 1986.

Bayer, Jane E. *A, My Name Is Alice.* Illustrated by Steven Kellogg. New York: Dial, 1984.

Beaumont, Karen. *I Ain't Gonna Paint No More.* Illustrated by David Catrow. New York: Houghton Mifflin Harcourt, 2005.

Becker, Aaron. *Journey.* Somerville, MA: Candlewick, 2013.

Boyd, Lizi. *Flashlight.* San Francisco, CA: Chronicle, 2014.

Brown, Margaret Wise. *Goodnight Moon.* Illustrated by Clement Hurd. New York: Harper, 1947.

Brown, Peter. *Mr. Tiger Goes Wild.* New York: Little, Brown, 2013.

Campoy, Isabel. *Maybe Something Beautiful: How Art Transformed a Neighborhood.* Illustrated by Teresa Howell. New York: Houghton Mifflin Harcourt, 2016.

Carle, Eric. *Eric Carle's ABC.* New York: Grossett and Dunlap, 2007.

Carle, Eric. *The Very Busy Spider.* New York: Philomel, 1984.

Cauley, Lorinda Bryan. *Clap Your Hands.* New York: Putnam, 1992.

Chin, Jason. *Gravity.* New York: Roaring Brook, 2014.

Cole, Joanna. *Anna Banana: 101 Jump Rope Rhymes.* Illustrated by Alan Tiegreen. New York: HarperCollins, 1989.

Collier, Bryan. *Uptown.* New York: Henry Holt, 2000.

Cordell, Matthew. *Hello! Hello!* New York: Little, Brown, 2012.

Cordell, Matthew. *Wolf in the Snow.* New York: Feiwel and Friends, 2017.

Crews, Donald. *Freight Train.* New York: Greenwillow, 1978.

Crews, Nina. *The Neighborhood Mother Goose.* New York: Greenwillow, 2004.

Cuevas, Michelle. *The Uncorker of Ocean Bottles.* Illustrated by Erin E. Stead. New York: Dial, 2016.

de la Peña, Matt. *Carmela Full of Wishes.* Illustrated by Christian Robinson. New York: Putnam, 2018.

de la Peña, Matt. *Last Stop on Market Street.* Illustrated by Christian Robinson. New York: Putnam, 2015.

Dewdney, Anna. *Llama, Llama, Red Pajama.* New York: Scholastic, 2005.

Donaldson, Julia. *The Gruffalo.* Illustrated by Axel Scheffler. New York: Dial, 1999.

Duvoisin, Roger. *Petunia.* New York: Knopf, 1950.

Ehlert, Lois. *Color Zoo.* New York: HarperCollins, 1989.

Ellis, Carson. *Du Iz Tak?* Somerville, MA: Candlewick, 2016.

Falconer, Ian. *Olivia.* New York: Atheneum, 2000.

Fleming, Candace. *Bulldozer's Big Day.* Illustrated by Eric Rohmann. New York: Atheneum, 2015.

Fleming, Candace. *Clever Jack Takes the Cake.* Illustrated by G. Brian Karas. New York: Schwartz and Wade, 2010.

Fleming, Candace. *Giant Squid.* Illustrated by Eric Rohmann. New York: Roaring Brook, 2016.

Fleming, Candace. *Honeybee: The Busy Life of Apis Mellifera*. Illustrated by Eric Rohmann. New York: Holiday House, 2020.

Fleming, Candace. *Oh, No!* Illustrated by Eric Rohmann. New York: Schwartz and Wade, 2012.

Fleming, Denise. *Count!* New York: Henry Holt, 1992.

Fleming, Denise. *In the Small, Small Pond*. New York: Macmillan/Square Fish, 1993.

Fleming, Denise. *Mama Cat Has Three Kittens*. New York: Macmillan/Square Fish, 2002.

Fogliano, Julie. *And Then It's Spring*. Illustrated by Erin E. Stead. New York: Roaring Brook, 2012.

Frazee, Marla. *The Farmer and the Clown*. New York: Simon and Schuster, 2014.

Graegin, Stephanie. *Little Fox in the Forest*. New York: Schwartz and Wade, 2017.

Gravett, Emily. *The Odd Egg*. New York: Simon and Schuster, 2008.

Gravett, Emily. *Orange Pear Apple Bear*. New York: Simon and Schuster, 2006.

Henkes, Kevin. *A Good Day*. New York: Greenwillow, 2007.

Henkes, Kevin. *Lilly's Purple Plastic Purse*. New York: Greenwillow, 1996.

Henkes, Kevin. *Wemberly Worried*. New York: Greenwillow, 2000.

Henkes, Kevin. *When Spring Comes*. New York: Greenwillow, 2016.

Hoban, Russell. *Bedtime for Frances*. Illustrated by Garth Williams. New York: HarperCollins, 1960.

Hoffman, Eric. *A Dark, Dark Cave*. Illustrated by Corey Tabor. New York: Viking, 2016.

Hutchins, Pat. *Rosie's Walk*. New York: Aladdin, 1971.

James, Simon. *Days Like This: A Collection of Small Poems*. Somerville, MA: Candlewick, 1999.

Jenkins, Emily. *A Greyhound a Groundhog*. Illustrated by Chris Appelhans. New York: Schwartz and Wade, 2017.

Jenkins, Steve. *Actual Size*. New York: Houghton Mifflin Harcourt, 2004.

Juster, Norton. *The Hello, Goodbye Window*. Illustrated by Chris Raschka. New York: Hyperion, 2005.

Kasza, Keiko. *The Wolf's Chicken Stew*. New York: Putnam, 1987.

Keats, Ezra Jack. *Peter's Chair*. New York: Harper, 1967.

Keats, Ezra Jack. *The Snowy Day*. New York: Viking, 1962.

Klassen, Jon. *We Found a Hat*. Somerville, MA: Candlewick, 2016.

Lê, Minh. *Drawn Together*. Illustrated by Dan Santat. New York: Hyperion, 2018.

Lewis, Kevin. *Chugga-Chugga Choo-Choo*. New York: Little, Brown, 1999.

Lionni, Leo. *Alexander and the Wind-Up Mouse*. New York: Knopf, 1969.

Lionni, Leo. *Frederick*. New York: Random House, 1967.

Mack, Jeff. *Look!* New York: Philomel, 2015.

Martin, Bill, Jr. *A Beasty Story*. Illustrated by Steven Kellogg. New York: Houghton Mifflin Harcourt, 1999.

Martin, Bill, Jr. *Brown Bear, Brown Bear, What Do You See?* Illustrated by Eric Carle. New York: Henry Holt, 1967.

McKissack, Patricia. *Let's Clap, Jump, Sing and Shout; Dance, Spin and Turn It Out! Games, Songs, and Stories from an African American Childhood*. Illustrated by Brian Pinkney. New York: Schwartz and Wade, 2017.

McNulty, Faith. *If You Decide to Go to the Moon*. Illustrated by Steven Kellogg. New York: Scholastic, 2005.

Medina, Juana. *1 Big Salad: A Delicious Counting Book*. New York: Viking, 2016.

Montanari, Susan McElroy. *Hip-Hop Lollipop*. Illustrated by Brian Pinkney. New York: Schwartz and Wade, 2018.

Mora, Oge. *Thank You, Omu!* New York: Little, Brown, 2018.

Mora, Pat. *Confetti: Poems for Children*. Illustrated by Enrique O. Sanchez. New York: Lee and Low, 1999.

Morales, Yuyi. *Niño Wrestles the World*. New York: Roaring Brook Press, 2013.

Morris, Richard T. *Bear Came Along*. Illustrated by LeUyen Pham. New York: Little, Brown, 2019.

Opie, Iona. *My Very First Mother Goose*. Illustrated by Rosemary Wells. Somerville, MA: Candlewick, 1996.

Orozco, José Luis. *Diez Deditos and Other Play Rhymes and Action Songs from Latin America*. Illustrated by Elisa Kleven. New York: Dutton, 1997.

Page, Robin. *Move!* Illustrated by Steve Jenkins. New York: Houghton Mifflin, 2006.

Pak, Soyung. *Dear Juno*. Illustrated by Susan Kathleen Hartung. New York: Puffin, 2001.

Pinkney, Jerry. *The Lion and the Mouse*. New York: Dial, 2009.

Quintero, Isabel. *My Papi Has a Motorcycle*. Illustrated by Zeke Peña. New York: Penguin Random House, 2019.

Rathmann, Peggy. *Officer Buckle and Gloria*. New York: Putnam, 1995.

Robinson, Christian. *Another*. New York: Atheneum, 2019.

Rohmann, Eric. *My Friend Rabbit*. New York: Roaring Brook, 2002.

Ryan, Pam Muñoz. *Mice and Beans*. Illustrated by Joe Cepeda. New York: Scholastic, 2001.

Santat, Dan. *After the Fall: How Humpty Dumpty Got Back Up Again*. New York: Roaring Brook, 2017.

Sarah, Linda. *Big Friends*. Illustrated by Benji Davies. New York: Henry Holt, 2016.

Schaefer, Carole Lexa. *The Squiggle*. New York: Penguin Random House, 1996.

Seeger, Laura Vaccaro. *Bully*. New York: Roaring Brook, 2013.

Seeger, Laura Vaccaro. *First the Egg*. New York: Roaring Brook, 2007.

Sendak, Maurice. *Chicken Soup with Rice*. New York: HarperCollins, 1962.

Sendak, Maurice. *Where the Wild Things Are*. New York: Harper and Row, 1963.

Shulevitz, Uri. *Snow*. New York: Farrar, Straus and Giroux, 1998.

Stead, Philip C. *Bear Has a Story to Tell*. Illustrated by Erin E. Stead. New York: Roaring Brook, 2012.

Stead, Philip C. *A Sick Day for Amos McGee*. Illustrated by Erin E. Stead. New York: Roaring Brook, 2010.

Steig, William. *Doctor de Soto*. New York: Simon and Schuster, 1982.

Stockdale, Susan. *Carry Me! Animal Babies on the Move*. Atlanta, GA: Peachtree, 2005.

Taback, Simms. *There Was an Old Lady Who Swallowed a Fly*. New York: Viking, 1997.

Tankard, Jeremy. *Grumpy Bird*. New York: Scholastic, 2007.

Thong, Roseanne Greenfield. *Green Is a Chile Pepper: A Book of Colors*. Illustrated by John Parra. San Francisco: Chronicle, 2014.

Velasquez, Eric. *Looking for Bongo*. New York: Holiday House, 2016.

Wellington, Monica. *Zinnia's Flower Garden*. New York: Puffin, 2007.

Wenxuan, Cao. *Feather*. Illustrated by Roger Mello. Translated by Chloe Garcia Roberts. New York: Elsewhere Editions, 2017.

Westcott, Nadine Bernard. *The Lady with the Alligator Purse*. New York: Little, Brown, 1988.

Wheeler, Eliza. *Home in the Woods*. New York: Nancy Paulsen, 2019.

Wiesner, David. *Tuesday*. New York: Clarion, 1991.

Willems, Mo. *Don't Let the Pigeon Drive the Bus!* New York: Hyperion, 2003.

Willems, Mo. *Knuffle Bunny: A Cautionary Tale*. New York: Hyperion, 2004.

Willems, Mo. *Leonardo the Terrible Monster*. New York: Hyperion, 2005.

Willems, Mo. *Today I Will Fly!* New York: Hyperion, 2007.

Williams, Karen Lynn, & Khadra Mohammed. *My Name Is Sangoel*. Illustrated by Catherine Stock. Grand Rapids, MI: Eerdmans, 2009.

Wood, Audrey. *King Bidgood's in the Bathtub*. Illustrated by Don Wood. New York: Houghton Mifflin Harcourt, 1985.

Wood, Audrey. *Silly Sally*. New York: Houghton Mifflin Harcourt, 1992.

Woodson, Jacqueline. *The Day You Begin*. Illustrated by Rafael López. New York: Penguin, 2018.

Woodson, Jacqueline. *The Other Side*. Illustrated by E. B. White. New York: Putnam, 2001.

Zelinsky, Paul O. *The Wheels on the Bus*. New York: Dutton, 1990.

CHAPTER 4

Scheduling and Conducting Read Alouds

Here are two questions to which we would all love to have definitive answers: How much time should I spend each day reading aloud? and When during the day should I read aloud to the children? Unfortunately, there are no simple answers to these "when" and "how much" questions about reading aloud. Let us just say upfront that it is impossible to specify a certain number of minutes each day that would be just right, or too much, or too little for reading aloud. Similarly, there is no one slot in your daily schedule that is best for reading aloud.

HOW MUCH TIME?

Like most teachers, you probably feel like there is never enough instructional time during a day to do everything you want. Perhaps a good way to think about the topic of how much time to spend reading aloud to your children is to consider this: What am I adding instructionally—and what am I giving up—when I choose to read aloud?

Even this is not an easy issue to resolve because such decisions are not part of a simple zero-sum game. For example, reading the book *Seeds Move!* (Page, 2019) to a group of children could be a way of covering the topic of plants while also working on basic concepts about print and fostering children's familiarity with how informational text structures work in books. Or a read aloud of *Llama Llama Misses Mama* (Dewdney, 2009) could be a vehicle for developing children's phonological awareness as well as addressing the beginning-of-the-school-year socioemotional issue of young children's separation from parents. And although we regard read alouds as an essential and robust instructional activity for children, we also recognize that read alouds alone cannot teach young children all they need to know, even when it comes to the language and literacy aspects of the curriculum, let alone the overall body of learning standards that need to be addressed. Children need to participate in read alouds, but they also need time for a variety of other instructional and interpersonal interactions during the school day.

We believe that no amount of research will ever yield a definitive answer to the question of how much of the school day should be spent reading aloud to children. Rather, the answer is dependent on child and classroom factors like the children's prior literacy knowledge and experience and how long the school day is. A good way to make the decision about this issue is to have conversations at your school/center with other teachers and your principal/director. This approach allows you to benefit from collegial discussions about the amount of reading aloud that seems appropriate for the needs of your children.

In general, however, we offer the following advice: typically, teachers should have at least one large group read aloud per day that serves the different kinds of instructional aims discussed later in this chapter. We have conducted studies with preschoolers that show that after about twenty minutes, their engagement in such an activity drops off quite a bit (Paciga et al., 2009), so we recommend a period of fifteen to twenty minutes be spent on reading aloud with younger children in a large-group setting. If it is the beginning of the school year or you have a group of children who have very little or no prior experience with read alouds, it would be a good idea to start with sessions of ten or so minutes. With first and second graders, a longer period can be appropriate, say up to twenty-five minutes. That gives enough time to get into substantive discussions but not so much as to begin losing a significant portion of children's attention.

Some teachers also schedule additional small-group or one-to-one read alouds for children who have not had much prior experience with books and therefore need additional support. Teachers may also slip in another short read aloud during certain times of the day as a means of transition or to provide a productive shift from one kind of activity to another.

▪ WHEN DURING THE DAY?

We see read alouds as times when important teaching takes place, so we like the idea of scheduling the read aloud for the morning because (a) children are fresh and in general more receptive then, and (b) the book can become something that serves to frame or integrate the content that is covered during the remainder of the day, thus emphasizing the central role of books in your classroom and in children's lives.

There may be other times when you want to conduct an additional read aloud on a particular day depending on the children's mood or needs—or even on something that comes up in the context of other activities, what many people call a teachable moment. For example, on a day when several of the children are especially squirrely, you might want to read a quiet book like *Daniel's Good Day* (Archer, 2019). Teachable moments can occur at any time. For example, a conversation that took place during lunch in one classroom led to readings of *Fry Bread* (Maillard, 2019) and *Bee-bim Bop* (Park, 2005) to recognize the culinary traditions of children from different cultures. Finally, we recommend that you keep books of poetry on the corner of your desk so that in those in-between moments when you have two or three minutes to fill, you can read a poem. Some poems for children take less than a minute to read. A routine like this will also help to ensure that poetry is not relegated to a once-a-year poetry unit.

Monitoring Your Decisions about the "When" of Reading Aloud

It is useful to periodically revisit decisions about when and how much to read aloud. As the year progresses, consider changes in your children's literacy development as well as their increasing maturity. Think about how reading aloud is actually functioning in the curriculum—what strategies and skills are you now emphasizing, and what role does listening to books being read aloud play in those? Follow-up monitoring and teacher reflection help guide teachers' decision-making about how much to read aloud, and that is probably the key to making sure that reading aloud is neither the tail that is wagging the early literacy instruction dog nor the neglected element in the language arts portion of your curriculum.

■ MAINTAINING A READING LOG

You might also find it helpful to maintain a log of what you are reading across the school year. A good way to keep track of the "book diet" you are offering your children through read alouds is by keeping a simple read-aloud log like this:

Date	Title	Genre	Culture or Ethnicity Represented	Focus of Read Aloud	Children's Reaction
10/6	Saturday	Story	African American	Inviting personal connections	
10/7	I Ain't Gonna Paint No More	Story	White	Rhyming words	
10/8					
10/8					
10/9					

A log like this helps to ensure that you have a good mix of books and poetry. We all have particular types of books we especially like and may become overly reliant on them. A reading log might reveal that you never share nonfiction books with the class. Or you might discover that you never read poetry or books portraying diverse characters.

Noting the focus of read alouds on a log can also help you monitor whether you are taking advantage of read alouds to promote the various foundational literacy skills that we talked about in chapter 2. Finally, including a brief note about how the children responded to each read aloud can provide you with a good record for the following year to remember which books worked well and which didn't.

■ HOW TO MAKE THE READ ALOUD A SUCCESS

To launch our thinking about how to read aloud, let's peek into two different classrooms. The first is that of Mr. Martin, who is reading aloud *A Dark, Dark Cave* (Hoffman, 2016). This book is frequently recommended as a quality book for young children, but most of the four-year-olds sitting on the rug do not appear to be engaged. Philipa has shifted her attention to a toy she brought to the rug. Several children are wiggling and looking about to other areas of the room. DeShante has wandered away from the rug completely. The read aloud is not going well.

Now let's look in on Ms. Lopez, who is reading aloud *Llama, Llama, Red Pajama* (Dewdney, 2005) to her preschoolers. The scene is quite different. Ms. Lopez reads, "Llama llama/Red pajama/In the dark without his mama."

"How is he feeling?" asks Ms. Lopez.

"He's scared, really scared," murmurs Juanita.

"How do you know?" probes Ms. Lopez.

"His eyes," responds Amber. "They're big."

When Ms. Lopez turns the page to reveal the wide-open mouth of the wailing little llama, the children burst into laughter. Conversation has been lively throughout this read aloud. Children make predictions, offer advice to Llama, and talk about their own bedtime rituals. After the read aloud, many of the children visit the book center to look at the copy of *Llama, Llama, Red Pajama* that Ms. Lopez has placed there.

Why were these two read alouds so different? Book choice was not likely the key factor; both books are highly recommended, quality pieces of literature. In talking to the two teachers afterward, we concluded that preparation was likely the major determinant of the success (or lack of success) of these two read alouds. Mr. Martin explained that he had pulled *A Dark, Dark Cave* from the school library shelf the morning of the read aloud and only had time to glance through the book before sharing it with the children. By contrast, Ms. Lopez had prepared carefully for her read aloud. She thought about different voices she could use for the little llama and his mother. She decided on stopping points for inviting predictions and the places in the book where she would invite children to discuss different issues and situations. The end results of the two teachers' approaches to preparing for their read alouds was telling.

Preparing to Read Aloud

The best read alouds are the ones for which a teacher thoughtfully prepares. If "select a good book" is the first rule for a successful read aloud, then the second rule must be "prepare your read aloud!" You not only want to avoid the mistake that Mr. Martin made of reading an unfamiliar book to your students; you should also try your hand at reading a book aloud *before* bringing it into the classroom. There is a good reason for this; sometimes you may read a book silently and really like it, but when you read it aloud, the book simply doesn't flow very well. For example, if you do not know Spanish, a practice read of a book like *Niño Wrestles the World* (Morales, 2015) will prepare you to handle phrases like "Niño vs. Cabeza Olmeca." Also, if you are unfamiliar with some of the "opponents" that Niño encounters (e.g., La Momia de Guanajuato or La Llorona), you can take a careful look at the information in the endpapers to talk with the children about these foes.

It is also important to practice pacing and expression before reading a book aloud. What is the mood of the story? Is it quiet and reflective or silly and energetic? Think about the characters. Is a character wise, clever, or cunning? How is a character feeling? Do those feelings shift during the story? Consider how you can use your voice to convey mood, emotion, and characterization. For example, *The Day You Begin* (Woodson, 2018) is a thoughtful book about feeling different but being brave enough to share yourself despite that. The book also contains lyrical language with a repetitive phrase: "There will be times . . . ." Consider how you can convey a thoughtful quality as you read the book. Evoking the mood of a book or bringing characters to life does not just happen; it happens when a reader has carefully prepared.

If the reading involves an informational book, examine not only the text of the book but also any end matter you find at the back of the book that provides background or additional information about the books' subject. For example, *¡Olinguito, de la A a la Z!/Olinguito, from A to Z!* (Delacre, 2016), a book in both Spanish and English, features the search for and discovery of the first new mammal species identified in the Americas in more than three decades. Organized with an alphabetical sequence using alliterative language, Spanish is presented first, with English text below. The end matter provides facts to support the illustrated introduction in the text.

Preparing for a read aloud also requires reading the book ahead of time with an eye toward how you can support children's comprehension and active engagement. Think about the degree to which you will need to build children's background before reading the book. A selection like *A Big Mooncake for Little Star* (Lin, 2018) is best appreciated by listeners who understand that the moon changes shape, so a teacher might need to provide basic background about the phases of the moon before reading. Other books may offer challenging concepts that can be addressed during the actual reading of the story. For example, in reading aloud *Hey, Water!* (Portis, 2019), talking about icebergs is probably more effective at the point where the author introduces the word rather than prior to the reading.

Also, as you prepare for a read aloud, be alert to stopping points where you can invite children's active engagement. Where might you want to invite predictions? In some books, page turns are set up as invitations to predict an upcoming word or phrase. In *I Ain't Gonna Paint No More* (Beaumont, 2005), for example, the final text on one opening is "Still I ain't complete til I paint my . . . ." Children will realize that the page turn is an invitation to predict a body part rhyming with *complete*. A turn of the page quickly confirms that the missing word is *feet*.

Seek out the stopping points that seem to demand listeners predict upcoming events. On one spread in *The Wolf's Chicken Stew* (Kasza, 1987), author/illustrator Keiko Kasza shows a wolf about to leap on a chicken who is oblivious to the wolf's presence. The accompanying text reads, "The wolf crept closer. But just as he was about to grab his prey . . . " (page turn). This is the perfect place for the reader to pause and ask children what they think will happen.

Finally, monitor your own responses to the book as you read it. Make a point of remembering what you notice or wonder about because these spontaneous responses can become conversation starters after the reading. For example, in reading *Good Night Owl* (Pizzoli, 2016), you might notice that Greg Pizzoli shows only one close-up of Owl's face. This happens at the point in the story when Owl's frustration with not being able to find the source of the "squeek" has reached a fevered pitch. This turning point can serve as the perfect place to talk with the children about character emotion, saying something like "Look closely at this picture. It is the first time we get to see a close-up picture of Owl's face. Look at his face. What do you think he might be feeling or thinking? What makes you think that?"

Introducing the Book

Once you are prepared to share the book, gather the children together in the space where read alouds take place in your classroom. Be sure to situate all the children so that everyone can see the illustrations. Some teachers seat children around the edge of the rug; others have the children cluster around them. There are advantages and disadvantages to each arrangement, but with young children, the cluster pattern has higher engagement for longer periods of time than children sitting around the edge of the rug, especially for children who are farthest away from the teacher (Paciga et al., 2009).

Your introduction to the book is important, but keep it short. If you spend too much time introducing the book, you might lose children before you even begin. The focus of read-aloud time and attention should be on reading the book and talking about it; however, a book introduction is a chance to help children acquire needed background knowledge and expand their store of literary understandings, and it primes them to listen to the book. Of course, you will want to introduce the book by title and tell the children the name of the author and illustrator to help them begin to develop a sense of what authors and illustrators do; but don't dwell on this.

Another way to support children's comprehension before beginning the read aloud is by reading the title of the book and inviting the children to look closely at the cover illustration and perhaps the book's endpapers and title pages. Illustrators often include important clues about the story in these features. For example, in *Saturday* (Mora, 2019), the front endpapers feature a calendar showing activities scheduled for various days across the month. Entries on the calendar suggest that Saturday activities might be different than those scheduled during the week. By taking advantage of clues such as these, you can build the children's expectations for what the book will be about. Finally, if appropriate, mention other books you and the children have read previously that are by the same author or illustrator, address the same topic or theme, or have the same character in them.

Some educators suggest taking a "picture walk" through the book to build children's curiosity and interest. Reading to Kids (2002) describes the picture walk this way: "Slowly flip through the book, page by page, without reading a single word. Ask them questions about each picture they see, and try to elicit responses that require them to make inferences based upon the images, and not the words, on each page" (http://readingtokids.org/ReadingClubs/TipPictureWalk.php).

We don't like this at all. This process can actually take away from children's engagement with and enjoyment of the book. It gives too much away before the children get to experience the text in conjunction with the illustrations, as the book was created to do.

Reading the Story

When you see the heading "Reading the Story," it is natural for you to think about what you will do during the reading. There are plenty of recommendations out there for how teachers should read to children to make read alouds interesting and effective, such as read with enthusiasm, use plenty of expression, use character voices where appropriate, make the book come alive, and ask questions about the book

These are all very good ideas, but we want to challenge you to go beyond these rather general suggestions and think in greater depth about what makes a good reading. First, instead of only considering what *you* will do in the reading, take a different perspective and think about what you *and* the children will do during the reading. We have noticed several features of highly effective readings that are not often discussed in books, articles, or websites on how to read aloud to young children.

What You, the Teacher, Are Doing

- Read the book in a way that recreates the excitement you felt the first time you read it.
- Think about pitch and volume. Many teachers are very excitable when reading to children. We have seen many teachers who read so enthusiastically that everything comes out in breathy excitement. It is much better to adjust your emotions and volume level to suit the content and language of the book.
- Vary the pace of your reading to capture shifts in mood and emotion.
- Remember the magic of the pause, especially at a page turn. This will leave the listeners anticipating what is to come.

Using these suggestions to read to children will make your read aloud more engaging, but perhaps more essential to the success of a storybook reading are children's opportunities to actively participate.

What the Children Are Doing

- Laughing
- Sharing their own thinking about the book
- Asking questions
- Joining in on repeated refrains

This is not to say the only successful read aloud is one in which children participate by laughing and talking. Sometimes silence signals deep engagement. Nonetheless, we know that two heads are often better than one, so we take it as a good sign when children come together to mull over a character's choice of action, ponder a question, or simply share observations.

Some teachers prefer to read a story straight through without interruption, believing that interruptions distract from the story line; however, this is probably not the best approach, especially with younger children who most likely will forget what they want to say if they have to wait until the end of the book before sharing their thinking. So if a child interrupts your reading to ask a question or contribute a response, value the interruption as an opportunity.

Although you will want to honor children's spontaneous responses during the reading, you will also want to be alert to opportunities to invite engagement and support understanding during the read aloud. When should you offer these invitations? To make that decision, pay close attention to the way in which the particular book you are reading is structured so you will recognize the best junctures for extending invitations. For example, in a structurally repetitive book like *Dear Zoo* (Campbell, 1986), once children become attuned to the basic pattern of the book, the book itself invites them to join in: "So they sent me a ___. He was too ___. I sent him back." A story like *Oh, No!* (Fleming, 2012) offers different opportunities. In this book one animal after another falls into a hole as it attempts to rescue other animals that have previously fallen into the hole. Children will be eager to join in the refrain of "Oh, no!" that accompanies each new animal's tumble into the "deep, deep hole."

In stories centered around problems, the point in the story line at which the problem emerges is ideal for inviting predictions. For example, when the first goat approaches the bridge in *The Three Billy Goats Gruff* (Pinkney, 2017), you can pause to ask the children what they think will happen next. And once a character makes an attempt to solve a problem, children can guess the outcome before you proceed with reading: Will that troll listen to the little billy goat and wait for the next larger goat to cross his bridge? The children are likely to have strong opinions.

Other storybooks may contain visual elements so crucial to the story's development that you might want to invite children to look closely at an illustration and talk about what they see. In Dan Santat's *After the Fall* (Santat, 2017), only visual information explains Humpty Dumpty's transformation at the end of the story. This is a perfect place to invite children's careful inspection of illustrations.

Concept books and informational books offer different opportunities for participation. In *What Do You Do with a Tail Like This?* (Jenkins & Page, 2003), the author uses a game-like format to engage readers. Pairs of pages are organized in such a way that the first page presents images of a targeted body part (e.g., nose, ears, eyes) belonging to different animals. These images are accompanied by a related question: "What do you do with a nose like this?" The question can be used as an invitation for readers to first guess the animals to which the body part belongs. The following page then reveals complete images of the featured animals and accompanying text explaining how the animal uses the targeted body part; however, before the teacher reads this text, children can share their own ideas about how the animal might use their nose (or ears or eyes).

Inviting Responses and Posing Questions

After reading the book aloud, there are many options for evoking children's responses and thus deepening their experience of the book. What you choose to do will determine the ways in which children extend their learning, so determining the purpose of the after-reading experience is the first decision to make. (See chapter 5 for ideas on different response opportunities.)

Following almost all readings, you will likely engage with the children in some question asking and discussion. Questions and discussion topics help teachers shape the ways in which children think about and beyond the book; therefore, you should first consider, "What do I want the children to think about in relation to this read aloud?" Your answer to that question will guide you in formulating what is important to have the children talk about.

It's easy to think of questions to ask after reading a book—sometimes *very* easy, and thus a teacher ends up with *too many* questions. Keep in mind, however, that if we want to encourage children's thinking, "known answer" questions won't do the job. We need to use purposeful questioning, questions that serve to "push" and guide children's thinking. Such questions help children accomplish learning goals in the following areas:

- Literary understanding: thinking about how character, setting, plot, and theme are revealed and developed throughout the book
- Socioemotional understanding: how elements of the book help children consider different emotions, social situations, interactions, and relationships
- Content understanding: learning information connected to subject areas like science and social studies
- Visual understanding: learning how to understand pictorially and graphically presented information

We offer sample questions related to these goals for *Bear Has a Story to Tell* (Stead, 2012). Stead's book is the story of Bear, who wants to share a story with his friends, but each friend is too busy preparing for winter to stop and listen. So instead, Bear helps each friend with winter preparations before he himself finally hibernates. When the friends gather in the spring, Bear has forgotten his story. Now his friends extend their hands to help Bear remember the forgotten story. A teacher might pose such questions as the following for *Bear Has a Story to Tell*:

- I think Bear is very kind. What are some things he does that show just how kind he is? (literary understanding/character)
- In this illustration, when Bear forgets his story, all his friends stand up. Why do you think they do this? (socioemotional understanding)
- What are the different ways that the animals spend their winters? (content understanding)

- How does the illustrator show us that the seasons of the year are changing from fall to winter to spring? (visual understanding)

Teachers often develop questions according to question taxonomies or hierarchies. The following is a simple one that can prove useful:

- Literal: Focus on details or important ideas directly stated in the text.
- Interpretive: Focus on what was meant by the text but was not directly stated.
- Critical/creative: Focus on the child's responses to or ideas about the meanings of the text.

The following are sample questions of each type for *Bear Has a Story to Tell*:

- Why does Duck tell Bear that he cannot listen to the story? (literal)
- When Bear first invites each friend to listen to his story, why do none of the friends want to listen? (interpretive)
- What important things about friendship can we learn from this story? (critical/creative)

There are two especially important things that a hierarchy like this helps us keep in mind:

- Literal details in a text matter, but the questions asked should focus only on details that are crucial for children to get the big ideas in the book.
- The hierarchy helps us remember that children need to go back to the book's text and/or visuals to find supports for their answers. This is especially important in the case of critical/creative questions that are typically thought of as higher-order thinking. Too often these questions can be answered without returning to the book at all. Ask higher-level thinking questions that stem from children's understanding of the book, not merely from their overall background knowledge.

Another way to deepen children's understanding of a book is discussion or questions that get them to connect the book to their own lives; connect the book to other texts; and connect the book to the world in general, their communities, states, or nations.

Here are examples of each of these types of questions:

- In what ways are you a good friend like Bear? (connection to children's own lives)
- How are the friends in this book like the friends in *A Sick Day for Amos McGee*? (connection to other texts)
- The animals all had special things they did to get ready for the winter. How do the people in our town get ready for the winter? (connection to the world)

Having your children discuss these kinds of connections makes both informational books and stories take on added significance, thus building in the children both deep comprehension and a deeper affinity for what books and reading can do for them.

Gauging the Success of the Read Aloud

Accomplished teachers continually monitor children's uptake and understandings throughout each day's activities. The read-aloud time is no exception. Researchers have found that it is not uncommon for younger children to become confused about what is happening in a book, what information the book is conveying, or what is depicted in an illustration from the book. This is an important issue because, as observations from classrooms have also shown, if teachers don't respond appropriately to what children say during read alouds, children may persist in their misunderstanding or misinterpretation (Paciga et al., 2009).

This is an important and challenging issue for teachers of young children to consider when planning a successful read aloud. Why? We think there are a few interrelated reasons. One is that teachers care deeply about their young children and want to be encouraging, so when a child makes a comment about the book's language or illustration that seems to be off the wall or wrong, it is common for a teacher to simply pass over what the child said and be happy that the child finally contributed by saying something. In other words, teachers sometimes think that to be supportive of children's efforts and strive for developmentally appropriate instruction, they shouldn't correct children's contributions during discussions like those that occur during read alouds. Another reason is that read alouds are most frequently done with the whole group, and it is difficult to monitor and be able to respond to every child's response. Finally, some teachers believe that any response from a young child should be acceptable, no matter how divergent from the book, because a main goal of the read-aloud activity is engagement.

We sympathize with the dilemma about what to do in these situations. Although there is no definitive research-based or "correct" way to handle these situations, there are several things that observations of classroom practice indicate are important for you as the teacher to think about and strategies that do and don't help.

First, different factors can lead to a child's misconception. Consider the following:

- Text language, text information
- Illustration features (e.g., details of the illustration, illustration design)
- Child's background knowledge and experiences

For example, on the two-page spread of *Don't Let the Pigeon Drive the Bus!* (Willems, 2003) where the pigeon has its meltdown ("LET ME DRIVE THE BUS!!!"), there are five different illustrations of a pigeon. Some children think the book is showing five different pigeons rather than one pigeon performing five different actions while screaming the words. A text factor that can easily lead to misconception may be a specific vocabulary word: *King Bidgood's in the Bathtub* (Wood, 1985) contains, "'Help! Help!' cried the Page." You'll likely need to help children understand what *page* means in this context. And sometimes children's misconceptions result from some combination of the above three factors.

What are some strategies to address children's misconceptions when they arise during a read aloud?

- Provide information: It's usually more complicated than this, but sometimes children just need to know what a word or phrase means, have an idea that is presented in the language of the book restated in words they understand, or even have the teacher gesture an action of a character that helps them understand a character's feelings.
- Reread and relook while drawing attention to relevant information: "Let me read those two pages again while you look at the illustration closely. What was it that the alligator said? What did she mean by that?"
- Model reasoning: Try to understand the child's point of view, and then model thinking that can help clarify the misconception. "I see what you are thinking. But notice that. . . . So, when I see what the girl has in her hand, I figure that she. . . . Let's read on a little bit more and see if it becomes clear."

And one thing that definitely *won't* be helpful: correct the child with no explanation.

Something to keep in mind: It's not that children can't use inferencing (higher-level thinking) strategies. Rather, their inferencing problems usually result from accessing inappropriate information or not having the necessary background information to reach the conclusion that is in line with what the book is actually saying or implying.

So, in addition to paying attention so that you help children clear up any misconceptions that occur during the read aloud, what are signs that it went well? One thing to consider is attention. Were almost all the children engaged throughout most of the book? How do you gauge that while you are reading the book?

- Notice where the children's eyes are—on the book or on you is what you hope to see.
- Did you have a minimum of nonbook-related language during the session (i.e., having to spend time settling children or handling a disruption)?
- Did children's spontaneous responses and answers to your questions indicate that they were following the story or understanding the information in the book?
- Did the children ask questions that displayed genuine curiosity? Good books often stimulate questions (e.g., I wonder what . . . ? Why did . . . ? Do you think that . . . ?).

The Teacher, the Assistant, and the Read Aloud

Finally, when it comes to the "how" of reading aloud in the classroom, it is important to consider the roles of the adults in the room during the read aloud. If your classroom is one in which both a teacher and an assistant teacher/instructional aide are present, then we see both adults playing important roles in the read aloud. In some classrooms, the teacher and the assistant each take responsibility for preparing and conducting the read aloud on different days. In other classrooms, only the teacher reads and discusses the book with the children, but the assistant performs the important role of sitting with the children and keeping the child or two who is easily distracted focused and on task, modeling for the children ways of responding to the reading, or otherwise facilitating the read-aloud experience of the children. In any case, it is important for the two of you to discuss who will do what because it is crucial for both adults to be present and involved in this important instructional activity.

To conclude, we want to reiterate that preparation for a read aloud may be the most important step to ensure that children are engaged during an actual read aloud. A particularly important part of preparation is looking closely at the book because the book can tell you what to do. In the compendium at the end of this book, we include our own recommendations for sharing each annotated book with children—ideas that emerged through this process of looking closely at the possibilities offered by each book.

▪ REFERENCES

Paciga, K. A., Lisy, J. G., & Teale, W. H. (2009). Examining Student Engagement in Preschool Read Alouds. In K. Leander, D. W. Rowe, D. K. Dickinson, M. Hundley, R. T. Jimenez, & V. J. Risko (Eds.), *58th Yearbook of the National Reading Conference* (pp. 330–47). National Reading Conference.

Reading to Kids. (2002, March 19). *The Picture Walk*. http://readingtokids.org/ReadingClubs/TipPictureWalk.php.

▪ RECOMMENDED CHILDREN'S BOOKS

Archer, Micha. *Daniel's Good Day*. New York: Penguin, 2019.

Beaumont, Karen. *I Ain't Gonna Paint No More*. Illustrated by David Catrow. New York: Houghton Mifflin Harcourt, 2005.

Campbell, Rod. *Dear Zoo*. New York: Little Simon, 1986.

Delacre, Lulu. *¡Olinguito, de la A a la Z!/Olinguito, from A to Z!* New York: Children's Book Press, 2016.

Dewdney, Anna. *Llama, Llama Misses Mama*. New York: Viking, 2009.

Dewdney, Anna. *Llama, Llama, Red Pajama*. New York: Scholastic, 2005.

Fleming, Candace. *Oh, No!* Illustrated by Eric Rohmann. New York: Schwartz and Wade, 2012.

Hoffman, Eric. *A Dark, Dark Cave*. Illustrated by Corey Tabor. New York: Viking, 2016.

Jenkins, Steve, & Robin Page. *What Do You Do with a Tail Like This?* New York: Houghton Mifflin Harcourt, 2003.

Kasza, Keiko. *Wolf's Chicken Stew*. New York: Putnam, 1987.

Lin, Grace. *A Big Mooncake for Little Star*. New York: Little, Brown, 2018.

Maillard, Kevin Noble. *Fry Bread: A Native American Family Story*. Illustrated by Juana Martinez-Neal. New York: Roaring Brook, 2019.

Mora, Oge. *Saturday*. New York: Little, Brown, 2019.

Morales, Yuyi. *Niño Wrestles the World*. New York: Square Fish, 2015.

Page, Robin. *Seeds Move!* New York: Beach Lane, 2019.

Park, Linda Sue. *Bee-bim Bop!* Illustrated by Ho Baek Lee. New York: Clarion, 2005.

Pinkney, Jerry. *The Three Billy Goats Gruff*. New York: Little, Brown, 2017.

Pizzoli, Greg. *Good Night Owl*. New York: Little, Brown, 2016.

Portis, Antoinette. *Hey, Water!* New York: Holiday House, 2019.

Santat, Dan. *After the Fall: How Humpty Dumpty Got Back Up Again*. New York: Roaring Brook, 2017.

Stead, Philip C. *Bear Has a Story to Tell*. Illustrated by Erin E. Stead. New York: Roaring Brook, 2012.

Stead, Philip C. *A Sick Day for Amos McGee*. Illustrated by Erin E. Stead. New York: Roaring Brook, 2010.

Willems, Mo. *Don't Let the Pigeon Drive the Bus!* New York: Hyperion, 2003.

Wood, Audrey. *King Bidgood's in the Bathtub*. Illustrated by Don Wood. New York: Houghton Mifflin Harcourt, 1985.

Woodson, Jacqueline. *The Day You Begin*. Illustrated by Rafael López. New York: Nancy Paulsen, 2018.

CHAPTER 5

Extending the Story Experience for Children

When the teacher reads the right book with enthusiasm and invites children to participate actively, read alouds are lively events. But keep in mind that the read-aloud experience does not end when the final page of the book is read. For readers young and old alike, engagement with a book often continues after the book is closed—and with the best books, sometimes long after. Rick DeTorie, the cartoonist who draws the *One Big Happy* comic strip, captured this phenomenon when he portrayed little Ruthie jumping out of bed, running into her mother's bedroom in the middle of the night, and announcing a solution to Hansel and Gretel's problem: they should have taken a cell phone with them into the forest! Like Ruthie, children often linger in the spell of stories, ideas, and information long after encountering them in a read aloud.

There are different ways to extend the read-aloud experience and promote children's continued engagement with books. One way is simply by rereading the book. Another is ensuring the books are available for children's independent use following read alouds. Finally, teachers can extend children's engagement with stories by involving them in different kinds of response activities that include talk, art, and drama.

▥ REPEATED READINGS

Young children love to return to books they have enjoyed—as evidenced by their frequent pleas to "read it again!" The rhythm and rhyme of *Brown Bear, Brown Bear, What Do You See?* (Martin, 1967) prompted one two-year-old to request twenty-five rereadings of the book in a single sitting! Another parent called the school and asked that a different book be sent home—she just couldn't read *Pete the Cat* (Dean, 2010) anymore.

Teachers (and parents) sometimes express frustration when children clamor to listen to the same book over and over, but researchers have looked closely at what happens during repeated readings at home and in the school. They have found that, on a first reading, children often appear to work mainly on understanding the story, as evidenced by the questions they ask. On subsequent readings, children typically begin to share their own observations and thinking. They also frequently shift to talking about parts of the story not previously discussed. They even share more complex thinking about books when the books are reread (Martinez & Roser, 1985; Morrow, 1988).

For some stories, the complexity of the visual storytelling is such that a full appreciation of the illustrations might not be possible on a first reading. For example, in *A Beasty Story* (Martin, 1999), illustrator Steven Kellogg integrates into the cover illustration, the endpapers, and the title page subtle clues about how the story will unfold, but it is not until a second reading that a child is likely to attend to (and appreciate) this foreshadowing. For older students, *The Mitten* (Brett, 1989) is an example of a picturebook with complex visual storytelling. In this book, Brett presents three story strands simultaneously through the use of borders surrounding the central illustration. A repeated reading is the ideal way to understand the complex visual crafting.

Repeated readings can also be a vehicle to heighten awareness of language usage. On a first reading of books like *The Uncorker of Ocean Bottles* (Cuevas, 2016), students are likely to focus largely on finding out what happens to the Uncorker, a lonely man who delivers messages to others but never receives any of his own. On a second reading, teachers can invite students to listen for the poetic language Cuevas infuses throughout the book, such as "loneliness as sharp as fish scales" and "a quill dipped in sadness."

■ CLASSROOM BOOK CENTER

Teachers can also set up the classroom environment to encourage children to return to books on their own. Every classroom should have its own book center—an inviting space where children can find an array of books to read (or pretend to read if they are not yet reading). But a word of warning: all classroom book centers are *not* created equal. In some classrooms children rarely visit the center, while in other classrooms it is one of the most popular spots—it's all about intentionally designed space.

Frequently visited book centers are likely to share a number of features. They are often partitioned off from the rest of the class, provide enough space to accommodate four or five children, and offer comfortable places to sit and read. These design features are important because they make the classroom library a special place all its own and encourage children to interact with each other.

One kindergarten teacher created such a space using PVC pipe as the framework for a "house." The roof and walls (which were low enough for the teacher to monitor what was happening inside) were made of bedsheets attached to the framework. Beanbags inside the house provided comfortable seating. The children in this classroom loved their cozy book center, and the physical design, which allowed for several children to visit the center at once, encouraged interaction around books.

Another teacher used beaded curtains to create a magical effect without having to give up visibility into the space. Keep in mind that young children's reading in the book area is usually anything but a silent activity. They share with each other and even pretend read to others. Such interactions should be encouraged.

Design features are important, but books are the real secret to the center's success. The main purpose of the center is to encourage children to interact with books independent of the teacher. That has implications for which books to include, how many books, and the way in which they are displayed and organized.

The types of books included in the classroom book center should mirror the recommendations in chapter 3 for read alouds. While you will want a variety of genres in the center, the majority of what is available for young children are stories. So these may form the backbone of the collection, but it is also important to include informational books and poetry. It is particularly important to include a range of diverse books that can serve as mirrors and windows for the children in your classroom (McNair, 2016).

We have frequently observed children sharing the discoveries they make as they peruse the pages of informational books such as *Seeds Move!* (Page, 2019). The bridge into informational books for many young children is the concept book, and they love opportunities to interact with this kind of book also. For example, children can explore colors and the names of train cars in a concept book like *Freight Train* (Crews, 1978).

Books that contain rhymes, songs, and wordplay are also ones that children like to read emergently, especially in collaboration with a classmate or two. For example, think of *There Was an Old Lady Who Swallowed a Fly* (Taback, 1997).

Finally, be sure to include predictable books to encourage younger children's independent engagement. Researchers have found that children are far more likely to engage in emergent reading with highly predictable books like *Ten Little Fingers and Ten Little Toes* (Fox, 2018) (Martinez & Teale, 1988).

And, of course, in first and second grade, it is critical to include books children can read independently. Books that appear on the Geisel Award list are good choices. This award is presented annually by the American Library Association to the writers and illustrators of the most distinguished American books for beginning readers. Titles like *Stop! Bot!* (Yang, 2019), winner of the 2020 Geisel Award, have minimal text, accessible language, supportive illustrations, and oftentimes humor to hook young readers.

When young children have available both unfamiliar books (ones never read to them) and familiar ones, they choose the familiar books—hands down. So you will want to include at least some familiar books in the center. Books you have read repeatedly are likely to be popular, especially with children who are not yet reading conventionally.

The way in which children actually use a book in the book center is at least partly dependent on how familiar they are with it. Emergent readings contribute to children's literacy development in important ways. So we certainly want to encourage children who are not yet reading on their own to pretend read books in the book center, and they are more likely to pretend read books that have already been read to them.

It's important to remember that children do not always read when they visit the book center. Sometimes they sit and quietly look through the pages of a book. Such sustained attention to books is something to be encouraged, and children are especially likely to linger over stories they love and informational books with intriguing pictures.

Yet another consideration in stocking the book center is how many books to include. There is no right number. Children need choices, but you don't want to present younger children with an overwhelming number of choices. You also want to make sure that they can find quality books; so these books should not be buried under a large number of mediocre books. With five-to-eight-year-olds, you will probably want at least three to four books per child; however, if you work with younger children, include fewer books so they are not overwhelmed with the number of choices. It's also important to rotate new titles through the book center on a regular basis throughout the year to keep the center fresh and interesting for the children.

Not only do you want the book center to be stocked with the right types of books; you will want to display the books in ways that draw children into the center. So be sure to display the covers of quality books that feature wonderful artwork. The lively images and bright colors will likely pull children into the center.

Finally, good book centers contain a variety of literature-related materials. Book posters can be hooks that pull children in. You can often get such posters from booksellers just by asking. Stuffed animals can add appeal to a center. Young children will frequently choose to read to the stuffed animals when they visit the center. Also, many characters from children's books are produced as puppets or stuffed animals.

■ TALKING ABOUT BOOKS

Talk is one way that children express their thinking about books, and with younger children, much of their talk occurs *during* the actual reading of the book or immediately thereafter. In chapter 4 we discussed strategies to evoke children's best thinking during the read aloud. In this section we focus on how you can encourage talk—and thus thinking—about books beyond that time.

While watching his mischievous brother play, we overheard a four-year-old comment, "He's just like Curious George!" For this child, the book was serving as a lens for thinking about the world—in this case for better understanding human behavior.

We can encourage children to use literature in this way by inviting them to apply familiar stories to think about new situations. For example, if children identify issues in their own immediate school world that they deem unfair, they could be reminded of what the rooster in *The Rooster Who Would Not Be Quiet!* (Deedy, 2017) did when he encountered injustice—he spoke out! The book could then become the impetus for thinking about the importance of speaking out to bring about change in children's own world.

Perhaps the best way to promote this kind of thinking is by modeling it. For example, when preparing for an upcoming trip to the zoo, a teacher might announce, "I am going to make a list of the things we need for our trip—just like Duck did in *Duck, Duck, Porcupine!*" (Yoon, 2016). Teachers can also encourage children to draw on books to solve problems, as one teacher did when a student became frustrated because there were no plates in the dramatic play center. The teacher reminded the child about *Not a Stick* (Portis, 2008), a story the class had read the previous day, in which a little pig turns a simple stick into a fishing pole, a drum major's baton, a paintbrush, and so forth. Soon the frustrated child was looking for a creative solution to her own problem.

▪ ART

Children create meaning in their lives through their artwork, and they also discover meaning in the art created by others. Epstein and Trimis (2002) have described art as a way of thinking about the world. Just as their art helps children think about the real world, we believe it can also help them think about *book worlds*; therefore, we want to create many opportunities to extend children's experiences with books through art.

Like language and motor skills, children's artistic abilities are developmental in nature. Older children can readily respond to literature through art. That is, they can express their thinking and feelings related to books through drawings, paintings, or various artistic constructions; however, art may not be as appropriate an avenue of response for younger preschoolers.

Children are able to respond to books through art only when they have developed the ability to think about something not present and to express it artistically. Furthermore, children must understand that their drawings (or scribbles) can be representational—that is, they can represent a person, object, or scene. Only then do invitations to respond to literature through art become meaningful.

Children typically produce their first representational drawings between the ages of two and three. If you work with very young children, you will want to carefully observe them in the art center to gauge whether they are developmentally ready to respond to literature through art. A child who points to a scribble she has created and says "That's a kitty" may also be ready to respond to an invitation to express her thinking about a story through art.

Both teacher-initiated responses and children's spontaneous responses are valuable—and connected. When you invite students to respond to literature through art, they will come to view art as a valued avenue for expressing their thinking. Soon they will be drawing in response to stories without any invitation at all.

Teacher invitations to respond to stories through art can range from open-ended invitations to more focused ones. An open-ended invitation to respond to *Just a Minute* (Morales, 2003) would be asking children to create their own picture about something that happened in the story. A focused invitation to *Daniel Finds a Poem* (Archer, 2016) might encourage children to create a picture of what they believe to be the most beautiful part of the poem that Daniel found on his visit to the park. Photography can also serve as a form of artistic response. After listening to *Don't Let the Pigeon Drive the Bus!* (Willems, 2003), children can take turns mimicking the facial expressions of the pigeon as his tantrum escalates while another child takes digital photographs.

You can also invite your students to express more personal responses to literature. For example, after reading *Carmela Full of Wishes* (de la Peña, 2018), children can draw a picture of something they would wish for on their birthday. Or in response to *Love* (de la Peña, 2018), they might draw a picture of something in their own lives that makes them feel love. The sharing of such artwork often leads to thoughtful talk about a story.

The kinds of response invitations we have talked about so far focus on the content of books, but children can also be encouraged to experiment with the artistic techniques used by the illustrators. When you share a picturebook with your students, talk with them about how the illustrator created his or her artwork—especially if the illustrator used a medium like collage with which your students could experiment.

Many picturebook illustrators work in watercolors, which are found in most art centers. Parts of *The Squiggle* (Schaefer, 1996) are done in colored chalk; children can try their hand with this medium on the sidewalk. Like Eric Carle, children can create tissue-paper collages, or they can construct the kind of three-dimensional collages created by Melissa Sweet in *Balloons over Broadway: The True Story of the Puppeteer of Macy's Parade* (Sweet, 2011). Or, after reading and talking about the artwork in *Knuffle Bunny: A Cautionary Tale* (Willems, 2004), children can experiment with mixed media, combining digital photographs with painting or drawing.

Several of the books mentioned above include digital photographs, and we'd like to take a minute to think about all the possibilities that such a medium offers for children. Many children regularly use cell phones or tablets to take photos at home, and even those who haven't had such experiences quickly learn how to take and manipulate digital images. We think that the opportunities for photography to extend read alouds in the classroom are limitless; so think about them as potentially being part of everything from digital language experience stories, to a way of capturing story dramatizations (see below) that can then be sent home in a newsletter, to class-constructed alphabet books. And if you really want to go digital, have your children prepare short (one- to two-minute) book talks (think *Reading Rainbow*) and video them to share with other classrooms in the school or with parents via the school YouTube channel.

In addition to using different kinds of media, children can also explore artistic techniques used by illustrators. For example, after the children see how Denise Fleming fills the pages of *In the Small, Small Pond* (D. Fleming, 1993) with bright colors, you can invite them to do the same in their own artwork. Or, like the illustrator of *Bear Has a Story to Tell* (Stead, 2012), your students can convey a sense of calm in their drawings by filling their work with greens and blues—colors associated with peacefulness.

When teachers regularly extend invitations to draw or paint in response to stories, children are increasingly likely to spontaneously choose to express their thoughts and feelings about stories through art. So provide a variety of accessible art materials for children to use—crayons, colored pencils, water-based markers, watercolors, chalk. Make interesting materials available for the children to use, especially after sharing books by illustrators like Melissa Sweet, who creates collages using a wide range of items. Include paper in varied colors and sizes in the center as well as papers with interesting designs and textures, such as wrapping paper, foil, and sandpaper. Children may even enjoy working with materials like fabric scraps, yarn, toothpicks, buttons, feathers, popsicle sticks, and string. Introducing new materials into the center from time to time encourages children to choose art as a medium for expressing their responses to literature.

▨ DRAMA

Not too long ago, we visited a kindergarten playground where we overheard a child invite her friends, "Let's do the billy goats!" Soon the children were vying for roles—most wanting to be the scary troll. Once parts were negotiated—with the promise of taking turns being the troll—the children moved to the play structure that offered a bridge that would serve as the setting for their story dramatization. One by one, the billy goats made their way across the bridge, using their wits or their brawn to outsmart the troll. The drama was enacted repeatedly so everyone could hide beneath the bridge and menace the goats passing overhead.

Because of its power to engage, drama is an ideal way to extend story experiences. After all, young children learn through play, and drama *is* play. As children reenact the parts of different characters in stories, they become those characters for a short while; they wear their boots and look at the world through their eyes. Dramatic experiences help children better understand the stories you share.

Such experiences can be spontaneous, as occurred in the playground episode of "The Billy Goats Gruff," or they can be teacher initiated. One teacher we know is masterful at incorporating impromptu dramatic activities in the midst of story-book reading. This is what happened one day as she read *Where the Wild Things Are* (Sendak, 1963) to her students. After reading the line "they roared their terrible roars and gnashed their terrible teeth and rolled their terrible eyes and showed their terrible claws," the teacher paused in her reading and invited the children to act out this scene. Soon all the children were standing to better roar their roars and show their claws and gnash their teeth. What better way, in the midst of a storybook reading, to ensure that the children understood the meaning of some demanding vocabulary?

Dramatic story experiences that occur during a read aloud can also be a means of fully engaging children at dramatic junctures of stories. For example, in *Oh, No!* (C. Fleming, 2012) Tiger chases animal after animal into a deep, deep hole. When the animals are finally rescued by Elephant, Tiger is the one who falls into that deep, deep hole. As the animals look down on Tiger, he wails, "Please, please, won't you help me out?" This is the perfect point to invite the children to become the other animals and take turns responding to Tiger's plea for help.

While mini-dramatizations can occur during a read aloud, children can also engage in dramatic activities following the reading. These after-reading dramatizations may involve acting out a scene from a story or even the complete story; however, dramatizations with younger children may be far less structured. For example, we recently watched a teacher read the concept book *Who Hops?* (Davis, 1998) to a group of three-year-olds. The pages of this book are a series of depictions of different animals that hop, fly, glide, swim, and crawl; it concludes by asking, what creature can do all these things? After discussing with the children that they could engage in all these actions—except for flying, that is—the teacher noted that children could *pretend* to fly, and that is exactly what they did—all the way to their music class.

Also keep in mind the power of suggestion—simple props or three-dimensional objects can remind children of a book and thereby prompt them in their informal dramatizations. For example, a red hat in the drama center might signal children to act out *I Want My Hat Back* (Klassen, 2011), and a purple plastic purse in the dress-up center could inspire children to become characters in *Lily's Purple Plastic Purse* (Henkes, 1996).

Story Theater

Dramatic play is typically informal, but there is also value in more structured, teacher-guided reenactments of scenes or entire stories. Story theater is one form of teacher-guided dramatization. In story theater, children mime a story or scenes from the story while the teacher narrates what is happening. Because story theater relies on miming rather than the creation of dialogue, it can be used with younger children as well as older ones. For the very young, you might choose to use nursery rhymes like "Los Pollitos," "Hey Diddle Diddle," or "Teddy Bear, Teddy Bear." Stories that invite the listener to join in the actions with story characters are also perfect for use with very young children. *Clap Your Hands* (Cauley, 1992) invites such participation: "Clap your hands,/stomp your feet./Shake your arms,/then take a seat." In a similar fashion, Eric Carle's *From Head to Toe* (Carle, 1997) is set up as dialogue between children and animals:

> I am a penguin and I turn my head. Can you do it?
>
> I can do it! (replies a child)
>
> I am a giraffe and I bend my neck. Can you do it?
>
> I can do it! (replies a child)

Young children will delight in making each move the animals make.

Story theater activities for older children can be built around longer, more complex books. Still, you will want to choose a story that offers action, relatively few characters, and minimal dialogue. A favorite of ours is *Caps for Sale* (Slobodkina, 1947). Each child can have a role in this story. One can play the peddler while the other children can become the monkeys who steal the caps and imitate the antics of the frustrated peddler. Children will beg to reenact the story again and again.

Creative Dramatics

Creative dramatics is another form of drama that you can use with children. In creative dramatics, children act out the book (or a scene) and also create dialogue for the characters. This is more challenging than story theater because children must remember the story events (instead of having the teacher narrate those events as occurs in story theater), and they must also create appropriate dialogue for characters. For these reasons, this is a form of drama that may not work particularly well with very young children.

For a successful creative dramatics activity, keep things simple. Remember, the reenactment is not being done for an audience. Rather, the goal is to have children spontaneously improvise the story, so there is no script to follow, no dialogue to memorize, and no need to practice. If props or costumes are used, they should be simple, but probably there is no need for them at all.

It *is* important, however, to carefully structure and support the activity. For example, rather than trying to have the children act out an entire story, focus on reenacting a single scene. One excellent way you can support the children is by becoming one of the characters in the scene. For example, in acting out the scene in "Goldilocks and the Three Bears" in which the three bears return home, you might play the part of the papa bear. This places you in the perfect position to feed the children dialogue that will help move the action along. You might also coach from the sidelines, prompting children with dialogue suggestions (e.g., "What do you think Baby Bear said when he found his broken chair?") or ideas about how to move the action along (e.g., "Should the three bears look in the bedroom after finding that broken chair in the living room?").

Stories that work best for creative dramatics reenactments are ones with strong action and numerous opportunities for dialogue. Folktales like "The Little Red Hen" and "The Three Little Pigs" work well. So do humorous stories like *I Want My Hat Back* (Klassen, 2011) and *Petunia* (Duvoisin, 1950).

Flannel Boards

Another way to extend children's engagement in stories is by setting up a flannel board story center in your classroom or putting the flannel board and props in the book center. Use large plastic storage bags, each of which contains a book and the flannel figures and objects needed to reenact the book. The best kind of stories for flannel board retellings are those with a clear sequence of events or characters, such as "The Gingerbread Man" or *The Napping House* (Wood, 1984). Once the children have watched you reenact a book using the flannel board, they will be lining up to try on their own.

Puppets

Young children also enjoy acting out stories using puppets. You can motivate children simply by modeling the use of puppets to enact stories. Although a wide variety of hand and finger puppets are available commercially, it is also easy to make puppets from paper plates, sticks, tongue depressors, cups, or other items. A formal puppet stage would be great for a puppet presentation, but a table with a sheet draped over it functions quite nicely as a platform for a puppet show. The kinds of stories that work well in creative dramatics also work well as puppet presentations.

▪ CONNECTING WITH THE FAMILY

So far our suggestions for extending children's experiences with stories have focused on the classroom, but you can also encourage children to share their story experiences with their families. Teachers can design craft activities based on stories that have been shared in school. By craft activities we mean activities in which the teacher provides precut pieces for children to assemble following teacher directions.

For example, after reading *The Very Hungry Caterpillar* (Carle, 1969), a kindergarten teacher might provide cut-out caterpillar segments for children to assemble and glue together. Activities like this do not promote the kind of thinking about literature that you are likely to see emerge from children's spontaneously generated artwork or teacher-initiated art activities; however, teacher-supplied concrete objects that are based on stories can serve to connect school and home, especially if children take the objects home with a note to parents: "Ask me about the caterpillar story we read at school."

You can also establish connections with families by sending a book home and inviting family members to read the story with their child. The book can be accompanied by a comments notebook for recording observations about the story. Family members can serve as the scribe, writing responses in the notebook. They can also encourage their children to add their own art responses or written responses. In launching a home read-aloud program, be sure to announce the program with fanfare, telling parents about its value and explaining how the program will be organized and what their role will be.

If you would like more detailed (but readable) discussions of some of these topics, see the list of resources at the end of this chapter.

▪ REFERENCES

Epstein, A., & Trimis, E. (2002). *Supporting Young Artists: The Development of the Visual Arts in Young Children*. Ypsilanti, MI: High Scope Press.

Martinez, M., & Teale, W. H. (1988). Reading in a Kindergarten Library Center. *Reading Teacher, 41*(6), 568–72.

Martinez, M. G., & Roser, N. (1985). Read It Again: The Value of Repeated Readings during Storytime. *Reading Teacher, 38*(8), 782–86.

McNair, J. C. (2016). #WeNeedMirrorsAndWindows: Diverse Classroom Libraries for K–6 Students. *Reading Teacher, 70*(3), 375–81. https://doi.org/10.1002/trtr.1516

Morrow, L. M. (1988). Young Children's Responses to One-to-One Story Readings in School Settings. *Reading Research Quarterly, 23*(1), 89–107.

▪ RECOMMENDED CHILDREN'S BOOKS

Archer, Micha. *Daniel Finds a Poem*. New York: Nancy Paulsen/Penguin, 2016.

Brett, Jan. *The Mitten*. New York: Putnam, 1989.

Carle, Eric. *From Head to Toe*. New York: HarperCollins, 1997.

Carle, Eric. *The Very Hungry Caterpillar*. Illustrated by Eric Carle. New York: Putnam, 1969.

Cauley, Lorinda Bryan. *Clap Your Hands*. New York: Putnam, 1992.

Crews, Donald. *Freight Train*. New York: Greenwillow, 1978.

Cuevas, Michelle. *The Uncorker of Ocean Bottles*. Illustrated by Erin Stead. New York: Dial, 2016.

Davis, Katie. *Who Hops?* San Diego: Harcourt Brace, 1998.

de la Peña, Matt. *Carmela Full of Wishes*. Illustrated by Christian Robinson. New York: Putnam, 2018.

de la Peña, Matt. *Love*. Illustrated by Loren Long. New York: Putnam, 2018.

Dean, James. *Pete the Cat: I Love My White Shoes*. Illustrated by Eric Litwin. New York: HarperCollins, 2010.

Deedy, Carmen Agra. *The Rooster Who Would Not Be Quiet!* Illustrated by Eugene Yelchin. New York: Scholastic, 2017.

Duvoisin, Roger. *Petunia*. New York: Knopf, 1950.

Fleming, Candace. *Oh, No!* Illustrated by Eric Rohmann. New York: Schwartz and Wade, 2012.

Fleming, Denise. *In the Small, Small Pond*. New York: Macmillan/Square Fish, 1993.

Fox, Mem. *Ten Little Fingers and Ten Little Toes*. Illustrated by Helen Oxenbury. New York: Houghton Mifflin Harcourt, 2018.

Henkes, Kevin. *Lilly's Purple Plastic Purse*. New York: Greenwillow, 1996.

Klassen, Jon. *I Want My Hat Back*. Somerville, MA: Candlewick, 2011.

Martin, Bill, Jr. *A Beasty Story*. Illustrated by Steven Kellogg. San Diego: Harcourt Brace, 1999.

Martin, Bill, Jr. *Brown Bear, Brown Bear, What Do You See?* Illustrated by Eric Carle. New York: Holt, 1967.

Morales, Yuyi. *Just a Minute: A Trickster Tale and Counting Book*. New York: Chronicle, 2003.

Page, Robin. *Seeds Move!* New York: Simon and Schuster, 2019.

Portis, Antoinette. *Not a Stick*. New York: HarperCollins, 2008.

Schaefer, Carole Lexa. *The Squiggle*. Illustrated by Pierr Morgan. New York: Crown, 1996.

Sendak, Maurice. *Where the Wild Things Are*. New York: HarperCollins, 1963.

Slobodkina, Esphyr. *Caps for Sale: A Tale of a Peddler, Some Monkeys and Their Monkey Business*. New York: HarperCollins, 1947.

Stead, Philip C. *Bear Has a Story to Tell*. Illustrated by Erin E. Stead. New York: Roaring Brook, 2012.

Sweet, Melissa. *Balloons over Broadway: The True Story of the Puppeteer of Macy's Parade*. Boston: Houghton Mifflin, 2011.

Taback, Simms. *There Was an Old Lady Who Swallowed a Fly*. New York: Viking, 1997.

Willems, Mo. *Don't Let the Pigeon Drive the Bus!* New York: Hyperion, 2003.

Willems, Mo. *Knuffle Bunny: A Cautionary Tale*. New York: Hyperion, 2004.

Wood, Audrey. *The Napping House*. Illustrated by Don Wood. San Diego: Harcourt, Brace Jovanovich, 1984.

Yang, James. *Stop! Bot!* New York: Viking, 2019.

Yoon, Salina. *Duck, Duck, Porcupine!* New York: Bloomsbury, 2016.

▪ RESOURCES

For an easy-to-read discussion of how preschoolers' responses to literature change as stories are read repeatedly, see the following:

Martinez, M. G., & Roser, N. (1985). Read It Again: The Value of Repeated Readings during Storytime. *Reading Teacher, 38*(8), 782–86.

You can find more detailed information about setting up your classroom book center in the following:

Martinez, M. G., Yokota, J., & Temple, C. (2017). *Thinking and Learning through Children's Literature*. Lanham, MD: Rowman & Littlefield.

If you would like to read more about how to engage young children in different forms of drama, we encourage you to read the following chapter:

Roser, N. L., Martinez, M., & Moore Carrell, H. (2013). Re-invite Drama into Classrooms: New Ways with an Old Form. In K. D. Wood, J. Paratore, B. Kissel, & R. McCormack (Eds.), *What's New in Teaching Literacy?* (pp. 1–9). Newark, DE: International Reading Association. doi:10.1598/e-ssentials.8043.

Picturebook Compendium

1 Big Salad: A Delicious Counting Book
Written and illustrated by Juana Medina
Viking, 2016
Ages: 3–6
Summary: This whimsical counting book offers children the opportunity to count radish mice, carrot horses, tomato turtles, and a host of other fruit and vegetable animals from one to ten. A simple recipe for a healthy salad appears at the end of the book.
Illustrations: Each number is illustrated with animals made (in part) with a real vegetable or fruit. For example, the number ten is illustrated by ten clementine kitties. The body core of each kitty consists of a section of a clementine orange. The tail, head, and legs of the kitty are created with simple black line drawings.

Reprinted with permission

Sharing *This* Book with Children:

- Show the children the cover of the book, and ask them to talk about what they see. Ask what seems to be different about this salad.
- As you turn each page, invite the children to identify the animal they see in the illustration before you read the name of the critter.
- Also, once it becomes apparent that each page features animals made with a particular vegetable or fruit, invite the children to try to identify the vegetable or fruit before you read the text.
- On each page invite the children to count the number of critters as you point to each one.
- The children are not likely to be familiar with each of the featured fruits and vegetables. So after reading the book, share the actual fruits and vegetables with the children, giving them the opportunity to try to identify each one.
- Then make a salad with the children!

Content Connections/Skills Connections: Counting, nutrition: fruits and vegetables, animals, cooking

Insider Tips: Drawing on her own experiences growing up in Columbia, Juana Medina has written two early (and humorous) chapter books with extensive illustrations. These are great books for introducing chapter book read alouds to young children.

Other Books by the Same Author/Illustrator:

- *Juana and Lucas*
- *Juana and Lucas: Big Problems*
- *Lena's Shoes Are Nervous: A First-Day-of-School Dilemma* by Keith Calabrese, illustrated by Juana Medina
- *I'm a Baked Potato* by Elise Primavera, illustrated by Juana Medina

A, My Name Is Alice
Written by Jane E. Bayer and illustrated by Steven Kellogg
Dial, 1984
Ages: 4–6

Reprinted with permission

Summary: This alphabet book is based on a playground game the author played as a child. Each letter is presented on a single-page spread using the following pattern:

- XX (featured letter) my name is XX (name beginning with featured letter) and my husband's name is XX (name beginning with featured letter). We come from XX (place beginning with featured letter) and we sell XX (object beginning with featured letter).

For the letter A, this is the text: "A my name is Alice and my husband's name is Alex. We come from Alaska and we sell ants." The text appears at the top of each page, and the featured letter appears in large, colored type.

Illustrations: Characters named in the text are represented as animals in the illustrations. Some of the animals will be unfamiliar to children (e.g., condor, emu); however, the text directly beneath the featured animal names the animal (e.g., "Alice is an APE." "Alex is an ANTEATER."). The featured item that the animals sell is also shown in the illustration.

Sharing *This* Book with Children:

- Before reading each page, point to the large featured letter and ask the children if they can identify the letter. If no one is able to do so, identify the letter for the children.
- On each page, after reading the patterned text, ask the children to look at the illustration and identify the type of animal the named characters are (e.g., Alice is an ape, and Alex is an anteater). If the children are unable to identify the animals, read the text that names both animals. You can also ask the children to try to identify the item that the featured animals sell.

- On subsequent readings of the book, the children may want to use the featured text pattern to make up their own alliterative sentences.

Content Connections/Skills Connections: Animals, alphabet, phonemic awareness
Insider Tips: At the end of the book, there is an author's note about playground games including the one on which the book is based. On the final page, there are also some facts about the less familiar animals featured in the book.
Related Book:

- *Alligator Arrived with Apple: A Potluck Alphabet Feast* by Crescent Dragon-wagon, illustrated by Jose Aruego and Ariane Dewey

Actual Size
Written and illustrated by Steve Jenkins
Houghton Mifflin Harcourt, 2004
Ages: 4–8

Reprinted with permission

Summary: Each page of this nonfiction picturebook features an illustration of either an animal in its entirety or part of an animal. Whether part or whole, whatever is shown is the *actual size*. For example, on one double-page spread, readers see the hand (and only the hand) of a gorilla, while a tiny pygmy mouse lemur appears in its entirety. On another page the giant walking stick stretches across the entire double-page spread. The author includes an interesting piece of information about each animal as well as information about its size. More detailed information about each animal is included in the final pages of the book.
Illustrations: The illustrations are collages, Steve Jenkins's signature medium.

Sharing *This* Book with Children:

- In introducing the title of the book, be sure the children understand the word *actual*.
- As you move through the book, give the children the opportunity to try to identify each animal before you read the text.
- The children can take turns placing their hands on the illustrations of the different animals to get a better idea of the actual size of each one.
- Depending on the age of the children, you may want to include some of the additional information about each animal that is found at the end of the book.
- After reading, bring out the measuring tape. Jenkins includes information about the size of each animal. For example, while the reader only sees the head of the Alaskan brown bear, Jenkins tells the reader that the creature is thirteen feet high. This is the perfect opportunity to measure the distance of thirteen feet to help the children envision the size of this creature.
- Be sure to place the book in the book center after reading.

Content Connections/Skills Connections: Animals, mathematics: measurement

Insider Tip: Jenkins's *Prehistoric Actual Size* is structured much like *Actual Size*.
Related Books:

- *Prehistoric Actual Size* by Steve Jenkins
- *Looking Down* by Steve Jenkins

After the Fall: How Humpty Dumpty Got Back Up Again
Written and illustrated by Dan Santat
Roaring Brook, 2017
Ages: 5–8

Reprinted with permission

Summary: This is the story of what happened to Humpty Dumpty after falling from the wall—his new fear of heights and the way he overcame that fear.

Illustrations: The visual text plays a critical role in story development. The illustration on the dust jacket gives clues to *why* Humpty Dumpty was on the wall. The cover illustration reveals the actual fall, while early illustrations in the story (rather than the words) reveal how the fall changed Humpty Dumpty. The final illustrations are critical to understanding the conclusion of the story. Throughout the book readers will see Santat's masterful shifting of perspective.

Sharing *This* Book with Children:

- Begin story time by sharing the nursery rhyme "Humpty Dumpty." On a second reading, invite the children to join you in reciting (or reading) the rhyme.
- Explain that you are going to read a story in which Humpty Dumpty *was* put back together again. Ask the children to predict how a fall from a wall might have changed Humpty Dumpty.
- In introducing the book, tell the children that it will be particularly important to look closely at all the illustrations. Show them the dust jacket, and read the title of the book. Ask them what clues they can find that reveal *why* Humpty Dumpty was sitting on a wall.
- Remove the dust jacket, and show the children the cover of the book.
- After reading the text "There were some parts that couldn't be healed with bandages and glue," ask the children to look closely to see if they can tell what couldn't be healed.
- As you move through the book, be sure to talk about the changing perspectives in the illustrations, and let the children speculate about why the illustrator makes these shifts.
- After reading the page "Hopefully, you'll remember me as the egg who got back up," invite the children to share what they notice in the illustration.
- On the following double-page spread, which contains no words, again pause and ask the children to talk about what is happening.
- After reading the story, invite the children to talk or write about times when they were afraid and how they overcame their fears.

Content Connections/Skills Connections: Emotions: overcoming fear, nursery rhymes

Insider Tip: Dan Santat received the Caldecott Medal for *The Adventures of Beekle*.

Awards and Recognition: NCTE Charlotte Huck Award Winner, Kirkus Best Picturebook, New York City Public Library Notable Best Book for Kids, Horn Book Fanfare Best Book

Related Books:

- *The Thing Lou Couldn't Do* by Ashley Spires
- *Humpty Dumpty* by Salina Yoon

Alexander and the Wind-Up Mouse
Written and illustrated by Leo Lionni
Dragonfly Books, 1974
Ages: 5–7

Reprinted with permission

Summary: Tired of being chased by humans, Alexander—a real mouse—wanted to be a wind-up mouse like his friend Willy who was loved by all the children. Then Alexander has the chance to make a wish—if he can bring a purple pebble to the magic lizard. Just as Alexander finds the sought-after pebble, he discovers that Willy has been thrown out with the other discarded toys. How will Alexander use his wish?

Illustrations: Rather than extending the written text, the illustrations in this book show key scenes described in the written text.

Sharing *This* Book with Children:

- Introduce the book by reading the title and showing the children the cover illustration. Ask the children how the two mice are different. Be sure that the children understand what a wind-up mouse is. If possible, bring in a wind-up toy to demonstrate.
- Character motivation and feelings and character relationships are particularly important in this book. You may want to stop at the following points to talk with the children:
  - ○ Stopping point: When Alexander tells Willy that the people do not like him, Willy explains he can only move when wound up but that all the people love him.
  - ○ Invitation: Ask the children to talk about which mouse they would want to be and why.
  - ○ Stopping point: When Willy tells Alexander about the magic lizard, Alexander asks if the lizard can change him into a wind-up mouse.
  - ○ Invitation: Why does Alexander want to become a wind-up mouse?
  - ○ Stopping point: Read the part of the text in which the magic lizard asks Alexander, "Who or what do you wish to be?"
  - ○ Invitation: What do you think Alexander is going to wish for? Why?

- ◦ Stopping point: Alexander discovers the empty box.
- ◦ Invitation: Why does Alexander feel sad?
- ◦ Stopping point: At the end of the story, Alexander and Willy dance until dawn.
- ◦ Invitation: Why do the two friends dance until dawn?

Content Connections/Skills Connections: Friendship, being yourself
Insider Tip: Leo Lionni used collage, his signature medium, in creating the illustrations.
Awards and Recognition: Caldecott Honor book
Related Book:

- *Beautiful Blackbird* by Ashley Bryan

Other Books by the Same Author:

- *Swimmy*
- *Tico and the Golden Wings*
- *Frederick*
- *Cornelius*

And Then It's Spring
Written by Julie Fogliano and illustrated by Erin E. Stead
Roaring Brook, 2012
Ages: 4–6
Summary: A little boy and his dog busily plant their garden—and then wait for spring to arrive.
Illustrations: The picture/text relationships are of particular note. The text is actually a poem—one that makes no mention of the little boy and his dog (or other animals). Nor does the poet mention all the things the boy does as he prepares his garden. This means that the illustrations convey a great deal of information that is critical to the story's development.

Reprinted with permission

Sharing *This* Book with Children:

- Because the illustrations contain so much important story information, be sure the children have time to carefully inspect each illustration before you turn the page.
- Before reading, ask the children to talk about their experiences planting gardens.
- As you move through the book, read the text on each page and then invite the children to talk about what they see happening in the illustrations.
- After reading the next-to-last page ("and then you walk outside to check on all that brown"), invite the children to predict what the boy will see.
- If it is early spring, plant a garden with the children (or seeds in indoor containers).

Content Connections/Skills Connections: Seasons, gardens
Insider Tips: *And Then It's Spring* has been translated into Spanish. Erin E. Stead won the Caldecott Medal for *A Sick Day for Amos McGee*.
Related Books:

- *Spring Is Here* by Will Hillenbrand
- *When Spring Comes* by Kevin Henkes

Anna Banana: 100 Jump-Rope Rhymes
Written by Joanna Cole and illustrated by Alan Tiegreen
Scholastic, 1989
Ages: 4 and up
Summary: This is a collection of jump-rope rhymes, both short and long.
Illustrations: The rhymes are accompanied by humorous line drawings.

Sharing *This* Book with Children:

- As is true of nursery rhyme collections, this is not a book to share with children in one sitting. Rather, it is important to become familiar with all the rhymes in order to select the right one for the right occasion.
- Rhymes are meant to be revisited many times. When returning to the book, ask the children to choose favorites for you to read. They can then join in reciting familiar rhymes.
- On repeated readings of rhymes, invite the children to clap to the beat of the rhyme or to listen for and identify rhyming words.

Content Connection/Skills Connection: Phonemic awareness: rhyming
Insider Tip: Jump-rope rhymes can be enjoyed as rhymes if jumping rope is not practical.
Related Books:

- *Miss Mary Mack and Other Children's Street Rhymes* by Joanna Cole
- *Lucy Cousins Treasury of Nursery Rhymes* by Lucy Cousins

Another
Created by Christian Robinson
Atheneum, 2019
Ages: 5–8

Reprinted with permission

Summary: This wordless book is visually complex and very imaginative. A little girl is sleeping with her cat when a portal opens in her bedroom wall. When a seemingly identical cat (differentiated only by the color of its collar) enters and steals the cat's stuffed mouse, the cat and girl follow the thief and find themselves in another world (or is it another dimension?).
Illustrations: The illustrations demand even more attention than in most wordless books. As the little girl and her cat move through the portal and into the other world, readers must rotate

the book more than once. And because so many elements of the other world mirror those in the little girl's world, attention to the color of the smallest details is required. Given the visual complexity of this book, the best way to prepare for a read aloud is by carefully inspecting the details in every illustration and making decisions ahead of time regarding when to rotate the book.

Sharing *This* Book with Children:

- Begin by showing the children the dust jacket, the book cover, and the endpapers. Then read the title and ask the children what the word *another* might refer to: Another what?
- As with any wordless book, move slowly through the book, giving the children ample time to talk about what they see and their interpretations of the illustrations.
- In the middle of the book are three double-page spreads filled with children of different ethnicities and from different races and cultures, all engaged in fun activities. Give the children the chance to talk about why they would like to join in this other world.
- Be sure to make this book available in the book center.

Content Connection/Skills Connection: Imagination

Insider Tip: Robinson's Instagram includes innovative art lessons and has eighty-six thousand followers.

Awards and Recognition: New York Times Best Children's Book, NYPL Best Book, Publishers Weekly Best Book

Related Book:

- *Sam and Dave Dig a Hole* by Mac Barnett

Balloons over Broadway: The True Story of the Puppeteer of Macy's Parade
Written and illustrated by Melissa Sweet
Houghton Mifflin, 2011
Ages: 5–8

Reprinted with permission

Summary: This is the biography of Tony Sarg, the man who created the puppets for the first Macy's Thanksgiving Day Parade. While the book largely focuses on Sarg's adult work with marionettes and puppets, it begins with his childhood and the inventions he loved to make.

Illustrations: Sweet's lively illustrations are done in her signature mixed-media style.

Sharing *This* Book with Children:

- Ask the students who has seen a parade and what they especially enjoyed about it.

- Ask who has seen the Macy's Thanksgiving Day Parade on television. Let students who have seen it talk about what makes this parade special. You can also introduce this famous parade: https://www.youtube.com/watch?v=LEwJ0l1_GUY.
- After reading, ask the children to identify some problems Tony Sarg encountered in creating puppets for the parade and how he solved them.
- Give the students time to talk about what they liked about Sweet's mixed-media creations. Then invite the children to create designs for puppets they would like to see in the Macy's Thanksgiving Day Parade. Encourage them to use mixed media for their creations.

Content Connections/Skills Connections: Celebrations, problem-solving
Insider Tip: Children can view a video of the 1931 Macy's Thanksgiving Day Parade: https://www.youtube.com/watch?v=AhLYjhmu2_s&feature=youtu.be.
Awards and Recognition: Sibert Award, Caldecott Honor book
Related Books:

- *Carmine: A Little More Red* by Melissa Sweet
- *How to Read a Book* by Kwame Alexander and illustrated by Melissa Sweet

Bear Came Along
Written by Richard T. Morris and illustrated by LeUyen Pham
Little, Brown, 2019
Ages: 4–8
Summary: One by one, animals living solitary lives along the river are caught up in a great adventure as the river sweeps them along—an adventure that culminates in creating community.
Illustrations: This oversized book is perfect for conveying the story of an oversized adventure. The design of the endpapers is of particular note. The front endpapers are painted in subdued colors. While all characters

Reprinted with permission

appear in the illustration, most are hidden, and only careful inspection will reveal them. The back endpapers present the same setting, but this time the scene appears in bright colors and the animals are clearly evident. Shifting perspectives are also of note.

Sharing *This* Book with Children:

- After showing the cover of the book and reading the title, turn to the front endpapers and invite the children to talk about what they see.
- Each time a page ends with "until," invite predictions.
- After reading, ask, "Do you think the animals would take this wild ride again? Why?"

- Show the final endpapers, and let the children compare them to the front endpapers. Ask why the illustrator chose to make the endpapers different.

Content Connection/Skills Connection: Community
Insider Tips: The illustrator describes the story as a "perfect metaphor for life." This description suggests the importance of talking with students about the theme of this book. Also, the illustrator created the book *Outside, Inside*, reflecting on essential workers, community, and people's kindnesses during the COVID-19 pandemic.
Related Book:

- *The Mitten* by Jan Brett

Bear Has a Story to Tell
Written by Philip C. Stead and illustrated by Erin E. Stead
Roaring Brook, 2012
Ages: 4–7
Summary: Winter is approaching, and Bear is getting sleepy, but he has a story he wants to tell. However, Bear's friends are too busy preparing for winter to listen, so instead Bear helps his friends with their preparations. When Bear awakens in the spring, ready to tell his friends the story, he has forgotten it! This time Bear's friends come to his aid.

Reprinted with permission

Illustrations: The illustrations convey important information about character. In particular, Bear's gentle nature is revealed through the illustrations. The illustrations also reveal changes in the seasons that are important to the story's development.

Sharing *This* Book with Children:

- Even though this story is a fantasy, the various animals do things that real animals do in the winter. Before reading, tell the children that many animals take steps to avoid very cold weather in the winter. In particular, explain to the children that bears spend the winter sleeping in their dens. Then, as you move through the story and new animals are introduced, encourage the children to talk about how the animals are preparing to spend the winter.
- Character is a particularly important element of this story. Stop at the following points in the story to talk about various facets of characterization:
  - After Bear helps Duck check the direction of the wind, ask the children what they know about Bear so far.
  - When you reach the illustration of Bear looking up at the falling snowflakes, invite the children to talk about how Bear might be feeling.
  - As each friend awakens in the spring, talk with the children about how Bear is again helping his friends.
  - When Bear forgets his story, it is time for his friends to help him. Talk with the children about how this problem is resolved in the story.

- Because this is a story about friendship, encourage the children to talk about ways in which they have tried to help their friends. Invite the children to do one special thing for someone this day. Then, at the end of the day, the children can share what they did.

Content Connections/Skills Connections: Friendship, seasons

Insider Tip: This book is available in Spanish with the title *Oso Quiere Contar una Historia.*

Related Books:

- *A Home for Bird* by Philip C. Stead, illustrated by Erin E. Stead
- *A Sick Day for Amos McGee* by Philip C. Stead, illustrated by Erin E. Stead

A Beasty Story
Written by Bill Martin Jr. and illustrated by Steven Kellogg
Harcourt Brace, 1999
Ages: 3–6

Reprinted with permission

Summary: Four little mice enter a dark, dark house, where they encounter a beast—a beast that floats through the air to an even darker house. Is this a dangerous threat, or is it a trick?

Illustrations: The book is oversized, a design element that is perfect for a "beasty" story. The cover, front endpapers, and title page offer important clues suggesting that the beast might actually be a trick. The text of the story is placed at the top of the double-page spreads, and speech bubbles are included on each page.

Sharing *This* Book with Children:

On a first read aloud:

- Even though the cover, front endpapers, and title page offer clues that the beast might be a trick, these same elements also offer clues that the story will be a scary one. Reading from the scary perspective is more fun for a first read, so when introducing the book, do not deliberately focus attention on the "trick" clues.
- After showing the cover and reading the title, invite predictions.
- On the copyright page, read the signs aloud as well as the speech bubbles. The clues on this page are designed to build suspense, so read the text using a suspenseful voice.
- Once you begin to read the actual story for the first time, read *only* the text at the top of the page. (On subsequent readings, you can read the speech bubbles.)
- Pause for predictions after reading the following text: "There is something inside the dark green bottle."
- Pause again for predictions after reading the following text: "Through the dark, dark wood, toward an even darker house."
- Pause again after reading "Into a dark orange room, where a white beast rises."

- After the first read aloud of the story, invite the children to closely inspect the cover, front endpapers, and title page to look for the clues the illustrator included in these story components that suggest a trick was being played.

On subsequent read alouds:

- On a second read aloud, the children will likely want to join in reading the repetitive text.
- On this read aloud, read the speech bubbles to the children. Much of the speech bubble commentary focuses on the colors the little mice are noticing.
- In each illustration, Mouse #1 is carrying a pad of paper and a pencil. In some illustrations the mouse is writing. Ask the children what Mouse #1 seems to be writing on the paper. In the illustrations where Mouse #1 is not writing, ask the children to think about why he might have stopped writing.
- On a re-reading of the story, direct the children's attention to the main text line and the color words that are actually printed in the corresponding color (e.g., the word *red* is printed with red ink). On a piece of chart paper, write all the color words from the story (red, blue, purple, green) using matching colored markers.
- After re-reading the story, give the children colored markers and pads of paper, and invite them to investigate the classroom to record the colors of different objects they find in the room. Tell the children they can use the class chart if they want help spelling the color words.

Content Connections/Skills Connections: Color, writing
Insider Tip: The repetitive text adds to the suspenseful nature of the story.
Related Books:

- *A Dark, Dark Cave* by Eric Hoffman
- *We're Going on a Bear Hunt* by Michael Rosen

Bedtime for Frances
Written by Russell Hoban and illustrated by Garth Williams
HarperCollins, 1960
Ages: 4–5
Summary: It is bedtime, and Frances, a little badger, cannot go to sleep. Everywhere she looks, Frances sees scary things in her bedroom.
Illustrations: Spot illustrations sprinkled throughout focus on character development rather than on action or setting. Expressive illustrations reveal Frances's emotions.

Sharing *This* Book with Children:

- After reading the title of the story, invite the children to talk about their bed-time routines.
- After reading the page about the giant, ask the children what the giant might be.
- When Frances first sees the crack in the ceiling, pause and ask the children why the crack might be a problem for Frances.

- After the first mention of the curtains blowing, ask the children why this might be scary.
- When finished, review all the problems that Frances encountered as she tried to go to sleep and the ways in which her parents helped to solve each problem.

Content Connections/Skills Connections: Bedtime, fears, comprehension: problem/solution

Insider Tip: Russell Hoban wrote a series of books about Frances the badger.

Related Books:

- *Can't You Sleep, Little Bear?* by Martin Waddell
- *Llama Llama Red Pajama* by Anna Dewdney

Bee-bim Bop!
Written by Linda Sue Park and illustrated by Ho Baek Lee
Clarion, 2005
Ages: 4–6

Reprinted with permission

Summary: A young girl helps prepare a Korean meal, called bee-bim bop, for her family. The book explains the whole process of making the meal, from going to the grocery store to preparing the meal to how it is served.

Illustrations: Realistic pictures show how the meal and even a rice cooker might look.

Sharing *This* Book with Children:

- The children can be invited to talk about cultural foods that are served in their house.
- Encourage the children to chime in while reading predictable text in the book "hungry, hungry, hungry for some BEE-BIM BOP."
- Talk about the different utensils used: chopsticks, rice cooker, bowls, spoons.
- In repeated readings of the book, provide the children with opportunities to practice phonological awareness (i.e., rhyming and wordplay).

Content Connections/Skills Connections: Culture, food, phonemic awareness: rhyming

Insider Tip: A recipe for bee-bim bop is included at the back of the book; it might be too difficult to do as a cooking activity with the children in class, but if appropriate, give copies of the recipe to the children so they can try it at home with their family.

Related Books:

- *A Big Mooncake for Little Star* by Grace Lin
- *Sip, Slurp, Soup, Soup/Caldo, Caldo, Caldo* by Diane Gonzales Bertrand

Big Friends
Written by Linda Sarah and illustrated by Benji Davies
Henry Holt, 2016
Ages: 3–6

Reprinted with permission

Summary: Birt and Etho are big friends. They play outside in large cardboard boxes, being kings, astronauts, and other things. One day Shu, a new boy, arrives, finds a "big enough box," and gets the courage to ask if he can join them. The three begin to play together, but Birt "feels strange" and eventually stops playing with them. Shu and Etho devise a unique box solution to get the three of them together as friends.

Illustrations: The gouache illustrations will be easily understood by the children and express the emotions of delight in companionship as well as the loneliness of being apart.

Sharing *This* Book with Children:

- Though it is easy to overlook, this book is an international book first written, illustrated, and published outside the United States, in the United Kingdom. Pointing this out to the children will help them begin to understand how some books are read by children in many countries.
- The height of action in this book is the two-page spread on which Shu asks Birt to come out because "we made you something." A good time to stop and ask for predictions is after reading "But it's much, much more than a box" on the right-hand page.

Content Connections/Skills Connections: Collaboration, friendship
Related Books:

- *My Friends* by Taro Gomi
- *My Friend Rabbit* by Eric Rohmann

A Big Mooncake for Little Star
Written and illustrated by Grace Lin
Little, Brown, 2018
Ages: 3–7

Reprinted with permission

Summary: After making a mooncake with her mother, Little Star is told not to eat any of the mooncake (placed in the sky) until her mother gives her permission. But night after night, Little Star creeps out of bed to have a snack from the mooncake. Soon the mooncake is gone!

Illustrations: On the endpapers the reader sees Little Star and her mother making a huge mooncake. The first sentence of the story says, "Little Star's mama laid the Big Mooncake onto the night sky to cool." However, it isn't evident from the illustrations that the mooncake is the moon in the sky. This becomes apparent only on the ninth spread, where the moon appears in the upper left-hand corner of the page and Little Star in the lower right-hand corner. The thirteenth spread shows the different phases of the moon as Little Star continues to nibble away night after night.

Sharing *This* Book with Children:

- After reading the title, turn to the front endpapers and encourage the children to talk about what they see. Ask the children what they like to cook with their family members.
- After reading the first page of the story, invite the children to predict what might happen.
- After reading the ninth double-page spread (the moon in the upper left-hand corner of the page and Little Star in the lower right-hand corner), invite the children to talk about how this illustration seems different from the earlier ones.
- On the thirteenth double-page spread (showing the different phases of the moon), invite the children to talk about what seems to be happening in this illustration.
- The story can be used to launch a lesson on the phases of the moon.

Content Connections/Skills Connections: Asian culture, moon

Insider Tips: On the back dust jacket, the author/illustrator writes about her favorite Asian holiday, the Mid-Autumn Moon Festival, when people eat mooncakes and tell stories about the moon. Asian children often hear stories about the "moon rabbit" rather than the "man in the moon." The rabbit is seen in the moon, pounding rice cakes using a mortar and pestle.

Awards and Recognition: Boston Globe Best Book, Caldecott Honor book

Related Books:

- *Kitten's First Full Moon* by Kevin Henkes
- *Moon: A Peek-Through Picturebook* by Britta Teckentrup

Boats

Written and illustrated by Byron Barton

HarperCollins, 1986

Ages: 3–5

Summary: This board book presents different types of boats and identifies the work they do.

Illustrations: As is typical of his style, in this book Barton uses bold colors and outlines objects with thick black lines. He uses simple geometric shapes to create the featured boats.

Sharing *This* Book with Children:

- Present the cover of the book to the children, and ask who has been on a boat. The children can talk about their experiences on boats.
- As you read through the book, encourage the children to act out being on the different types of boats. For example, the children can pretend to row the rowboat. They can be the firefighters on the fireboat and use hoses to put out a fire.

- After reading, stock the art center with colorful geometric shapes that the children can glue to paper to make their own boats. These can be displayed in the classroom.

Content Connection/Skills Connection: Transportation: boats
Insider Tips: Byron Barton is well known for the many books he has written about different types of machines and modes of transportation. Many of his books are available as board books.
Related Books:

- *My Bus* by Byron Barton
- *My Car* by Byron Barton
- *Planes* by Byron Barton
- *Trains* by Byron Barton
- *Trucks* by Byron Barton
- *Boats Go* by Steve Light

Brown Bear, Brown Bear, What Do You See?
Written by Bill Martin Jr. and illustrated by Eric Carle
Henry Holt, 1967
Ages: 3–6
Summary: In this highly patterned, rhyming book, each page turn features a new animal described by its color.
Illustrations: Each of Eric Carle's signature tissue-paper collages features a brightly colored animal that fills a double-page spread.

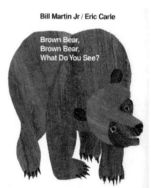

Bill Martin Jr / Eric Carle

Brown Bear, Brown Bear, What Do You See?

Reprinted with permission

Sharing *This* Book with Children:

- Children will ask you to read this book over and over. On these repeated readings, children can each take the part of a different animal and answer the question posed for that animal.
- Revisit the book with younger children, but instead of reading the text, ask the children to identify the animals and their colors.
- Because the book is so rhythmic, you can use it to help older children develop phonemic awareness. On repeated readings, encourage the children to join you in clapping along with the text—one clap for each syllable.
- Children can make their own collages using colored tissue paper.

Content Connections/Skills Connections: Colors, phonemic awareness
Insider Tips: The book is also available as a board book. This was the first book Eric Carle illustrated for children.
Related Books:

- *Panda Bear, Panda Bear, What Do You See?* by Bill Martin Jr., illustrated by Eric Carle

- *Polar Bear, Polar Bear, What Do You Hear?* by Bill Martin Jr., illustrated by Eric Carle

Bulldozer's Big Day
Written by Candace Fleming and illustrated by Eric Rohmann
Atheneum, 2015
Ages: 3–5

Reprinted with permission

Summary: Bulldozer can hardly wait to invite his friends from the construction site to his birthday party. But all the work machines have no time for Bulldozer; they are too busy scooping, sifting, stirring, and mashing. Bulldozer becomes more and more downcast—until his friends surprise him with the gigantic cake they have been constructing.

Illustrations: The illustrations are block prints that feature bold black lines and primary colors.

Sharing *This* Book with Children:

- On the first reading of the story, focus mainly on the story problem (no one seems to remember that it's Bulldozer's birthday), Bulldozer's reactions, and the resolution.
- Introduce the story by showing the cover of the book and reading the title. Ask the children what might happen on Bulldozer's big day.
- After reading the first page, invite the children to predict once again.
- As Bulldozer moves from friend to friend, each one keeps working. Invite the children to talk about how Bulldozer feels when this happens.
- After reading the page in which the construction whistle blows, invite predictions.
- After finishing the story, invite the children to share memories of their birthday parties.
- Following the reading of the story, go back through the book, showing the children the illustrations of the different machines. Ask the children to identify each one and talk about the kind of work each does. The children can pretend to be each machine and act out the identified action.
- To extend children's experience with the book, make it available in the book center along with as many toy work machines as possible so children can reenact the story.

Content Connections/Skills Connections: Birthdays, construction, machines

Insider Tips: The story is filled with wonderful verbs that describe the actions of the machines. Illustrator Eric Rohmann was awarded the Caldecott Medal for *My Friend Rabbit.*

Related Books:

- *Bulldozer Helps Out* by Candace Fleming
- *Goodnight, Goodnight, Construction Site* by Sherri Duskey Rinker

Bully
Written and illustrated by Laura Vaccaro Seeger
Roaring Brook, 2013
Ages: 4–7
Summary: After being bullied, a young bull *becomes* a bully.
Illustrations: The cover of the book is a bold red. This same bold red is used on the title page for the title of the book. The story actually begins with illustrations that appear before the title page, and

Reprinted with permission

the illustrations in the book play a critical role in telling the story. In particular, the changes in the size of the bull tell the reader how the bull is changing and how he is feeling. Changes in the size of the print in the speech bubbles also convey important story information.

Sharing *This* Book with Children:

- Show the cover of the book and read the title. Then ask the children what a bully is.
- Invite the children to predict what might happen in the story.
- Stop after reading the double-page spread that appears before the title page, and ask the children how the little bull feels when the big bull says, "Go away." Be sure and ask the children what they see in the illustration that supports their responses.
- On the first double-page spread after the title page, the rabbit asks the little bull if he wants to play. On the following page, the bull says "NO!" Invite the children to think about why the bull responded in this way.
- As you move through the story, encourage the children to talk about how the bull is feeling. Ask the children what they see in the illustration that supports their responses.
- Toward the end of the story, we see the bull (who is now huge) beginning to grow smaller and smaller. Invite the children to talk about *why* this is happening.
- After reading the book, show the children the cover of the book once again. Invite the children to speculate why such a bold red was used for the cover of the book. Share the old saying "seeing red" with the children, explaining that it means feeling very angry.
- After reading the story, talk with the children about the things they can do to help if they see someone being bullied or if they are being bullied.

Content Connections/Skills Connections: Bullying, peer relationships
Insider Tips: Bullying is a serious problem in our society. The National Association for the Education of Young Children offers resources for teachers related to bullying. You can find this information at http://www.naeyc.org/search/apachesolr_multisitesearch/bullying.

Related Books:

- *Llama and the Bully Goat* by Anna Dewdney
- *Stick and Stone* by Beth Ferry, illustrated by Tom Lichtenheld

Caps for Sale: A Tale of a Peddler, Some Monkeys and Their Monkey Business
Written and illustrated by Esphyr Slobodkina
HarperCollins, 1947
Ages: 3–6
Summary: Awakening from his nap, a peddler discovers that the caps he was carrying on top of his head have mysteriously disappeared.
Illustrations: The straightforward illustrations and story line correspond well.

Sharing *This* Book with Children:

- Before reading, show the children pictures of isolated pioneer homes and talk about the role of peddlers in earlier times when people often had limited access to stores.
- After reading the story, talk with the children about the meaning of the old saying "monkey see, monkey do." The children can take turns being the leader who engages in actions (such as pretending to brush teeth) that the "monkeys" (the other children in the class) can imitate.
- The peddler carried gray, brown, blue, and red caps on his head. Young children can count the number of caps of each color that the peddler carried.
- Once introduced, this story begs to be acted out. Invite the children to take the part of the peddler and the monkeys and act out the story as you reread the text. The children can supply some of the dialogue of the peddler ("Caps! Caps for sale. Fifty cents a cap.") and the monkeys ("Tsz, tsz, tsz."). Children will enjoy using real caps when acting out this story.

Insider Tip: First published in 1938, *Caps for Sale* is a book that has passed the test of time. Slodobkina illustrated many books written by children's author Margaret Wise Brown.
Content Connections/Skills Connections: Dramatization, counting
Related Books:

- *Circus Caps for Sale* by Esphyr Slobodkina
- *More Caps for Sale* by Esphyr Slobodkina

Carmela Full of Wishes
Written by Matt de la Peña and illustrated by
Christian Robinson
Putnam, 2018
Ages: 5–8

Reprinted with permission

Summary: It is Carmela's birthday, and she is finally old enough to go with her brother to the neighborhood laundromat. When she picks a dandelion on the way to the laundromat, her brother tells her she can make a wish before blowing away the dandelion's fuzz. Finding the right wish becomes Carmela's goal.

Illustrations: Robinson's acrylic paintings capture the richness of a Latino community.

Sharing *This* Book with Children:

- Ask the children to talk about birthday wishes and what they would wish for.
- Show the children the cover of the book and read the title. Ask them what Carmela seems to be doing on the cover illustration. This will provide an opportunity to see if the children are familiar with the tradition of making wishes before blowing on dandelions.
- After reading, ask the children to talk about Carmela's relationship with her brother: Why doesn't her brother want Carmela to run errands with him? How does Carmela respond? At what point does the relationship between Carmela and her brother change?
- Review all the things that Carmela considered wishing for. Invite the children to talk about what they believe Carmela actually wished for at the end of the story.
- The author mentions that Carmela thought about her dad getting his papers fixed so he could come back home. While the book is not primarily about immigration issues, this mention provides an excellent opening to talk with children about an important issue in our society—families separated due to immigration regulations.

Content Connections/Skills Connections: Birthdays, sibling relationships, wishes
Insider Tips: There is also a Spanish version of this book. *Last Stop on Market Street* by Matt de la Peña was awarded the Newbery Award and was also named a Caldecott Honor book.
Related Books:

- *Last Stop on Market Street* by Matt de la Peña
- *My Rotten Redheaded Older Brother* by Patricia Polacco

Carry Me! Animal Babies on the Move
Written and illustrated by Susan Stockdale
Peachtree, 2005
Ages: 3–6
Summary: This simple informational book features a wide range of ways in which baby animals from around the world are carried.

Reprinted with permission

Illustrations: Each double-spread features a different animal, and the simplicity of the acrylic paintings makes it easy for children to focus on the baby animal being carried by its mother.

Sharing *This* Book with Children:

- As you turn each page, ask the children to look closely to find the baby animal. Then ask them if they can identify the featured animal.
- Before reading the accompanying text, ask the children to describe how the animal mother is carrying the baby animal.
- After reading the book, review each double-page spread and the strong verb featured on that page that is likely to stretch children's vocabulary—verbs like *cling* and *perch*. The illustrations offer rich clues to the meaning of the verbs. The children can take turns acting out these verbs.

Content Connection/Skills Connection: Animals
Insider Tip: Though the text on each page is simple, the book will be challenging because some of the featured animals will be unfamiliar to children. However, a two-page guide at the end of the book identifies each featured animal and tells more about it.
Related Books:

- *Babies on the Go* by Linda Ashman
- *Move!* by Robin Page and Steve Jenkins

Chicken Soup with Rice
Written and illustrated by Maurice Sendak
HarperCollins, 1962
Ages: 4–7
Summary: With verses organized by month, this book celebrates chicken soup with rice.
Illustrations: For each month, there is a pen-and-ink drawing with a bit of color.

Sharing *This* Book with Children:

- Before reading, ask the children to talk about their favorite foods, including soup.
- Point out to the children that each month of the year has a verse. After naming the featured month, ask the children to use the illustration clues to talk about the kind of weather the illustrator shows for that month.

- With its rhythm and rhyme, this book begs to be reread. On repeated readings, children will want to join in on the final four lines of the verse (e.g., Happy once/happy twice/happy chicken soup/with rice).
- If possible, make chicken soup with rice with the children.

Content Connections/Skills Connections: Food, months of the year, seasons
Insider Tip: This book was originally published as part of the Maurice Sendak's Nutshell Library, a four-volume boxed set of small books that children will enjoy: *Alligators All Around*, *Chicken Soup with Rice*, *One Was Johnny*, and *Pierre*.
Related Books:

- *¡Hola! Jalapeño* by Amy Wilson Sanger
- *Sip, Slurp, Soup, Soup/Caldo, Caldo, Caldo* by Diane Gonzales Bertrand

Chugga-Chugga Choo-Choo
Written by Kevin Lewis and illustrated by Daniel Kirk
Hyperion, 1999
Ages: 3–5
Summary: The text features the sounds, journeys, and work of a train.

Reprinted with permission

Illustrations: The illustrations feature the toys of a child with a particular focus on the toy train.

Sharing *This* Book with Children:

- As you read, invite the children to talk about what the illustrations reveal. For example, when the text reads, "Hurry! Hurry! Load the freight," the freight being loaded is toy blocks.
- The text is filled with onomatopoeia (e.g., "chugga-chugga choo-choo" and "Whoooooooooo! Whoooooooooo!"), and the children will enjoy joining in on these phrases.
- The children can re-create the story in the block center.

Content Connections/Skills Connections: Language play, transportation, trains
Related Books:

- *Freight Train* by Donald Crews
- *The Little Train* by Lois Lenski

Clap Your Hands
Written and illustrated by Lorinda Bryan Cauley
Putnam, 1992
Ages: 3–5
Summary: A zany cast of characters—animals and children—clap their hands, rub their tummies, and pat their heads. This rhyming book invites joyous movement.

Reprinted with permission

Illustrations: Animals and children demonstrate the actions named in the text.

Sharing *This* Book with Children:

- Practice reading aloud so you can effectively convey the rhythm and rhyme of the book.
- In sharing the book, first read it in its entirety to highlight the rhythm and rhyme.
- On subsequent readings, invite the children to join the characters in acting out the featured movements. This is a book the children will want to act out again and again.
- Reread and let the children identify the rhyming words on each double-page spread.
- Make the book available in the drama center so the children can do the actions on their own.

Content Connections/Skills Connections: Movement, phonemic awareness: rhyming
Insider Tip: This book is available as a board book.
Related Books:

- *Eyes, Nose, Fingers and Toes* by Judy Hindley
- *From Head to Toe* by Eric Carle

Clever Jack Takes the Cake
Written by Candace Fleming and illustrated by G. Brian Karas
Schwartz and Wade, 2010
Ages: 5–8
Summary: Jack has been invited to the princess's birthday party, but he has no money for a gift. Jack is clever though, so he decides to bake the princess a cake and decorate it with a strawberry on top. But as he makes his way to the castle, Jack encounters obstacle after obstacle and arrives at the castle with only the strawberry. But fortunately, Jack is clever . . .

Reprinted with permission

Illustrations: The front and back endpapers give clues about how the story will develop.

Sharing *This* Book with Children:

- Read the title and ask what the word *clever* means. Encourage the children to share examples of clever things they have done. Ask them to remember clever things Jack does in the story.
- The story has a problem/solution structure that provides multiple opportunities for children to make predictions. As problems emerge, encourage the children to predict how Jack might try to solve the problem.
- Be sure to stop at the end of the story for predictions about what Jack will say when the princess asks what present he has brought.
- After reading, remind the children of the title. Ask them what *clever* things Jack did.

Content Connections/Skills Connections: Comprehension: problem/solution, vocabulary

Insider Tip: This book has extensive text, and the illustrations are not critical to understanding the story. These features make the book a good candidate for promoting sustained listening (see chapter 3).

Related Books:

- *Borreguita and the Coyote* by Verna Aardema, illustrated by Petra Mathers
- *One Grain of Rice* by Demi

Color Zoo
Written and illustrated by Lois Ehlert
HarperCollins, 1989
Ages: 2 and up
Summary: A combination of shapes and colors reveals different zoo animals.
Illustrations: The book features a series of cut-outs stacked so that with each page turn a layer is removed to reveal a picture of a different animal.

Sharing *This* Book with Children:

- Before reading the book, talk about the different zoo animals that might be in the book.
- Talk about the colors and shapes used to make each animal.
- Talk about the characteristics of shapes (e.g., on the page with the square, triangle, and circle, ask how a circle is different from a triangle or from a square).
- Talk about similarities and differences with shapes (e.g., sides, no sides).

Insider Tips: *Color Farm* is the companion book made in the same format. Both books are available as sturdy board book versions as well as the original version.
Awards and Recognition: Caldecott Honor book, Hornbook Fanfare Honor List, ALA Notable Book
Content Connections/Skills Connections: Animals, colors, shapes
Related Books:

- *Oodles of Animals* by Lois Ehlert
- *Planting a Rainbow* by Lois Ehlert

Confetti: Poems for Children/Confeti: Poemas para Niños
Written by Pat Mora and illustrated by Enrique O. Sánchez
Spanish edition translated by Queta Fernández and Pat Mora
Lee and Low, 1996
Ages: 4–7
Summary: This collection of quiet poetry largely celebrates the everyday world that surrounds children—sun, wind, clouds, dance, a grandmother's lap.

Reprinted with permission

Illustrations: The illustrations are composed of images that are both concrete and abstract, and the composition of the illustrations conveys the sense of confetti.

Sharing *This* Book with Children:

- This isn't a book to read straight through. Rather, it's one to visit time and again.
- Be sure you become familiar with the poems so you can select the right one for the right day. For example, when there are clouds floating in a blue sky, share the poem "Cloud Dragons."
- Children can request repeated readings of favorite poems.
- When you share a poem, invite the children to talk about how the illustrator interpreted the poem. Encourage the children to create their own visual interpretation of the poem.

Content Connections/Skills Connections: Nature, poetry

Insider Tips: There is also a Spanish version of this collection. Pat Mora is a tireless advocate of poetry for children. She initiated Children's Day/Book Day, a literacy initiative that now falls under the auspices of the American Library Association: http://www.patmora.com.

Related Books:

- *Book Fiesta!: Celebrate Children's Day/Book Day* by Pat Mora
- *Celebremos El día de los niños/El día de los libros* by Pat Mora
- *Yum! MMMM! Que Rico!* by Pat Mora

Count!
Written and illustrated by Denise Fleming
Henry Holt, 1992
Ages: 2 and up

Reprinted with permission

Summary: This counting book uses vibrantly colored double-page spreads to feature the numbers one to ten as well as twenty, thirty, forty, and fifty. Each set of pages is accompanied by a set of animals or creatures representative of the number present on the pages.

Illustrations: Fleming uses a papermaking technique to create her distinctive images. Cotton rag fiber beaten to a fine pulp and suspended in water is the basic material. Chemicals and pigments are added to the pulp, and the pulp then becomes her paint. Cups and squeeze bottles are her brushes; hand-cut stencils are her underdrawings. By building layers and layers of colored pulp or handmade paper, a "pulp painting" is created.

Sharing *This* Book with Children:

- Children are encouraged to participate in this story as they encounter each number and the accompanying salutations or commands. For example, when learning the number seven, the text states, "Wiggle, worms!," and children can wiggle like a worm.

- This book counts from one to ten and by tens until fifty. Choose the appropriate counting concept depending on the level of your students.

Content Connection/Skills Connection: Numbers: counting one to ten and by tens to fifty

Insider Tip*:* Fleming created this book to help her daughter Indigo learn how to count. Point out the similarity of collaged illustrations in Denise Fleming's books.

Related Books:

- *My Very First Book of Numbers* by Eric Carle
- *Ten Tiny Babies* by Karen Katz

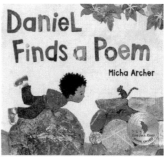

Reprinted with permission

Daniel Finds a Poem
Written and illustrated by Micha Archer
Nancy Paulsen/Penguin, 2016
Ages: 4–7
Summary: When Daniel sees a sign announcing poetry in the park, he sets out to learn what poetry is by talking to animals in the park. Each has a different answer. For example, spider explains that poetry "is when morning dew glistens." Daniel uses the answers he collects to create his very own poem.
Illustrations: Archer created the collages in this book using tissue paper, patterned papers, and oil. Be sure to show the children the cover illustration that is revealed when the dust jacket is removed.

Sharing *This* Book with Children:

- Ask the children to name poems they like. Ask them what makes something a poem.
- Read the title and show the children the illustrations on the dust jacket and book cover. Ask them how someone might *find* a poem.
- Read the book and return to the question posed before reading: How did Daniel *find* a poem?
- Take the children on a nature walk to look for poems. Explain that while they won't be able to find poems by talking to animals, they can look closely at the world and perhaps see poems. For example, "A poem is the bright blue sky with a shining sun."
- After the nature walk, create a class poem based on what the children have seen.

Content Connections/Skills Connections: Animals, nature, perspective, poetry
Insider Tip: To learn more about how Micha Archer creates her artwork, visit her website: https://www.michaarcher.com/how-does-she-do-that-video.
Related Books:

- *Daniel's Good Day* by Micha Archer
- *Frederick* by Leo Lionni

Daniel's Good Day
Written and illustrated by Micha Archer
Nancy Paulsen/Penguin, 2019
Ages: 3–7

Reprinted with permission

Summary: As Daniel walks through his diverse neighborhood on the way to his grandmother's house, people along the way tell him to have a "good day." So Daniel sets out to understand what makes a good day for the people he meets and discovers that each one has a different explanation. The story culminates with Daniel's poem about what makes a good day.

Illustrations: Archer's brightly colored collages infuse Daniel's neighborhood with vibrancy. Be sure to peek under the dust jacket.

Sharing *This* Book with Children:

- Before sharing the book, ask the children to talk about what makes a good day for them.
- Show the book's dust jacket as well as the cover of the book. Invite the children to predict what might happen in the book.
- As Daniel's neighbors tell him what makes a good day for them, they do not explain *why* it makes a good day. Readers must make these inferences. For example, the baker tells Daniel that birthdays make a good day for him. Invite the children to talk about *why* each person answers as she or he does.
- After reading, show the children the cover of the book once again and let them see which of the people Daniel meets along the way are pictured on the book's cover.
- Invite the children to visit the writing center to write their own poem or story about a good day.

Content Connections/Skills Connections: Comprehension: inferences, neighborhoods, perspective, poetry

Insider Tips: To learn more about how Micha Archer creates her artwork, visit her website: https://www.michaarcher.com/how-does-she-do-that-video. There are Chinese editions of the Daniel books.

Related Books:

- *Daniel Finds a Poem* by Micha Archer
- *Saturday* by Oge Mora

A Dark, Dark Cave
Written by Eric Hoffman and illustrated by Corey R. Tabor
Viking, 2016
Ages: 3 and up

Summary: Two children move cautiously through a dark, dark cave, encountering bats, crawling creatures, shining eyes—when suddenly their father demands they play more quietly.

Illustrations: The illustrations become increasingly scary as pages are turned—until the lights come on. Details in the illustrations of the cave mirror elements appearing in the children's room.

Reprinted with permission

Sharing *This* Book with Children:

- As you read, ask the children to look closely at the illustrations and talk about what they see.
- Invite the children to join in on the repetitive refrain "a dark, dark cave."
- When you get to the double-page spread of the children's room, again ask the children to look closely at all the things that appear in the room. Ask if the things they see in the room remind them of things they saw in the cave.
- In the following double-page spread, we see close-ups of the little boy and little girl. A dark cloud appears over the boy's head, and a shining sun appears over the girl's head. Invite the children to think about why these items appear over the heads of the children.
- Invite the children to discuss why the final scenes of the book take place on a sunny farm.

Content Connection/Skills Connection: Imagination

Insider Tip: Children will want to re-read this book and join in on the repetitive refrain.

Related Books:

- *Not a Box* by Antoinette Portis
- *Not a Stick* by Antoinette Portis
- *Regards to the Man in the Moon* by Ezra Jack Keats

The Day You Begin
Written by Jacqueline Woodson and illustrated by Rafael López
Penguin Random House, 2018
Ages: 4–8

Reprinted with permission

Summary: This book is about the times a person feels different for whatever reason—because of their skin color or language or because of their background experiences. It is also about taking the courageous step of sharing who you are and thereby making connections to others.

Illustrations: Rafael López's vibrant mixed-media art conveys wide-ranging emotions.

Sharing *This* Book with Children:

- Invite the children to talk about times when they felt different from others. Focus on the many different ways in which people might feel like they are different.
- Children might also want to share personal connections as you read the story.
- After reading, invite the children to talk about how Angelina solved her problem.
- Encourage the children to share what they would say about themselves if they were newcomers in the class.
- Talk about how they can make newcomers feel welcome—whether the person is a newcomer to the class or to their neighborhood.
- The poetic language in this book is notable. Talk about the repeating phrase in the book: "There will be times." Consider using this phrase to create a class book with the students.

Content Connections/Skills Connections: Diversity, social and emotional development

Insider Tips: Jacqueline Woodson is the winner of the National Book Award, a National Ambassador for Young People's Literature, and the IBBY Hans Christian Andersen Award.

Related Books:

- *Each Kindness* by Jacqueline Woodson
- *The Other Side* by Jacqueline Woodson

Days Like This: A Collection of Small Poems
Written and illustrated by Simon James
Candlewick, 1999

Ages: 3–6
Summary: This is a collection of small poems about ordinary things—going on hikes, sledding, rain, sleeping outdoors.
Illustrations: Each poem is accompanied by an illustration that fills a single page or even the double-page spread. For some poems the content of the illustration reflects the content of the poem, but for other poems the illustration extends the meaning of the poem.

Reprinted with permission

Sharing *This* Book with Children:

- This is not a book to share with children in one sitting. Rather, it is important to become familiar with all the poems in order to select the right poem for the right time.
- Poetry is all about sound and images. So when sharing these poems, invite the children to listen for words that "paint pictures" for them or words whose sound they like.

Content Connection/Skills Connection: Vocabulary
Insider Tip: Too often we only share nursery rhymes with children. The poems in this collection are very accessible and can help to extend children's interest in poetry.
Related Books:

- *A Child's Book of Poems* by Gyo Fujikawa
- *Read Aloud Rhymes for the Very Young* by Jack Prelutsky

Dear Juno
Written by Soyung Pak and illustrated by Susan Kathleen Hartung
Puffin, 2001

Ages: 4–7
Summary: One day, Juno receives a letter from his grandmother in Korea. Although he can't read the letter, the picture and flower his grandmother sent him tells Juno what the letter says. He decides to write back using his own drawings.

Reprinted with permission

Illustrations: The illustrator uses realistic pictures created with oil-paint glazes on sealed paper to attract readers to the story. Use the illustrations to talk about what Juno was trying to "write" to his grandmother and different writing systems.

Sharing *This* Book with Children:

- Before reading this book, use a map to discuss with the children how far away Korea is.

- Encourage the children to think of different ways Juno could have communicated with his grandmother and why writing letters was the best way for him.
- Talk with the students about what Juno was "writing" in his letter to his grandmother by having them look at the pictures that he drew. Also, have the children talk about what the materials Juno's grandmother sent to Juno meant. What was she trying to communicate?
- Ask the children to share stories of family members who live far away.

Content Connections/Skills Connections: Communication, culture, family
Awards and Recognition: Ezra Jack Keats Book Award
Related Books:

- *Dear Mr. Blueberry* by Simon James
- *Halmoni's Day* by Edna Coe Bercaw

Dear Zoo: A Lift-the-Flap Book
Written and illustrated by Rod Campbell
Little Simon, 1982
Ages: 3–6

Reprinted with permission

Summary: An unnamed narrator writes to the zoo, asking for a pet. The zoo responds by repeatedly sending inappropriate pets—until finally the perfect pet arrives. This patterned book is also a lift-the-flap book. Double-page spreads focus on a single request: "So they sent me a _____. He was too tall! I sent him back." The animal can be identified by lifting the flap on the right-hand page of the spread. The text contains clues to the identity of the animal (e.g., "too tall").

Illustrations: The double-page spreads are simply designed. Only text appears on the left side of the spread: the first part of the pattern ("So they sent me a _____"). On the facing page appears the final part of the pattern (e.g., "He was too tall! I sent him back.") accompanied by the flap, which, when lifted, reveals the animal.

Sharing *This* Book with Children:

- Introduce the book by sharing the front cover, the title, and the name of the author/illustrator.
- On each double-page spread, first read the text on the left side of the spread and pause for the children to guess what the animal might be. Before lifting the flap, read the text on the right side of the spread and let the children use the verbal clue in the text to make a second guess about the identity of the animal. Then lift the flap to reveal the animal.
- About halfway through the book, let the children talk about animals they think might make the narrator happy.
- Be sure to make this patterned book available in the classroom book center.

Content Connections/Skills Connections: Animals, patterned books
Insider Tip: A Dear Zoo app is available for iPads.

Related Books:

- *Dear Zoo Animal Shapes* by Rod Campbell
- *I Went Walking* by Sue Williams

Diez Deditos/Ten Little Fingers: And Other Play Rhymes and Action Songs from Latin America
Selected by José-Luis Orozco and illustrated by Elisa Kleven
Dutton, 1997
Ages: 3–5

Summary: Finger rhymes and action songs from Latin America are introduced with background notes. The rhyme appears in Spanish on the left side of the page and in English on the right side. Simple drawings demonstrate accompanying motions for each line of the rhyme. For the songs, the same format is used with easy-to-follow musical accompaniment.

Reprinted with permission

Illustrations: Bursts of fireworks fill the endpapers and help to establish a festive mood. Each rhyme is accompanied by either a full-page collage filled with colorful details or by a small colorful collage related to the focus of the rhyme.

Sharing *This* Book with Children:

- This isn't a book to read straight through. Rather, it's one to visit time and again. Perhaps you will choose to share a rhyme or song (or two) daily.
- Be sure to demonstrate the hand motions that accompany the rhyme or song.
- After learning the song/rhyme in one language, children will enjoy learning it in the other language.

Content Connections/Skills Connections: Phonemic awareness: rhymes, songs
Insider Tip: You can see José-Luis Orozco performing "Diez Deditos/Ten Little Fingers" on YouTube: https://www.youtube.com/watch?v=VZQFU_xAZ6I.
Related Books:

- *De Colores and Other Latin American Folksongs for Children* selected by José-Luis Orozco
- *¡Pío Peep!* selected by Alma Flor Ada and F. Isabel Campoy

Doctor de Soto
Written and illustrated by William Steig
Scholastic, 1982
Ages: 5–8
Summary: Doctor de Soto, a mouse dentist, runs his office with his wife. One day they treat a fox with a rotten tooth. The fox behaves on his initial visit, but on his follow-up appointment, he decides that he is going to eat the mice. Doctor and Mrs. de Soto must find a way to outfox the fox.
Illustrations: William Steig's detailed illustrations support vocabulary development and are crucial to the development of the plot.

Reprinted with permission

Sharing *This* Book with Children:

- On the page where Doctor and Mrs. de Soto are lying in bed, they come up with a plan to solve their problem. Encourage the students to explain the problem in the story. Then have them predict Doctor and Mrs. de Soto's plan to solve the problem.
- Children can talk about some of the interesting words in this story (e.g., *patient, dainty, timid, pitiful, extractor, chortled, stunned, dignity*).

Content Connections/Skills Connections: Jobs, dentist/teeth, problem-solving, vocabulary
Insider Tip: This book is available in Spanish.
Awards and Recognition: Newbery Honor book
Related Books:

- *Doctor de Soto Goes to Africa* by William Steig
- *The Amazing Bone* by William Steig

Don't Let the Pigeon Drive the Bus!
Written and illustrated by Mo Willems
Hyperion, 2003
Ages: 4 and up
Summary: A bus driver must leave and tells the readers, "Don't let the pigeon drive the bus." Once the driver is gone, the pigeon begs and pleads with the reader to have the chance to drive the bus but is unsuccessful in his attempts.
Illustrations: Willems uses simple line drawings.

Reprinted with permission

Sharing *This* Book with Children:

- Since the pigeon is talking to the reader, encourage the students to chime in to answer the pigeon's questions.

- Invite the children to look closely at the page where the pigeon says, "LET ME DRIVE THE BUS!!!" Ask the students to look at the illustrations to see what the pigeon does when he has his tantrum. Let the students talk about reasons children sometimes have temper tantrums.
- On one page there are multiple images of the pigeon trying to convince the reader to let him drive the bus. Have the students identify the pigeon's emotion in each illustration. For example, the first image on the left-hand page is of the pigeon saying, "I'll be your best friend!" and the pigeon's body language shows that the bird is trying to win the reader over.
- At the end of the book, the pigeon's eyes are closed, and in a thought bubble the reader sees three big eighteen-wheelers. Invite the children to predict what the pigeon is thinking.

Content Connections/Skills Connections: Emotions, inferring: using illustrations to infer emotions, predicting

Insider Tip: Mo Willems's website has some great information about his books and his work: http://www.mowillems.com/.

Awards and Recognition: Caldecott Honor book

Related Books:

- *No, David* by David Shannon
- *When Sophie Gets Angry—Really, Really Angry* by Molly Bang
- *Sometimes I'm Bambaloo* by Rachel Vail

Other Books by the Same Author/Illustrator:

- *The Pigeon Finds a Hot Dog!*
- *The Pigeon Wants a Puppy*
- *The Pigeon Has Feelings, Too!*
- *The Pigeon Loves Things That Go!*
- *Knuffle Bunny: A Cautionary Tale*
- *Knuffle Bunny Too*

Don't Throw It to Mo!

Written by David A. Adler and illustrated by Sam Ricks

Penguin, 2015

Ages: 5–7

Summary: Mo is the smallest member of his football team, so he doesn't get to play much. And the members of the rival team make fun of him. One day, when the team is losing, the coach sends in Mo, telling him to go deep—but the coach also tells the team not to throw the ball to Mo. Then, on the last play of the game, the coach again tells Mo to go deep—only this time the coach says to throw the ball to Mo, and Mo makes the winning play!

Illustrations: The cartoon-style illustrations have child appeal.

Reprinted with permission

Sharing *This* Book with Children:

- Bring in a small football and ask the children if they know what game uses it.
- Ask the children if any of them are on a football team. If some of the children are on a team (or have background knowledge about the game), ask them to talk about some of the skills football players need. Depending on the children's responses, you might need to talk about the meaning of "going deep."
- Introduce the book by sharing the front cover, the title, and the author/illustrator.
- Read through page 10, and ask the children if Mo enjoys being on a football team. Ask the students to explain their responses.
- After reading page 11, ask the children why the coach thinks it is important for Mo to practice catching a butter-covered ball.
- After page 15, ask why they think the coach tells the team not to throw the ball to Mo.
- After page 19, talk about what the members of the other team are saying about Mo.
- After page 20, ask the children to predict what will happen when the ball is thrown to Mo.
- After finishing the book, ask the children who they think is the hero of the story—the coach or Mo. Ask them to support their thinking.

Content Connections/Skills Connections: Persevering, sports
Awards and Recognition: Geisel Award winner
Related Books:

- *Get a Hit, Mo!* by David Adler
- *Kick It, Mo!* by David Adler

Door
Created by JiHyeon Lee
Chronicle, 2018
Ages: 3–7
Summary: A boy finds a key next to an insect that nobody around seems to notice. A small colored insect leads the boy from his black-and-white world to a seemingly unused door covered in cobwebs. Entering the door, the boy encounters a variety of creatures enjoying life. When he returns home, the boy decides to leave the key in the lock with the door open. Perhaps he will return again? Or, having left the door open for others, is he sharing his surprise find?

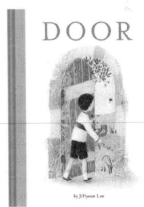

Reprinted with permission

Illustrations: This wordless book tells its story entirely through black and colored pencil illustration. Viewers looking closely will not only follow the main story line but also find clues that signal what is going to happen. The front endpapers and the title page illustration offer visual cues that lead into the story. While almost all pages show the protagonist moving farther and farther toward the right, which compels each page turn, the final two illustrations show the boy facing back toward the beginning of the book. What might that signal to the viewer about the book's ending?

Sharing *This* Book with Children:

- Begin by introducing the fact that the author/illustrator is South Korean and the book was first published there.
- Tell the students they will need to look at the illustrations to create the text for the story through their own descriptions of what they see happening. Details are important and often lead from page to page. Read the notes in the illustration section for ideas on how you might guide students to notice details that propel the story forward.
- Discuss: What visual cues are used to signal the human world in reality versus an imaginary fantasy world?
- The fantasy creatures dress like humans and seem to live experiences that parallel human experiences: picnicking, attending a wedding, swinging, playing, and partying. The speech bubbles reveal an undecipherable language; however, close inspection reveals patterns in this "language"—observe and note what those are.

Content Connections/Skills Connections: Observation skills, oral language development

Insider Tips: The protagonist is an Asian boy. In some Asian countries, boys wear shorts in all weather until they graduate from elementary school and move into junior high school.

Awards and Recognition: *New York Times* Editors' Choice book, *School Library Journal* starred review

Related Books:

- *Another* by Christian Robinson
- *Pool* by JiHyeon Lee

Drawn Together
Written by Minh Lê and illustrated by Dan Santat
Hyperion, 2018
Ages: 4–8

Reprinted with permission

Summary: A little boy is not happy about being dropped off at his grandfather's house—the two do not speak the same language. But when the boy pulls out his art supplies and begins to draw, the grandfather brings out his sketchbook. Soon the two are collaborating in the creation of a wonderful wordless adventure.

Illustrations: The illustrations are critical to the development of the story because it is through drawing that grandson and grandfather communicate. The design of the book deserves careful inspection. Two different styles/mediums of art are evident on the dust jacket. Underneath the dust jacket appears a black cover with a single word written on it—"Sketch." The front and back endpapers are also of note. They contain artwork that is stylistically different. The front endpaper presents a colorful, fantastical scene, while the illustration on the back endpapers is created in black and white and is done in a decidedly Asian style.

Sharing *This* Book with Children:

- Ask the children if they know someone who *only* speaks a language other than the one they speak. If any have had this experience, ask them how they communicate with that person. If no one responds, invite the students to reflect on how they might try to communicate.
- Tell the students you will be reading a story about a little boy who must spend the day with his grandfather, who does not speak English.
- Introduce the book by showing the peritextual features of *Drawn Together*, including the dust jacket, the book cover, and the endpapers (front and back). After asking the students what they notice, invite them to make predictions about what might happen in the story.
- Encourage the students to look closely at the title and talk about what the little boy seems to be thinking as he arrives at his grandfather's house.
- Because so much of the story unfolds only through illustrations, encourage the students to share what they are observing and thinking about as they view the illustrations. You will especially want to encourage thinking about character emotions.
- After reading the page that says "We see each other for the first time," invite the children to think about why the boy says this—and why the pictures on the facing pages are so different.
- Pause on the page that says "That old distance," and invite the children to think about what has happened and to predict what might happen next.

Content Connections/Skills Connections: Art, communication, grandparents
Insider Tip: You can listen to Dan Santat talking about his artwork and art process for *Drawn Together* in the YouTube video: https://www.youtube.com/watch?v=QpNR28w6cN4.
Awards and Recognition: Asian Pacific American Award for Literature, Charlotte Huck Award for Outstanding Fiction for Children
Related Books:

- *Mango, Abuela, and Me* by Meg Medina, illustrated by Angela Dominguez
- *Sitti's Secrets* by Naomi Shihab Nye, illustrated by Nancy Carpenter

Du Iz Tak?
Created by Carson Ellis
Candlewick, 2016

Reprinted with permission

Ages: 5 and up
Summary: A tiny shoot begins to grow, and at first two damselflies wonder what it is—"du is tak?" More creatures come to look. Eventually, with the help of a pill bug named Icky, they put a ladder up the plant and build a "tree" fort. Still more creatures get involved as the season moves on through summer; there is a dramatic event just before the plant flowers magnificently, and eventually come autumn and winter—and finally the next spring. A fascinating story with complex illustrations and text that is all a made-up language.

Illustrations: The illustrations have many details, and the details on one page become important or are further revealed on subsequent pages. This book is a great example of visual storytelling.

Sharing *This* Book with Children:

- Plan to spend a lot of time with this book to keep track of everything that is going on, both with the language/text and the illustrations, which are very detailed and shift in interesting ways from one two-page spread to another.
- You and the children will likely read this book not just from beginning to end. That's because when something happens or some insect/animal appears on one page, it was almost always foreshadowed on a previous page. This makes putting the visual narrative together very engaging for children because it is like figuring out a puzzle.
- Every page of this book is an opportunity for children to create what they think the insect characters are saying to each other.

Content Connections/Skills Connections: Seasons/life cycle, comprehension: sequence of events, cause/effect

Insider Tips: *Du Is Tak?* is the first book with invented language to become a Caldecott Honor book. *Du Is Tak?* is published in many countries, and the invented language has been "translated" to have the syntax and flow of the target language.

Awards and Recognition: Caldecott Honor book

Related Book:

- *Mr Wuffles* by David Weisner

Duck, Duck, Porcupine!
Written and illustrated by Salina Yoon
Bloomsbury, 2016
Ages: 3–6

Reprinted with permission

Summary: This book contains three different stories about the humorous adventures of Big Duck, Little Duck, and Porcupine.

Illustrations: The illustrations are done in bright, bold colors that match the cheery, humorous tone of the stories.

Sharing *This* Book with Children:

- Since the book contains three different stories, you can share the term *chapter* in introducing the book.
- The text appears (almost entirely) as speech bubbles. In stories one and three, the text in the speech bubbles is a dialogue between Big Duck and Porcupine. In story two, the text in the speech bubbles is essentially a monologue by Big Duck. Be sure to explain to the children what speech bubbles represent.
- Little Duck has no dialogue in the three stories, but he is an important character. Be sure the children look closely at the illustrations to see what Little Duck is doing.
- At the end of story one, invite the children to talk about how Little Duck saved the day.
- At the end of story two, invite talk about how Little Duck tried to help Big Duck.
- At the end of story three, ask which character they would go camping with and why.
- At the end of each story, the illustrator has Little Duck looking directly at the reader. Invite the children to think about why the illustrator might have done this.

Content Connection/Skills Connection: Friendship
Insider Tips: The author's book *My Kite Is Stuck! And Other Stories* received a Geisel Honor award.
Related Books:

- *My Kite Is Stuck! And Other Stories* by Salina Yoon
- *Penguin's Big Adventure* and other Penguin books by Salina Yoon

Elephants Can Paint Too!
Written and photographed by Katya Arnold
Atheneum, 2005
Ages: 5–8

Reprinted with permission

Summary: The central focus of this informational book is on elephants that paint. The author has created an engaging format for children by presenting comparisons between children and elephants (e.g., both children and elephants like cookies; both children and elephants like bright colors; both children and elephants make messes when the teacher is not looking). The author also includes text boxes with additional information about elephants.

Illustrations: The book is illustrated with photographs. Many of the double-page spreads feature a child on the left side and an elephant on the right side of the page. Endpapers feature paintings done by elephants.

Sharing *This* Book with Children:

- The book offers two textual pathways. The pathway written in large font offers one or two simply written sentences related to the featured photograph. The second pathway is presented through text boxes that include more detailed factual information.
- Deciding which pathway to follow with the children will depend on the ages and interests of your students. Even very young children will enjoy listening to text in the first pathway. With older children you may be able to read all the information in the text boxes.
- After sharing the book with the children, invite them to visit the art center and try out one of the various styles of elephant painting seen in the photographs.

Content Connections/Skills Connections: Animals: elephants, art
Insider Tip: An author's note provides information about how the author became involved in teaching elephants in Thailand how to paint.
Related Books:

- *Natumi Takes the Lead* by Gerry Ellis
- *Tarra and Bella* by Carol Buckley

Ella Sarah Gets Dressed
Written and illustrated by Margaret Chodos-Irvine
Harcourt, 2003
Ages: 4–6

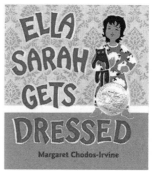
Reprinted with permission

Summary: Ella Sarah knows just what she wants to wear—and it isn't what her family members select. Why is Ella Sarah so determined?

Illustrations: These brightly colored illustrations were created with a print-making technique.

Sharing *This* Book with Children:

- Introduce the book by sharing the front cover, the title, and the name of the author/illustrator.
- Invite a few volunteers to briefly describe their favorite outfits.
- After reading the first page, ask the children to close their eyes, and as you reread the page, ask them to imagine what Ella Sarah's outfit will look like.
- After each family member offers a new suggestion for Sarah Ella's apparel, the children may choose to join in on Ella Sarah's response.
- After Ella Sarah rejects her sister's suggestion, ask the children why they think Ella Sarah is so determined to wear her pink polka-dot pants, her dress with orange-and-green flowers, her purple-and-blue-striped socks, her yellow shoes, and her red hat.
- When Ella Sarah looks at her outfit in the mirror, she thinks it is "just right." Ask the children if they agree with Ella Sarah and why or why not.
- After reading, ask once again if the children think Ella Sarah's outfit was "just right."
- After reading the story, leave the book in the dress-up center and encourage the children to select their own outfits for a tea party. Be sure to have teacups and saucers readily available for staging the tea party.
- In the art center, the children can design their own special outfits.

Content Connections/Skills Connections: Getting dressed, independence
Awards and Recognition: Caldecott Honor book
Related Books:

- *The Girl with the Parrot on Her Head* by Daisy Hirst
- *Froggy Gets Dressed* by Jonathan London

Eric Carle's ABC
Written and illustrated by Eric Carle
Grosset and Dunlap, 2007
Ages: 3–5
Summary: This lift-the-flap alphabet book features animals.
Illustrations: A single letter is featured on each spread. The illustration on the right side lifts up to reveal the next letter. On each page the uppercase letter is featured prominently. In the lower portion of the page, an animal

Reprinted with permission

beginning with the featured letter appears as well as a word that identifies the featured animal. The letters in this book were created using marbleized paper. The corresponding animals are collage creations.

Sharing *This* Book with Children:

- Page by page, either the teacher or the children can identify the letter and the corresponding animal(s).

Content Connection/Skills Connection: Alphabet
Insider Tip: Hand-painted tissue paper collage is Carle's signature style of illustration.
Related Books:

- *Eating the Alphabet* by Lois Ehlert
- *Chicka Chicka Boom Boom* by Bill Martin Jr. and John Archambault

The Farmer and the Clown
Created by Marla Frazee
Simon and Schuster, 2014
Ages: 3–8
Summary: In this wordless book, a little clown falls
off a circus train and is befriended by a grumpy (or
so it seems initially) old farmer. Soon though, a bond
develops between the pair as the farmer watches over
and works to cheer up the little clown until his circus
train returns.

Reprinted with permission

Illustrations: Browns and grays dominate scenes of the farm and the farmer. A clear
contrast is established when the little clown dressed in red and yellow appears on the
scene. On many pages, montages show the interactions of the farmer and the clown.

Sharing *This* Book with Children:

- Explain to the children that the book is wordless, so their job will be to read
  the illustrations very carefully.
- Begin by sharing the illustration on the dust jacket and asking the students to
  talk about what they see. Then invite predictions.
- Move slowly through the book, encouraging the students to talk about what is
  happening. In particular, encourage the children to talk about the emotions of
  the two characters.
- After the children talk about the page in which the little clown is reunited with
  the other clowns, invite the children to predict how the story will end.
- On the final page, encourage the children to think about what might happen if
  Marla Frazee were to write a second book about the farmer—but focus on the
  farmer and the monkey.

Content Connection/Skills Connection: Friendship
Insider Tip: Two of Frazee's books have been recognized as Caldecott Honor books.
Related Books:

- *The Farmer and the Monkey* by Marla Frazee
- *The Farmer and the Circus* by Marla Frazee

Feather
Written by Cao Wenxuan and illustrated by Roger Mello
Translated from the Chinese original edition by Chloe Garcia Roberts
Elsewhere Editions, 2017
Ages: 5–9

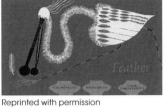

Reprinted with permission

Summary: A single feather, swept along by the wind, wonders to whom he belongs. On his journey to discover the answer, he asks the question of "to whom he belongs" to a variety of birds encountered along the way.

Illustrations: The illustrations are boldly and brilliantly colored. Each page provides a background color block and double-spread illustrations featuring each bird. The birds are presented from different perspectives and even on porcelain vases. What makes this book unique is the illustrator's use of a fold-over flap to show the single feather, split down the center. One half remains constant across the pages. The other half changes in color but retains its shape across the story. In a dramatic double spread, the single feather arcs across and fills both pages. Therefore, the book's design becomes part of the storytelling and the underlying theme of our constant search for identity.

Sharing *This* Book with Children:

- Begin by introducing the book as one created by two people living on opposite sides of the world from each other: one in China and the other in Brazil. Use a globe or a map to demonstrate the distance. The book was first published in Chinese and then translated from the original. Explain the role of the translator—the person who brings a story to its new language audience.
- All the birds in the book can be found in China, the country in which the book was first published. Yet many of the birds can also be seen in other parts of the world. Engage the students in discussion about the kinds of birds they see around them, and see if any of the birds in the book are also in their environment.
- If possible, invite someone from the local birdwatchers group to come to your classroom to discuss the birds in the book and how they compare to birds in the local environment.
- After the close of the book, ask the children how they might summarize what question was important to the feather throughout the book. Then emphasize that, despite the book's origin on opposite sides of the globe, the main idea of this book is one that humans all over the world think about: a sense of home and belonging. "Do I belong to you?"

Content Connections/Skills Connections: Belonging, patterned story
Insider Tips: Watch a video introduction here: https://www.youtube.com/watch?v=-JEItaf0Cte8. And an audio of the illustrator's philosophy in creating this book: https://www.teachingbooks.net/book_reading.cgi?id=17733.

Cao Wenxuan is the winner of the 2016 IBBY Hans Christian Andersen Author Award and the Chinese National Book Award. Roger Mello is the winner of the 2014

IBBY Hans Christian Andersen Illustrator Award and three-time winner of the IBBY Luis Jardim Award.
Related Books:

- *A Mother for Choco* by Keiko Kasza
- *Are You My Mother?* by P. D. Eastman

First the Egg
Written and illustrated by Laura Vaccaro Seeger
Roaring Brook, 2007
Ages: 3–6

Summary: This simple book focuses on transformations in nature (e.g., first the egg, then the chicken). Die cuts provide a peek at the next change that will be revealed by the turn of the page.

Illustrations: Seeger uses paint and die cuts to craft this exquisite book in which the design of the book is an important guiding element.

Reprinted with permission

Sharing *This* Book with Children:

- Introduce the book by sharing the dust jacket illustration, the title, and the name of the author/illustrator. Point out the die cut in the dust jacket and then remove the dust jacket to reveal the chicken on the front cover. Invite the children to talk about why the illustrator might have placed a chicken beneath the die cut.
- As each new creature or plant is first revealed, invite the children to predict the transformation before you turn the page.
- The author reminds us that the story begins with a word and the picture with paint. So invite the children to create their own picture or their own story.

Content Connections/Skills Connections: Nature, transformations
Awards and Recognition: Caldecott Honor book, Geisel Honor book
Related Books:

- *Why?* by Laura Vaccaro Seeger
- *Dog and Bear* by Laura Vaccaro Seeger

Flashlight
Created by Lizi Boyd
Chronicle, 2014
Ages: 5–8

Summary: This wordless book is an exploration of nature. A boy uses his flashlight to highlight the wonders of nature that surround him—bats, skunks, night blossoms, and much more.

Illustrations: The illustrations are done almost exclusively in black and gray. Only when the boy

Reprinted with permission

shines his flashlight on an animal or plant does it appear in color. Peek holes (or die cuts) also serve to focus the reader's attention on small but lovely details in these night scenes.

Sharing *This* Book with Children:

- This book demands close inspection of visual details, so it needs to be shared in very small groups.
- Introduce the book by inviting the children to talk about any experiences they have had outside in nature at night.
- Tell the children that the little boy in this book is outside at night with a flashlight. Invite them to predict what the boy will see with his flashlight.
- Move slowly through the book, encouraging the students to talk about what they see.
- Challenge the children to look for the moth on each page. It is the one creature that appears in color on each page, even though the flashlight is not shining on it.
- The double-page spread in which the boy drops his flashlight marks a turning point in the story. Challenge the children to talk about how the story has changed (with the animals now in charge of the flashlight).
- If your students live in a place where they might be able to access nature in the evening (e.g., a backyard), encourage them to go out with a flashlight to see what they can see in their own surroundings. The students can share their discoveries the following day.

Content Connections/Skills Connections: Observation, nature
Insider Tip: A version of the book has been set to music: https://www.youtube.com/watch?v=NeDgkfYFdy8.
Related Books:

- *Explorers* by Matthew Cordell
- *Float* by Daniel Miyare

Frederick
Written and illustrated by Leo Lionni
Pantheon, 1967
Ages: 5–8
Summary: While the field mice busily gather food for the winter, Frederick collects sunrays, colors, and words. Once all the food is gone, the mice ask Frederick where his supplies are. Frederick shares his poetry—warming hearts with thoughts of sun and bright colors.
Illustrations: Collages of marbled, textured paper appear against a white background.

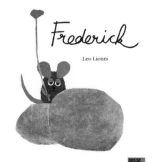

Reprinted with permission

Sharing *This* Book with Children:

- To introduce the book, talk with the students about how animals prepare for winter.

- Discuss the characteristics of the four seasons: fall, winter, spring, summer.
- Talk with the students about how mice prepare for the winter ahead.
- Reread Frederick's poem and invite the children to consider why the other mice were so pleased with what Frederick had given them.

Content Connections/Skills Connections: Poetry, seasons, social skills: working together
Insider Tip: This book is available in Spanish.
Awards and Recognition: Caldecott Honor book, ALA Notable Children's Book, New York Times Best Illustrated Book
Related Books:

- *Bear Has a Story to Tell* by Philip C. Stead, illustrated by Erin E. Stead
- *Maybe Something Beautiful* by F. Isabel Campoy and Theresa Howell, illustrated by Rafael López

Freight Train
Written and illustrated by Donald Crews
Greenwillow, 1978
Ages: 3–5
Summary: This simple concept book introduces different types of cars typically pulled by freight trains. Each type of train car is depicted in a different color.
Illustrations: The illustrations of the train are done in bold colors. Changes in the depiction of the smoke coming from the train's smokestack signal changes in the speed of the train.

Sharing *This* Book with Children:

- Introduce the book by sharing the front cover, the title, and the author/illustrator.
- The poetic text of this simple book deserves to be read straight through on an initial read.
- On a subsequent read, invite very young children to identify the colors of the different cars as you move through the book. Older children can identify the names of the different cars.
- Talk with the children about the function of the different kinds of train cars.
- As you reread the book, discuss the meaning of words such as *tunnels* and *trestles*.

Content Connections/Skills Connections: Color, trains, transportation
Insider Tips: The book is available in a bilingual format and as a board book. In the tablet app version, finger movements can swipe to move the train along. There is also a manipulative board version of this book, *Inside Freight Train*, in which the doors of the train cars can slide open to reveal the contents.
Awards and Recognition: Caldecott Honor book
Related Books:

- *School Bus* by Donald Crews
- *Trains* by Byron Barton

From Head to Toe
Written and illustrated by Eric Carle
HarperCollins, 1997
Ages: 3–5
Summary: This predictable book consists of double spreads on which an animal appears on the left side, demonstrating a particular movement such as waving its arms or thumping its chest, while on the right side of the spread a child mirrors the same movement.
Illustrations: This oversized book features large, brightly colored collage images created in signature Eric Carle style.

Sharing *This* Book with Children:

- Introduce the book by sharing the front cover, the title, and the name of the author/illustrator. Ask the children to identify the animal on the cover.
- In initially sharing the book, first read the book in its entirety. Because the book is so highly patterned, the children may begin to join in by posing the repeated question ("Can you do it?") or responding with the repeated response ("I can do it!").
- On subsequent readings, invite the children to act out the featured movements.

Content Connections/Skills Connections: Animals, movement
Insider Tip: Many of Eric Carle's picturebooks have nature themes.
Related Books:

- *Clap Your Hands* by Lorinda Bryan Cauley
- *Eyes, Nose, Fingers and Toes* by Judy Hindley

Fry Bread: A Native American Family Story
Written by Kevin Noble Maillard and illustrated by Juana Martinez-Neal
Roaring Brook, 2019
Ages: 5–8
Summary: Fry bread is a Native American food. Each page of this book begins with a statement about fry bread that is written in red (e.g., "Fry bread is shape." "Fry bread is sound."). Each of these statements is followed by a simple verse that elaborates on the statement. Some of the statements allude

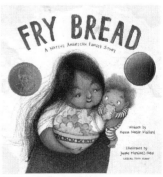

Reprinted with permission

to complex topics, including Native American history and the complexity of Native American cultures. The author's recipe for fry bread appears at the end of the book.
Illustrations: Illustrations depict warm scenes of family life. Endpapers are filled with the names of the many Native American tribal groups and can be used to help older children begin to appreciate the complexity of Native American culture.

Sharing *This* Book with Children:

- In introducing the book, ask the children if they have tasted fry bread. Invite those who know about fry bread to tell peers what is special about it. If no one is familiar with fry bread, explain that it is a special food eaten by Native Americans.
- In a second reading of the book, share with the children some of the more detailed information found in the back of the book.
- Following the reading, if possible, engage the students in making fry bread.

Content Connections/Skills Connections: Cooking, Native American culture
Insider Tip: This is the first book of Kevin Noble Maillard, a member of the Seminole Nation.
Awards and Recognition: Robert F. Sibert Informational Book Medal; American Indian Youth Literature, Picturebook Honor winner
Related Books:

- *Bee-bim Bop!* by Linda Sue Park
- *Dim Sum for Everyone* by Grace Lin

Giant Squid
Written by Candace Fleming and illustrated by Eric Rohmann
Roaring Brook, 2016
Ages: 5–8
Summary: With poetic text and intriguing illustrations, this informational book explores the mysterious giant squid, which lives deep in the ocean.
Illustrations: Scientists have learned about this mysterious creature by the clues they leave behind—a tentacle, a beak, an eye—and this is how the creature is introduced in both text and illustration. As we move through

Reprinted with permission

the book, each illustration features a single part of the giant squid until we reach the remarkable center foldout, which reveals the creature in its entirety (almost). The dark blue of the endpapers mirrors the depths of the ocean where giant squids live.

Sharing *This* Book with Children:

- Invite the children to share what they know about sea creatures. If no one mentions the giant squid, talk about the incredible depth of the ocean, which makes it very difficult for people to explore. It is a mysterious place.
- As you read, give the children opportunities to share responses.
- After reading, invite the children to help you compile a chart with information about this mysterious creature. Later the children may want to add drawings to the chart.
- The book deserves a second reading, probably on a different day given its length. On this reading, tell the children you want them to listen for words the

author uses to describe the giant squid. Invite them to "collect" words that help them see the giant squid.

- Compile a list of the words that the children can use to write about giant squids.

Content Connections/Skills Connections: Mysteries of nature, giant squid

Insider Tips: The creative structure of the book is unusual, with the text beginning several pages prior to the title page. The language is lyrical, filled with rich vocabulary laid out like poetry. Footage of giant squids is extraordinarily rare. You can show children footage of the creature on YouTube: https://www.youtube.com/watch?v=eOXkUrhclcc.

Awards and Recognition: Robert F. Sibert Honor book

Related Books:

- *Ocean: A Photicular Book* by Dan Kainen
- *The Big Book of the Blue* by Yuval Zommer

A Good Day
Written and illustrated by Kevin Henkes
Greenwillow, 2007
Ages: 3–5
Summary: Something happens to turn a bad day into a good day for each character in this gentle story.
Illustrations: The layout of the illustrations is of note. On the double-page spreads in the first half of the book, the text is on the left page and the illustrations appear on the right. Then, following the turning point in the story, the placement of text and illustrations is reversed. The illustrator uses colorful stripes in a creative way. If you look under the dust jacket of the book, you find that these stripes completely cover the front and back covers. Stripes also appear in the middle of the book to signal the important change that occurs midway.

Sharing *This* Book with Children:

- Introduce the book by sharing the front cover, the title, and the name of the author/illustrator.
- The first page says, "It was a bad day." Encourage the children to talk about how the illustrations help them know the animals in the first half of the book are having a bad day.
- In the second half of the book, following the text that reads, "But then," the placement of text and illustrations is reversed. Draw the children's attention to this reversal, and ask them why the illustrator might have done this.
- Encourage the children to look closely at the final page, which shows all the animals that have been mentioned in the story.
- The story ends with the little girl having a good day—just like the animals. Invite the children to talk about what can turn a bad day into a good day for them.
- Encourage the children to visit the writing center to write or draw stories about their own good days (or bad days or "turnaround days").

Content Connection/Skills Connection: Social and emotional development
Insider Tips: Kevin Henkes has published more than fifty books for children. He won the Caldecott Medal for *Kitten's First Full Moon*.
Related Books:

- *Egg* by Kevin Henkes
- *Waiting* by Kevin Henkes

Good Night Owl
Written and illustrated by Greg Pizzoli
Disney/Hyperion, 2016
Ages: 4–6
Summary: Every time Owl tries to go to sleep, he hears a "squeek." Determined to find the source of the squeak, Owl begins to dismantle his house—first the cupboard, then the floorboards, next the roof, and so forth.
Illustrations: Owl does not know what is making the squeak, but the reader is in on the joke because the culprit—a little mouse—appears in almost every illustration.

Reprinted with permission

Sharing *This* Book with Children:

- Introduce the book by asking the children about their bedtime routines.
- The cover of the book shows Owl in bed and a little mouse peeking over the top of the bed's headboard. After reading the title, ask the children to predict what might happen in the story.
- After Owl takes his cupboard apart, stop each time he hears the squeak and invite the children to predict what Owl will do to try to find the source of the noise.
- The illustrations reveal Owl's growing agitation. Ask the children to find the visual clues that show Owl's frustration.

Content Connection/Skills Connection: Goodnight stories
Insider Tips: Throughout the story, the author spells the word *squeak* as "squeek." We suspect he did this because so often people say "eek" when they see a mouse!
Awards and Recognition: Geisel Honor book
Related Books:

- *The Going to Bed Book* by Sandra Boynton
- *Good-Night, Owl!* by Pat Hutchins

Goodnight Moon
Written by Margaret Wise Brown and illustrated by Clement Hurd
Harper and Row, 1947
Ages: 2–5
Summary: This classic book depicts a room in which a child and mother (shown as rabbits) are saying goodnight to the objects in the room in a soothing bedtime ritual.

Illustrations: The front cover illustration signals the time of day as the full moon and stars are shown outside the window. The first illustration shows half of the room, and viewers can see many of the objects to which the text later refers. References to a popular nursery rhyme and folktale appear in the room. On the first double-spread illustration, the other half of the room is shown, and on the second double-page illustration, the entire room is shown. The closing double spread shows a shift in the darkness of the room, and the "old lady" has gone.

Sharing *This* Book with Children:

- Cover: Ask the children to notice the illustration detail that signals this is a bedtime book.
- Illustrations: On the first page, ask the children what objects they see, and tell them to try to remember those objects as you read the book aloud.
- Cow over the moon picture: What nursery rhyme does this picture remind them of?
- Three bears framed picture: What story does this picture remind them of?
- First color double spread, showing the other half of the room: What objects can the children see in this picture?
- "Mush": the children might not know the meaning of this word and might need an explanation. Ask them to guess what object in the picture is "mush" and what they think it is.
- The "quiet old lady" enters the book visually at this point. What is she doing?
- Color double spread showing entire room: Ask the children how they can tell the lamp has been turned on (the shadows and lines that show the projection of the lamp's light).
- Note the angle of the moon entering the window scene at this point, and then note how the moon moves across the window as time passes in the book.
- Kittens and mittens: What nursery rhyme does this picture remind them of?
- Rhyming words used on opposing pages of the double spreads in many cases: Ask the children to signal when words do rhyme and when they do not.
- Observe: Details that change—at the end, the mouse and cat are in different places, the only two living things in the room.

Content Connections/Skills Connections: Bedtime rituals, object identification, observation

Insider Tips: Despite the fact that it was dubbed "overly sentimental" and therefore not included in any of the New York Public Library branches for the first twenty-five years of publication, the book sold about forty-eight million copies by 2017, its seventieth anniversary. It has been translated into at least eleven languages. There is a video of this book that is narrated by actress Susan Sarandon as well as a board book and big book versions and numerous related stuffed toys.

Awards and Recognition: Parents' Choice Gold Award, National Education Association Teacher's Top 100 Books for Children, *School Library Journal's* Top 100 Picturebooks

Related Books: Margaret Wise Brown created numerous books for preschool children, and when she died in 1952 at age forty-two, she had sixty unpublished manuscripts of which twenty-seven have been published posthumously, one as recently as 2017.

- *Goodnight Moon 1 2 3* by Margaret Wise Brown
- *Goodnight Moon A B C* created by the original illustrator's son, Thacher Hurd
- *Goodnight Moon* interactive app created by Loud Crow in 2015

Gravity
Written and illustrated by Jason Chin
Roaring Brook, 2014
Ages: 4–8

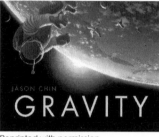

Reprinted with permission

Summary: This book explains the abstract concept of gravity in an accessible way. Essentially what the author does is *show* what would happen without gravity.
Illustrations: Illustrations are critically important to understanding the concept.

Sharing *This* Book with Children:

- Introduce the book by sharing the front cover, the title, and the name of the author/illustrator. Encourage the children to describe what they see in the cover illustration. Perhaps you could model "wondering" (which readers naturally do) by saying, "I wonder what 'gravity' is?"
- Each of the first two double-page spreads of the story show a portion of a book, but one must look closely to identify it as such. If children do not identify the object as a book, you can again wonder aloud. On the following spread, the book falls to earth and then, in the next illustration, it has landed. In the illustration in which the book has landed, the title of the fallen book appears (*Gravity*). Be sure to read it aloud.
- The following two double-page spreads are filled with interesting objects floating away. On the page with the text "FLOAT AWAY," if no one mentions that the letters in the words are also floating away, draw the children's attention to this detail.
- Continue reading, providing opportunities for the children to share their responses and questions.
- On the final page, if no one mentions the surprised looks on the children's faces, ask the children about this.

Content Connection/Skills Connection: Gravity
Insider Tips: You can find YouTube videos of astronauts floating in space: search "astronauts floating in space" and "astronauts floating weightless." More detailed information about gravity appears on the final double-page spread of the book.
Related Books:

- *Coral Reefs* by Jason Chin
- *Redwoods* by Jason Chin

Green Is a Chile Pepper: A Book of Colors
**Written by Roseanne Greenfield Thong and illus-
trated by John Parra**
Chronicle, 2014
Ages: 3–7

Reprinted with permission

Summary: This concept book introduces colors but does so in a decidedly Mexican American context— the pink of piñatas, the orange of marigolds for Day of the Dead, the yellow of masa. One or two double-page spreads are devoted to each color, and each double-page spread contains a simple rhyme highlighting the color: "Red is a ribbon, Red is a bow and skirts of *baile folklórico.*" Color words are introduced in English and Spanish.

Illustrations: Parra's illustrations are filled with details reflecting Latino culture. For example, orange is linked to marigolds for Day of the Dead, and brown is for the tasty treat churros. The illustrations are filled with calavera (skeleton) musicians.

Sharing *This* Book with Children:

- As you turn each page, ask the students to guess which color the rhyme will focus on. (Illustrations give plenty of clues.)
- If reading to Mexican American students, give them the opportunity to talk about the cultural details they find in the illustrations.
- If the class is not familiar with Mexican American culture or Spanish, there will be words that require explanation. After reading each rhyme, encourage the students to use illustration clues to understand unfamiliar words.
- Be sure that the children have the opportunity to repeat each color word in English and Spanish.
- You can extend by having the students create a class color book in English and Spanish with different children drawing pictures highlighting different colors.

Content Connections/Skills Connections: Colors, Mexican American culture
Insider Tip: A glossary at the back of the book provides explanations related to various words.
Awards and Recognition: Pura Belpré Award, Illustrator Honor
Related Books:

- *Color Zoo* by Lois Ehlert
- *Mouse Paint* by Ellen Stoll Walsh

A Greyhound, a Groundhog
Written by Emily Jenkins and illustrated by Chris Appelhans
Schwartz and Wade, 2017
Ages: 4–6

Reprinted with permission

Summary: This is a wordplay book. *Round, hound, ground, sound, hog,* and *dog* all get combined and twisted and turned about in a book that shows friendship and the joy of play.
Illustrations: The illustrations use a limited range of colors—gray and brown—to go along with the limited number of sounds and words that comprise the book.

Sharing *This* Book with Children:

- Make sure the children know what a hound/greyhound and a groundhog are before you read the book.
- On a first read, simply read the book aloud and share your delight in the wordplay.
- When you reread this book, stop from time to time and have the children fill in the words.

Content Connection/Skills Connection: Phonemic awareness: rhyming
Related Books:

- *In the Small, Small Pond* by Denise Fleming
- *In the Tall Tall Grass* by Denise Fleming
- *Orange Pear Apple Bear* by Emily Gravett

The Gruffalo
Written by Julia Donaldson and illustrated by Axel Scheffler
Dial Books, 1999
Ages: 4–6

Reprinted with permission

Summary: A mouse takes a stroll through the deep, dark wood and encounters a series of animals that eat mice. Mouse frightens each of them away by saying that a horrible, scary gruffalo is coming to meet Mouse and that each of them is the favorite thing that a gruffalo likes to eat. Of course, there is no such thing as a gruffalo—until one comes along and decides to eat Mouse. Can Mouse trick his way out of this?
Illustrations: Notice how the illustrations of the gruffalo change from appearing mean and large when he first comes into the book to small and more scared-looking by the end.

Sharing *This* Book with Children:

- Introduce the book by sharing the front cover, the title, and the name of the author/illustrator. Let the children know that children in many other countries have enjoyed this book too.
- Discuss the trickster strategies Mouse uses throughout the book.
- After Fox runs away ("'Good-bye, little mouse,' and away he sped."), discuss with the children what Mouse just did to trick Fox.
- After "'It's frightfully nice of you, Owl, but no—'" have the children predict what Mouse will try to say to Owl to get away.
- After Snake says, "Come for a feast in my log-pile house," ask, "What's Mouse going to do?"
- After "There's no such thing as a gruffal . . . " ask, "Why do you think Mouse stops in the middle of the word *gruffalo?*"
- Following the previous stop, ask the children to pay attention to how the Gruffalo looks in the illustrations all the way to the end of the book.

Content Connection/Skills Connection: Trickster tales
Insider Tip: This book has sold over thirteen million copies and has been published in more than forty countries around the world. It won several children's book awards in the United Kingdom.
Related Books:

- *The Gruffalo's Child* by Julia Donaldson
- *The Wolf's Chicken Stew* by Keiko Kasza

Grumpy Bird
Written and illustrated by Jeremy Tankard
Atheneum, 2007
Ages: 3–5
Summary: Bird wakes up grumpy—too grumpy to eat, play, or even fly. So he walks instead. And on his walk, Sheep, Rabbit, Raccoon, Beaver, and Fox end up keeping him company. Grumpiness gradually gives way to happiness as his friends lead Bird to say, "Hey, this is fun!"
Illustrations: The illustrations feature bold black lines and primary colors that change from dark to bright as the book goes on.

Reprinted with permission

Sharing *This* Book with Children:

- Introduce the book by sharing the front cover, the title, and the name of the author/illustrator. Let the children know that children in Canada enjoy this book too.
- This is a book that begins and finishes on the endpapers, so be sure to give the children the chance to look closely at those pages.

- Starting with the beginning endpapers, draw the children's attention to the expression on Bird's face and set them up to pay attention to that as the book goes along.
- After reading the first page of the story, ask, "How grumpy do you think Bird is?" Next page: "Wow! That's grumpy!"
- Notice how, as each animal friend asks Bird what he's doing, Bird becomes increasingly angry in how he replies. After Raccoon asks and Bird "snapped" his reply, on each of the next two pages, you can have the children predict how Bird will reply to Beaver and after that to Fox.
- If the children don't notice on their own what happens to Bird's expression as you go from the "Bird walked. The other animals walked." page to the "Bird stopped. The other animals stopped." page, take them back over those two pages and ask what they see.
- Whatever way children come to notice the change in Bird's expression, follow up by asking them to predict what they think will happen next.
- Facial expressions are important to the meaning of this book. You can take the children back through the book to see what they notice about the characters' expressions. One good opportunity for this is the final endpapers—"What do you think the other animals think about Bird's offering a worm to eat?"

Content Connections/Skills Connections: Feelings/emotions, friendship
Insider Tip: The author/illustrator is from Canada, but the book was published in the United States, so it is not considered an international book by publishing definition.
Related Books:

- *Boohoo Bird* by Jeremy Tankard
- *How Are You Peeling?* by Saxton Freymann

The Hello, Goodbye Window
Written by Norton Juster and illustrated by Chris Raschka
Hyperion, 2005
Ages: 4 and up
Summary: The kitchen window at Nanna and Poppy's house is not only where a little girl says hello and goodbye to her grandparents but also the entry to a seemingly magical getaway.
Illustrations: With swirling lines and rich colors, Raschka's mixed-media illustrations bring this special place to life. In many ways the artwork is reminiscent of the art of children.

Reprinted with permission

Sharing *This* Book with Children:

- Explain that Nanna and Poppy are the names the child calls her grandparents. Have the students discuss the names that they call their grandparents.
- Ask what they think is special about the little girl's visit with her grandparents.
- Have the students discuss activities that they do with their grandparents.

Content Connection/Skills Connection: Family
Insider Tip: The mixed-race family in the story is too infrequently seen in children's books.
Awards and Recognition: Caldecott Medal winner
Related Books:

- *A Ball for Daisy* by Chris Raschka
- *Full, Full, Full of Love* by Trish Cooke, illustrated by Paul Howard

Hello! Hello!
Created by Matthew Cordell
Disney/Hyperion, 2012
Ages: 5–8

Reprinted with permission

Summary: A little girl grows bored with her technology but is unable to engage her family members, who are themselves focused on various technological devices. So she goes outside—where the magical world of nature opens up for her.

Illustrations: Much of this story is told through illustrations. Of particular note is the illustrator's use of color to differentiate between the world of technology and the world of nature. The shift in the type of font used in the book is a further clue to the difference between the two worlds. The story begins on the two double-page spreads that appear before the title page.

Sharing *This* Book with Children:

- In introducing the story, invite the children to look carefully at the cover illustration and talk about what they see. Invite predictions based on the clues found on the cover.
- Remove the dust jacket to reveal the cover illustration. Remind the children that usually the illustration on the dust jacket is the same as the one on the cover. Invite them to speculate about why the illustrator created a totally different illustration for the book cover.
- Share the illustrations that appear prior to the title page, and ask the children how the little girl might be feeling and why.
- Invite the children to talk about why the illustrations shift from mainly black and white to full color when the little girl goes outside.
- A shift from realism to fantasy occurs once the little girl starts to ride the horse. Ask the children why animals such as a buffalo and dinosaur join the little girl on her ride.
- After reading the story, take the children on a nature walk to look for special things they find in nature. Then write a group story about these special things.

Content Connections/Skills Connections: Imagination, nature
Related Books:

- *Wish* by Matthew Cordell
- *Wolf in the Snow* by Matthew Cordell

Hey, Water!
Written and illustrated by Antoinette Portis
Holiday House, 2019
Ages: 4–7

Reprinted with permission

Summary: Using minimal words, the author conveys information about water—the forms in which it occurs (e.g., rivers, streams, puddles, oceans) and the states in which it occurs (e.g., steam, snow, ice). Each page presents a word that refers to the shape of water (e.g., dewdrop) as well as a sentence or phrase about the word. An endnote provides more information.

Illustrations: Portis's simple illustrations are drawn with a brush and colored digitally.

Sharing *This* Book with Children:

- After introducing the title of the book, encourage the children to talk about the different forms of water they have seen and why water is important in their own lives.
- As you turn each page, invite the children to identify the form of water featured on the page.
- On a second reading, highlight the rich vocabulary the author uses to talk about water.
- Drawing on information in the endnote, talk with the children about the water cycle and the importance of water conservation.

Content Connections/Skills Connections: Water cycle, advocacy: water conservation

Awards and Recognition: Robert F. Sibert Honor book, ALA Notable Children's Book

Related Books:

- *All the Water in the World* by George Ella Lyon
- *Water* by Melissa Stewart

Hip-Hop Lollipop
Written by Susan McElroy Montanari and illustrated by Brian Pinkney
Schwartz and Wade, 2018
Ages: 3–7

Reprinted with permission

Summary: In this bedtime story, a little girl named Lollipop is dancing hip-hop and just can't stop moving. The book language is filled with rhythm and rhyme and what for many children is the rhythm of a beloved style of music—hip-hop.

Illustrations: The swirling lines that fill Pinkney's illustrations reflect Lollipop's movement as she heads to bed. Also of note is the layout of the text (which mirrors

Lollipop's movement) and the use of enlarged (and colorful) font to emphasize particular words.

Sharing *This* Book with Children:

- Invite the children to talk about their bedtime routines.
- After reading the story through, ask the children what they noticed about the language in the story. If no one mentions rhyming words, reread and ask the children to listen for rhymes.
- Show the children a page of text (e.g., "At Big Sister's doorway, Lollie stops to say "Hey!"), and tell them you noticed that the words are not laid out in straight lines the way they usually are. Ask the children why that might be.
- Give the children the opportunity to talk about how Lollipop's bedtime routine is similar to or different from their own.

Content Connections/Skills Connections: Bedtime routines, phonemic awareness: rhyming

Related Books:

- *Hip Hop Speaks to Children: A Celebration of Poetry with a Beat* by Nikki Giovanni
- *Sleep Like a Tiger* by Mary Logue

Home in the Woods
Written and illustrated by Eliza Wheeler
Penguin Random House, 2019
Ages: 5–8

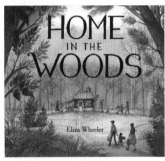

Reprinted with permission

Summary: It is the Great Depression, and when a mother and her eight children are evicted from their house in town, they move into a tarpaper shack in the woods. Readers follow the family through four seasons as together they make the shack into a home, learn to grow their own food, and find laughter and joy despite the hardships they face.

Illustrations: The book's dust jacket shows the home in the woods in the summer, while the cover shows a winter scene of the home.

Sharing *This* Book with Children:

- Explain to the children that this book tells the story of something that really happened to the author's grandmother a long, long time ago.
- Briefly explain that the Great Depression was a difficult time when many people did not have jobs and were unable to stay in their homes.
- Invite the children to imagine what living in the woods might be like.
- After reading, invite the children to talk about ways in which the characters' lives were different from their own. Record responses on a T-chart.

Content Connections/Skills Connections: Family, Great Depression

Insider Tip: Many works of historical fiction are too complex for young children, but this story is simply told and quite accessible.

Related Book:

- *Miss Maple's Seeds* by Eliza Wheeler

Honeybee: The Busy Life of Apis Mellifera
Written by Candace Fleming and illustrated by Eric Rohmann
Holiday House, 2020
Ages: 5–8

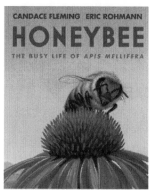
Reprinted with permission

Summary: This informational book covers the life span of the honeybee, delineating the many tasks the honeybee does from the time it first emerges from its solitary cell until it is strong enough to fly away from the hive in search of nectar until the day it dies. The life cycle lasts thirty-five days.

Illustrations: Rohmann's oil paintings do what would be difficult for words alone to achieve. His remarkable close-ups take us *inside* the hive to show us the varied activities of the honeybee—emerging from her solitary cell as a brand-new bee, cleaning the hive's nursery, feeding "the grub-like larvae," and attending to numerous other chores. When the honeybee finally leaves the hive, a centerfold spread opens to thirty-eight inches.

Sharing *This* Book with Children:

- Begin by asking the students to talk about what they know about honeybees. Record this information under the "K" column of a KWL chart—what they know.
- Then invite the students to talk about what they want to know about honeybees. Record their questions in the "W" column of the KWL chart—what they want to know.
- Read the book through the title page. Pause to mention that the book is unusual because the author begins sharing important information *prior to* the title page.
- In the first half of the book, as the reader learns about the various jobs of the honeybee, the author ends each page by posing a question about what the honeybee might do next (e.g., "Flying?"). Give the students time to respond to each of these questions.
- At the conclusion of the read aloud, invite the students to collaborate in completing the "L" column of the KWL chart—what they learned.
- The back matter is filled with useful information, much of which is intended for the teacher or older students. Included in the back matter is a double-page spread featuring a drawing of a honeybee with body parts labeled. Following each label is information about the body part. There is also additional information about helping to save honeybees.

Content Connection/Skills Connection: Honeybees

Insider Tips: The creative structure of the book is unusual, with the text beginning several pages prior to the title page. Also, the illustration on the title page offers critical information—it shows the "teeming trembling flurry" described so elegantly on the previous page.

Related Books:

- *Beehive* by Jorey Hurley
- *UnBEElievables* by Douglas Florian

How Are You Peeling? Foods with Moods
Written by Saxton Freymann and illustrated by Joost Elffers
Arthur A. Levine Books/Scholastic, 1999
Ages: 3–6

Reprinted with permission

Summary: Photographs of carved and decorated fruits and vegetables showing a range of different emotions are presented.

Illustrations: Children will likely want to study the photographs in this book in more detail, so be sure that you make it available through the classroom library.

Sharing *This* Book with Children:

- Introduce the book by sharing the front cover, the title, and the name of the author/illustrator. Discuss with the children the word *moods* that appears in the book's subtitle. Be sure children understand that it means how you feel or what your emotion is.
- The main reason for reading this book to children will be to focus on emotions, but follow-up sharings could be a way of discussing fruits and vegetables or even colors.

Content Connection/Skills Connection: Social and emotional learning
Insider Tip: "A Note about the Art" paragraph near the end of the book explains how the fruits and vegetables seen in the book were created.
Related Books:

- *Today I Feel Silly—And Other Moods that Make My Day* by Jamie Lee Curtis
- *Feelings* by Aliki

I Ain't Gonna Paint No More!
Written by Karen Beaumont and illustrated by David Catrow
Houghton Mifflin Harcourt, 2005
Ages: 4–7

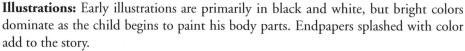

Reprinted with permission

Summary: A little boy promises not to paint anymore, but he just can't help himself. Soon his entire body is painted—much to his mother's frustration.

Sharing *This* Book with Children:

- Pause before turning each page so the children can use rhyme clues to guess the body part the boy will paint next (e.g., "So I take some red and I paint my . . . ").
- After reading the book, make a body outline on newsprint for each child, and let the children paint their own body parts—on paper!

Illustrations: Early illustrations are primarily in black and white, but bright colors dominate as the child begins to paint his body parts. Endpapers splashed with color add to the story.

Content Connections/Skills Connections: Body parts, phonemic awareness: rhyming

Insider Tip: The text of this story can be sung to the tune of "It Ain't Gonna Rain No More."

Related Books:

- *No, David!* by David Shannon
- *Oh, Were They Ever Happy!* by Peter Spier

I Want My Hat Back
Written and illustrated by Jon Klassen
Candlewick, 2011
Ages: 4–7

Reprinted with permission

Summary: A bear has lost his hat, so he asks each animal he meets if they have seen his hat. An unexpected turn of events occurs when the bear realizes *he* has seen his hat.

Illustrations: The endpapers feature all the animals that Bear meets as he searches for his hat. Klassen's illustrations are simple and uncluttered. The background of each illustration is a neutral cream color; however, when Bear realizes that he has seen his hat, the background of the illustration is a bright red—mirroring Bear's anger.

Sharing *This* Book with Children:

- Show the cover of the book and read the title. Ask the children to predict what the problem will be in the story and how Bear might try to solve the problem.

- Show the endpapers to the children, and ask them to identify the animals. Ask them to talk about why the illustrator might have included all these animals in the endpapers.
- Much of the story is written as a dialogue. On the pages where Bear is talking with another animal, use a different voice for the other animal to signal that a dialogue is taking place.
- After reading the page where Bear realizes he has seen his hat, ask the children why they think the illustrator made the illustration background red. Also ask the children why Bear says that he has seen his hat.
- The conclusion of the story is very open-ended. Bear *might* have eaten the rabbit that stole his hat, but the text never tells the reader this. So invite the children to talk about what they think happened at the end of the story. Be sure to ask them to support their thinking.
- After reading and discussing the book, return to the cover and ask the children why they think the title is written in red letters.

Content Connection/Skills Connection: Problem-solving
Insider Tip: This is the first of Jon Klassen's three "hat books."
Awards and Recognition: Geisel Honor book
Related Books:

- *This Is Not My Hat* by Jon Klassen
- *We Found a Hat* by Jon Klassen

If You Decide to Go to the Moon
Written by Faith McNulty and illustrated by Steven Kellogg
Scholastic, 2005
Ages: 5 and up
Summary: This is a book containing factual information about travel to the moon and about the moon itself. However, the information is presented using an imaginative framework device—a child traveling to the moon.
Illustrations: The oversized illustrations and use of

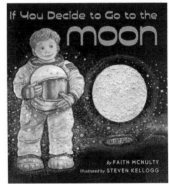
Reprinted with permission

many double-page spreads help to convey the vastness of space. Black is the background color of most of the illustrations of scenes set in space, whereas scenes on earth are done in color. This use of colors helps readers visualize differences between the earth and the moon.

Sharing *This* Book with Children:

- The book is long, so you may choose to share it across several read alouds.
- Before reading the book, create a chart containing three columns: K, W, and L. Before reading, ask the children what they know about the moon. Write their answers on the chart under the first column—K: What I Know.

- Then ask them what they want to know about the moon. Record responses under the second column—W: What I Want to Know.
- The subject matter is presented in a child-friendly way but is nonetheless complex, so encourage the children to talk both during and following the read aloud.
- As signaled by the title, the author invites readers to imagine they might go to the moon. In keeping with this approach, you might want to stop at key points in the read aloud and invite the children to imagine themselves in particular situations. For example, the children might suggest activities they could do on the spaceship as they travel to the moon and then think about how weightlessness might affect that activity.
- After reading the book (or parts of the book), return to the chart to add to the third column—L: What I Learned.

Content Connections/Skills Connections: Moon, space travel
Insider Tip: Listeners are pulled into the story because it is written in second person.
Related Books:

- *I Want to Be an Astronaut* by Byron Barton
- *The Moon Book* by Gail Gibbons

In the Small, Small Pond
Written and illustrated by Denise Fleming
Henry Holt, 1993
Ages: 3–7
Summary: The book describes the movements of pond animals across the seasons.
Illustrations: In many of the illustrations, the text is laid out in such a way as to mirror the movement of the animals portrayed in the illustration. For example, when the reader is told that herons lash, lunge, and plunge, the three verbs are positioned at sharp

Reprinted with permission

angles. The frog is the only animal that appears in each illustration including the cover of the book. Fleming shifts perspective from illustration to illustration. Sometimes we get a close-up view of a scene, and other times we look at the pond from afar or from above. Finding the frog in each illustration is a good way to gauge the perspective of the illustration.

Sharing *This* Book with Children:

- Introduce the book by sharing the front cover and the title. If the children do not know what a pond is, explain the word and perhaps even show a photograph of a pond.
- The first time you share the book with the children, read the story straight through—unless, of course, the children share observations or ask questions.

- There are numerous reasons you might choose to revisit the book. If the children did not notice the frog in each illustration, you can go back through each page and challenge them to find the frog.
- If no one has talked about the layout of the print, select a few pages to revisit and invite the children to observe how the print is laid out and to think about why the author did this. The second spread ("wiggle, jiggle, tadpoles wriggle") could be a good page to revisit because the children are likely to be familiar with the meaning of these words.
- While it is readily evident that the season represented on the first page of the book is different from the final page, the other seasonal changes are more subtle. To help the children identify these changes, begin by first talking about the season represented in the first and last pages. Then move through the book to see if they can identify other seasonal changes.
- The book is filled with rich, dynamic movement words. Select your favorites, and invite the children to dramatize the movements.

Content Connections/Skills Connections: Animals, habitat: pond, seasons
Insider Tip: Fleming uses vivid verbs throughout the book.
Related Books:

- *And Then It's Spring* by Julie Fogliano
- *When Spring Comes* by Kevin Henkes

It's Our Garden: From Seeds to Harvest in a School Garden
Written and photographed by George Ancona
Candlewick, 2013
Ages: 5–8
Summary: Text and photographs detail the work of students and teachers (and even families) as they create, care for, and harvest produce from their school garden in New Mexico.
Illustrations: Ancona's photographs provide a close look at the work done by children, teachers, and family members. Pages of the book also contain artwork created by the children.

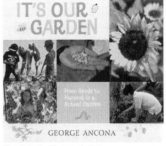
Reprinted with permission

Sharing *This* Book with Children:

- Begin by asking the students to share any experiences they have had with gardening.
- Before beginning to read, tell the children the class will create a chart of what they believe to be the most important steps in creating the garden.
- After reading, record the children's ideas about the important steps on a chart.
- If feasible, involve the students in creating their own school garden. If this is not feasible, bring seeds for the children to plant in small containers.
- Have the children document the growth of the plants in a class journal.

Content Connections/Skills Connections: Community, gardening

Insider Tips: This book is also available in Spanish. George Ancona has written many informational books for children, many focusing on diverse cultures.

Related Books:

- *Our School Garden* by Rick Swann
- *Up in the Garden and Down in the Dirt* by Kate Messner

Journey
Created by Aaron Becker
Candlewick, 2013
Ages: 5–8

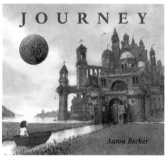

Reprinted with permission

Summary: In this wordless book, a bored girl enters another world, where she is swept up in a dramatic struggle of good versus evil.

Illustrations: The early pages of the story take place in the real world and are dominated by shades of brown with occasional (but important) bits of color. The illustrator uses color shifts throughout the book to signal important story events.

Sharing *This* Book with Children:

- As in any wordless book, move slowly through the pages of the book, giving the children ample time to talk about what they see and their interpretations of the illustrations.
- The story begins on the copyright/dedication page, so give the children time to look closely at this page. There are three items that appear in a color other than brown. If no one mentions these, invite the children to look for the spots of color in this illustration.
- The third-page spread is filled with color. Ask, "Why did the illustrator make this shift?"
- Important color shifts appear throughout the story. For example, the aircraft of the "evil forces" is all gray in contrast to the girl's bright red balloon. If children do not talk about these shifts, draw their attention to them and invite the children to think about how the illustrator uses color shifts in telling the story.
- At the end of the story, draw the children's attention to the "links" between the fantasy adventure and life in the real world (e.g., the purple bird and the red crayon).
- The adventure in the fantasy world centers around a conflict between good and evil. With the children, construct a story map to represent this portion of the story. Story map components include characters (good characters versus evil characters), story problem, attempts to solve the problem, outcomes of attempts, *and* resolution.

Content Connections/Skills Connections: Literary genre: wordless fantasy, visual literacy

Insider Tips: This is the first book in a trilogy created by Aaron Becker. The other two books in the trilogy are *Quest* and *Return*.

Awards and Recognition: Caldecott Award winner

Related Books:

- *Another* by Christian Robinson
- *Flotsam* by David Wiesner

Just a Minute: A Trickster Tale and Counting Book
Written and illustrated by Yuyi Morales
Chronicle, 2003

Reprinted with permission

Ages: 4–7

Summary: Señor Calavera arrives to take Grandma Beetle away, but Grandma Beetle is tricky. Each of Señor Calavera's requests for Grandma Beetle to leave are met by a "just a minute" response from Grandma Beetle as she busily prepares food for an upcoming celebration.

Illustrations: Morales's illustrations are filled with elements from Mexican culture, including *papel picado*, traditional clay pots and baskets, a machete for cutting fruit, wooden cooking spoons, piñatas, and a variety of traditional Mexican foods. And, of course, Señor Calavera (Mr. Skeleton) is the figure that playfully mimics the living in Day of the Dead celebrations in Mexico. In addition, Morales fills her illustrations with humorous details, such as Grandma Beetle winking at readers to let them in on her trick.

Sharing *This* Book with Children:

- In sharing the title of the book, be sure and read the subtitle: *A Trickster Tale and Counting Book*. Ask the children to talk about tricks they have played on other people. Explain that in a trickster tale, there is one character that outsmarts another character.
- Señor Calavera appears on the cover of the book. If you have Mexican or Mexican American children in the classroom, ask them if their families celebrate the Day of the Dead. If the answer is yes, invite them to talk about this celebration and the role of skeletons in the celebration.
- Looking at the cover, let the children predict who the trickster is and who is the one who is tricked.
- The trickster pattern emerges early in the story. Each time Señor Calavera asks Grandma Beetle to leave, invite the children to predict what she will say and do.
- Invite the children to look closely at the illustrations and talk about how Señor Calavera responds each time Grandma Beetle says "just a minute."
- At the end of the story, talk with the children about why Señor Calavera decided not to take Grandma Beetle away.
- On a subsequent reading of the story, children who do not know Spanish will enjoy learning the number words from one to ten that are used in organizing

the story. If you have Spanish speakers in the class, they can take the lead in teaching classmates the numbers in Spanish.

- If possible, let the children try some of the foods Grandma Beetle prepares.

Content Connections/Skills Connections: Birthdays, Mexican culture, trickster tales

Insider Tips: Yuyi Morales grew up in Mexico. Although she is now an American citizen, she spends part of the year in Mexico. She has written several books for young children, all of which are filled with rich cultural elements.

Awards and Recognition: Pura Belpré Award for Illustration

Related Books:

- *Just in Case* by Yuyi Morales
- *Niño Wrestles the World* by Yuyi Morales

King Bidgood's in the Bathtub
Written by Audrey Wood and illustrated by Don Wood
Harcourt, 1985
Ages: 4–6
Summary: The king won't get out of the bathtub! Who can solve the problem?
Illustrations: The illustrations are richly detailed, especially the bathtub scenes. In fact, these scenes unfold through the illustrations rather than the text.

Reprinted with permission

Sharing *This* Book with Children:

- Introduce the book by sharing the front cover, the title, and the name of the author and illustrator.
- The book might have words the children do not know but that are critical to understanding the story. One such word is *page*. Explain to the children that a royal page is the person with the job of waiting on the king.
- As you begin the book, pause on the dedication page to identify the boy as the king's page. Ask the children what the page seems to be doing. Encourage the children to watch for the page as you read the book.
- At the end of the book, ask the children how the page was able to solve the problem.

Content Connection/Skills Connection: Phonemic awareness: rhyming
Insider Tip: The book has a rollicking rhythm, so be sure to practice reading the book aloud before reading it to the children.
Awards and Recognition: Caldecott Honor book
Related Books:

- *Silly Sally* by Audrey Wood
- *The Napping House* by Audrey Wood, illustrated by Don Wood

Knuffle Bunny: A Cautionary Tale
Written and illustrated by Mo Willems
Hyperion, 2004
Ages: 4–6

Reprinted with permission

Summary: When Trixie loses her beloved stuffed animal, Knuffle Bunny, she desperately uses gibberish and flailing arms to communicate the problem to her father, but her efforts are to no avail. Only when her mother intervenes does a mad search through the laundromat turn up the missing bunny. And Trixie says her very first word: Knuffle Bunny.

Illustrations: The illustrations consist of black-and-white photographs on which bright cartoon drawings of people have been superimposed.

Sharing *This* Book with Children:

- Use the illustrations to talk about character emotions and intentions. For example, on the page where Trixie realizes that she has lost her bunny, ask the students, "What has Trixie realized? What is she thinking? How is she feeling? What will she do now?"
- The word *boneless* appears on the page where Trixie is having a meltdown. Invite the children to talk about what the word means.

Content Connections/Skills Connections: Feelings, facial expressions, predicting
Insider Tips: Mo Willems hides the pigeon somewhere in the pages of his nonpigeon books. In this book you can find the pigeon on the page where Mom, Dad, and Trixie are running back to the laundromat to find Knuffle Bunny. If children do not spot the pigeon during the first reading, encourage them to look for him on the second reading. Mo Willems is also the creator of the Elephant and Piggie books.
Awards and Recognition: Caldecott Honor book
Related Books:

- *Knuffle Bunny Too* by Mo Willems
- *Knuffle Bunny Free* by Mo Willems

The Lady with the Alligator Purse
Written and illustrated by Nadine Bernard Westcott
Little, Brown, 1988
Ages: 3–6

Reprinted with permission

Summary: In this nonsense rhyme, when Miss Lucy's baby tries to eat the bathtub, help comes in the form of the doctor (who recommends penicillin), the nurse (who recommends castor oil), and the lady with the alligator purse—who offers pizza!

Illustrations: The illustrations are filled with humorous details for children to discover.

Sharing *This* Book with Children:

- The rhythm and rhyme make the book one that must be read more than once. Invite the children to join in chanting and clapping on repeated readings.
- On repeated readings, as the teacher reads the narration, the children can take turns delivering the simple lines of the doctor, the nurse, and the lady with the alligator purse.

Content Connections/Skills Connections: Phonemic awareness, nonsense verse
Insider Tip: This is a jump-rope rhyme and has the typical features of this genre—rhythm, rhyme, and nonsense lines—features that make the genre so very appealing to young children.
Related Books:

- *Anna Banana* by Joanna Cole
- *Spider on the Floor* by Raffi

Last Stop on Market Street
Written by Matt de la Peña and illustrated by
Christian Robinson
Putnam, 2015
Ages: 5–8

Reprinted with permission

Summary: CJ is unhappy about having to take the bus across town every Sunday with his grandmother. His complaints are countered by Nana, who helps him discover beauty in unexpected places and realize how lucky he is to have the chance to help out at the local soup kitchen each Sunday.
Illustrations: Robinson's endpapers provide clues about some of what is to come in the story. His vibrant and energetic illustrations reveal the beauty that can be found in an urban setting.

Sharing *This* Book with Children:

- Invite children to talk about special things they do with a grandparent. Explain that this book is about a little boy who does something with his grandmother every Sunday.
- Open the book so the children can see both the front and back covers at the same time. Invite them to share their observations about what they see.
- After reading the line "How come we always gotta go here after church?," ask the children where CJ and Nana might be going.
- The author never uses words to identify the destination of CJ and Nana. Instead, the answer is found in the final illustration. Talk with the children about what they see in this illustration, what CJ and Nana are doing, and where they seem to be.
- After reading, make a T-chart. Have the children some up with a list of CJ's complaints and/or questions on the left side of the chart (e.g., why they don't have a car, CJ's wish for an iPod). On the right side, have the children identify

Nana's response. Follow this activity with this prompt: "What do you think was special about CJ's Nana?"

- de la Peña's includes rich language throughout the story. Share some of your favorite language (e.g., "He saw sunset colors swirling over crashing waves."). Reread the story, asking the children to listen for things the author says that they especially like. After reading the story, invite the children to share their favorite language from the story.

Content Connections/Skills Connections: Helping, grandparents

Insider Tip: It is very infrequent that a picturebook is recognized by the Newbery Committee, but *Last Stop on Market Street* was the winner of the 2016 Newbery Medal.

Awards and Recognition: Newbery Award, Caldecott Honor book, Coretta Scott King Illustrator Honor book

Related Books:

- *Carmela Full of Wishes* by Matt de la Peña, illustrated by Christian Robinson
- *Nana in the City* by Lauren Castillo

Leonardo the Terrible Monster
Written and illustrated by Mo Willems
Hyperion, 2005
Ages: 4 and up
Summary: Leonardo is a terrible monster; after all, he cannot scare anyone. So he sets out to find the most "scaredy-cat kid" in the whole world and try to scare him. In the end, Leonardo decides it is best to be a wonderful friend instead of a terrible monster.

Illustrations: Willems uses his familiar cartoon drawing style. The illustrations are on pastel backgrounds, and the font is large. The color of selected words is manipulated for emphasis. In most illustrations, Willems places characters in the lower corner of the spread to convey feelings of sadness.

Reprinted with permission

Sharing *This* Book with Children:

- Discuss with the students the qualities of a good friend.
- As you read, focus the students' attention on characters' feelings—and changes in feelings—by drawing their attention to the body language of the characters and their placement on the page.
- Ask, "How and why does Leonardo change from the beginning to the end of the book?"
- Discuss the idiom "I finally scared the tuna salad out of someone."

Content Connections/Skills Connections: Friendship, monsters

Insider Tip: Visit Mo Willems's website to learn more about this prolific author and illustrator: http://mowillems.com/.

Related Books:

- *Bear's New Friend* by Karma Wilson
- *Where the Wild Things Are* by Maurice Sendak

Let's Clap, Shout, Sing and Shout; Dance, Spin and Turn It Out!: Games, Songs and Stories from an African American Childhood
Collected by Patricia C. McKissack and illustrated by Brian Pinkney
Random House/Schwartz and Wade, 2017
Ages: All ages
Summary: This collection of rhymes, songs, and stories, well known and beloved by many African American families, has been brought together in a lively volume illustrated by Brian Pinkney. McKissack explains that from our youngest days, when our hands, feet, and voices were readily available for playful chanting, grow-

Reprinted with permission

ing up gave access to hand clapping, games, jump-rope rhymes, and more. McKissack's introductions to the entries offer explanations of historical and cultural significance, often sharing her own experiences as examples.

Illustrations: Pinkney explains how the rhymes brought back memories from playing on the playground to Sunday school stories he learned as a child. He describes how in listening to his memories, they danced onto the page. His illustration lines are energetic and full of movement.

Sharing *This* Book with Children:

- This is not a book to share with children in one sitting. Rather, it is important to become familiar with the contents of each chapter in order to determine the right selection for the right occasion.
- Chapter 1, "From Hand to Hand: Handclaps": The introduction explains that hand claps were often based on popular songs of the time, and this one (pp. 14–16) was based on a 1960s hit by R&B group Little Anthony and the Imperials: https://www.youtube.com/watch?v=4DOFw3SJrd0.
- Chapter 2, "Turn About: Jump Rope Rhymes and Games": A jump rope, a limbo stick, and a tug-of-war rope are the supplies needed for trying out the rhymes and games in this chapter.
- Chapter 3, "Shake Yo' Body: Circle Games and Ring Shouts": "Dem Bones" will be particularly fun for children to participate in (pp. 46–47). Weston Woods has taken the book by Bob Barner and turned it into a video production with music.
- Chapter 4, "Follow the Drinking Gourd: Songs Inspired by the Underground Railroad": Children will need support in this section. The numerous picturebooks on this topic will be helpful.

- Chapter 5, "Make a Joyful Noise: Spirituals, Hymns, and Gospel Music," and Chapter 6, "Pearls of Wisdom: Proverbs, Psalms, and Parables": These chapters are based on religious beliefs. The type of school in which you teach will determine whether you can include references to religion in school settings.
- Chapter 7, "A Word to the Wise: Superstitions, Fables, and Mama Sayings": This chapter is full of sayings that will be understood across cultures. The idea of "mama sayings" invites children to share wise sayings they have heard from their own mothers.
- Chapter 8, "On Program: Performance Pieces Inspired by African American Writers": This chapter might be conceptually difficult for young children.
- Chapter 9, "On the Porch or by the Fire: Folktales and Storytelling": The first story, Anansi, offers many connections to various versions of Anansi stories. There are many examples of African American folktales and storytelling to bring in as connections.

Content Connections/Skills Connections: Music, phonemic awareness, games

Insider Tips: Both the author and illustrator have a rich legacy of working with family members. Early in her career, Pat McKissack wrote many books in partnership with her husband, Frederick McKissack. Illustrator Brian Pinkney is married to author/editor Andrea Pinkney, and his father, Jerry Pinkney, is a highly awarded illustrator who has partnered with Brian's mother to create some picturebooks.

Awards and Recognition: Patricia McKissack and Brian Pinkney are frequent recipients of starred reviews and winners of numerous awards.

Related Books:

- *Flossie and the Fox* by Patricia McKissack
- *Mirandy and Brother Wind* by Patricia McKissack

Lilly's Purple Plastic Purse
Written and illustrated by Kevin Henkes
Greenwillow, 1996
Ages: 5–8
Summary: Lilly is so eager to share her new purse with her classmates that she doesn't wait until the appropriate time to share. So her teacher confiscates the purse, which makes Lilly furious. The story unfolds as Lilly seeks revenge and then must make amends.
Illustrations: Henkes's watercolor and ink illustrations very effectively convey Lilly's emotions—particularly through her eyes.

Sharing *This* Book with Children:

- Invite the children to talk about what they want to be when they grow up and why.
- Show the children the cover of the book, and ask them what the cover tells them about Lilly.

- This book is about emotions—what our emotions make us do and the consequences of those actions. This will make for a good focus as you move through the story. Consider stopping to talk with the children about these topics at the following points in the story:
  - when Lilly takes her purse to school
  - when Mr. Slinger takes the purse away from Lilly
  - when Lilly discovers the note Mr. Slinger wrote
  - when Lilly goes home
- As you talk about Lilly's shifting emotions, ask the children what they see in the illustrations that supports their responses.

Content Connections/Skills Connections: Emotions, family, school

Insider Tips: Henkes has written fifty books for children, including many about his mouse characters. He was awarded the Caldecott Medal for *Kitten's First Full Moon.*

Related Books:

- *Chrysanthemum* by Kevin Henkes
- *Wemberly Worried* by Kevin Henkes

The Lion and the Mouse
Created by Jerry Pinkney
Little, Brown, 2009
Ages: 5–8

Reprinted with permission

Summary: This is an almost wordless adaptation of Aesop's fable about a ferocious lion and a cowering mouse, with the moral that no act of kindness is ever wasted.

Illustrations: The watercolor illustrations in this book are stunning. The front endpapers establish the setting on the African savannah.

Sharing *This* Book with Children:

- The front cover of this book has neither title nor author/illustrator name—only a close-up of the lion's face, an unusual presentation. Have the children talk about the lion's expression.
- Open the book all the way so the children can see Pinkney's overall book design. Remove the dust jacket to reveal the different illustration on the cover of the book.
- Take the children through the whole book to get the arc of the entire story. Provide the children with plenty of time to look closely at each illustration.
- As you take the children back through the book, draw their attention to and discuss the different perspectives that Pinkney uses to tell the story:
  - Notice the close-ups; what kinds of feelings do they arouse in the children?
  - Some of the illustrations are two-page spreads; have the children talk about why Pinkney chose to do some of the pages this way.
  - One illustration looks down on the lion from above; why is it done this way?

- Don't forget to look at the endpapers in this book with the children. They're beautiful!

Content Connections/Skills Connections: Traditional literature, kindness
Awards and Recognition: Boston Globe Horn Book Award Honor book, Caldecott Award
Related Books:

- *Aesop's Fables* by Jerry Pinkney
- *The Little Red Hen* by Jerry Pinkney

Little Fox in the Forest
Created by Stephanie Graegin
Schwartz and Wade, 2017
Ages: 4–8

Reprinted with permission

Summary: This wordless book focuses on a little girl who has taken her beloved stuffed fox to school for show and tell. The first bit of color is introduced in an illustration when an actual fox steals the stuffed fox from the school playground. As the girl and her friend follow the fox into the woods, they enter a colorful fantasy world of animals, where their hunt for the stuffed fox continues, eventually reaching a satisfying ending. The structure of this picturebook is somewhat more complex than many. Most picturebooks have one major character with a problem, and the story revolves around the character's attempts to solve the problem. In this story, readers not only become caught up in the little girl's problem but also develop sympathy for the little fox who longs to have his own stuffed fox.

Illustrations: A careful inspection of the book cover reveals all major and minor characters. The early pages, set fully in the real world, are done in grayscale. The shift to full color occurs only when the girl and her friend enter into the "animal town" deep in the forest. This manipulation of color is a technique seen in many wordless picturebooks. A key difference between the beginning and the final endpapers serves as a clue to the story's resolution.

Sharing *This* Book with Children:

- Open the book to show both the front and back of the dust jacket. Invite the students to describe what they see and to predict what might happen in the story.
- On the first double-page spread, direct the children's attention to the left side of the page and talk about what is happening in the various frames. Be sure the students realize that the girl and boy are friends.
- On the facing page, read aloud the announcement that appears on the board in the classroom.
- On the next double-page spread, talk about what the illustrations reveal about the girl.

- Continue to move slowly through the book, encouraging the students to talk about what is happening in the story. As the children move deeper into the forest, more and more color appears in the illustrations. Ask the children why the illustrator might be adding more color.
- Pose this question at the end of the story: Why did the little girl give her beloved stuffed animal to the fox? Ask the children what they might do in this situation.

Content Connection/Skills Connection: Social and emotional development: sharing
Insider Tip: While Stephanie Graegin has illustrated picturebooks written by others, this is the first book she has both "written" and illustrated.
Related Books:

- *Float* by Daniel Miyare
- *Wave* by Suzy Lee

Llama Llama Red Pajama
Written and illustrated by Anna Dewdney
Viking, 2005
Ages: 3–5
Summary: When Mama Llama turns out the light and says goodnight, Baby Llama suddenly thinks of all kinds of reasons he needs his mama.
Illustrations: Up-close views of Llama convey the full range of emotions he is experiencing.

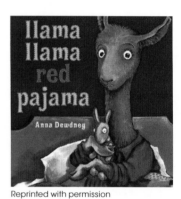
Reprinted with permission

Sharing *This* Book with Children:

- Before reading the book, ask the children to talk about their bedtime rituals.
- Encourage the children to look at the illustrations and talk about what they reveal about Baby Llama's feelings.
- Be sure to highlight all the words that describe how Baby Llama is feeling— words like *fret*, *whimper*, *moan*, *pout*, and *stomp*. Children can even act out these words.
- Children can also identify the rhyming words on each page.

Content Connections/Skills Connections: Bedtime, families
Insider Tip: This is one of a series of books about Llama.
Related Books:

- *Bedtime for Frances* by Russell Hoban
- *Don't Let the Pigeon Stay Up Late!* by Mo Willems

Look!
Written and illustrated by Jeff Mack
Philomel, 2015
Ages: 4–6

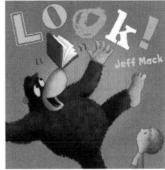
Reprinted with permission

Summary: In this book, which contains only two words—*look* and *out*—a gorilla is intent on enticing a little boy to play, but the little boy only has time for television.

Illustrations: This story is told almost entirely through illustrations.

Sharing *This* Book with Children:

- Because the story is *almost* a wordless book, it is important to move slowly through the illustrations, giving the children time to look closely.
- Invite the children to talk about how the gorilla tries to get the boy's attention and about the shifting feelings of the characters.
- At the end of the story, ask, "What have the gorilla and boy discovered about books?"
- The two featured words appear repeatedly throughout the story. Because they are always written in large font, you can direct students' attention to the words and invite them to read the words. Talk with the children about how they might interpret the words at different points in the story. Children will enjoy delivering the words differently as they read the story.

Content Connection/Skills Connection: Love of reading

Insider Tips: The book is designed with a vintage look. Jeff Mack's book *Playtime!* features the same characters and contains only three words: *playtime*, *bedtime*, and *shh*.

Related Books:

- *Playtime!* by Jeff Mack
- *Reading Makes You Feel Good* by Todd Parr

Looking for Bongo
Written and illustrated by Eric Velasquez
Holiday House, 2016
Ages: 4–6

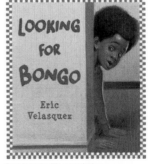
Reprinted with permission

Summary: A little boy looks all over for Bongo (a favorite stuffed animal). Finally, he discovers Bongo (and at the same time the reader discovers just what Bongo is). But the mystery is not fully solved. The little boy must find out *how* Bongo was lost.

Illustrations: The oil illustrations convey critical information about character emotions and key story events. The illustrations also contain hints about the family's African heritage, while the Spanish integrated throughout the book reveals the family's Latino heritage.

Sharing *This* Book with Children:

- Part of the fun of this book is discovering who/what Bongo is, so it is important not to give the children any clues that suggest Bongo is a favorite stuffed animal. In introducing the book, show the children the cover, read the title, and invite predictions about who Bongo might be and what the little boy on the cover might do to find Bongo.
- If you have Spanish speakers in the class, invite them to explain the Spanish phrases found throughout the story.
- After reading the page where the boy sees "a little brown arm," ask, "Who is Bongo?"
- After reading the page where the boy announces that he will "hold on to Bongo so he won't run away again," ask the children what the little boy might do to make sure he doesn't lose Bongo again.
- At the end of the story, ask the children if they have ever had problems with younger siblings taking their things. If yes, invite them to talk about their own solutions to the problem.

Content Connections/Skills Connections: Problem-solving, stuffed animals
Insider Tip: The final page in the book includes a variety of interesting information you may want to share with the children, including information about other meanings of *bongo*.
Related Books:

- *Corduroy* by Don Freeman
- *Monkey and Me* by Emily Gravett

Love
Written by Matt de la Peña and illustrated by Loren Long
Putnam, 2018
Ages: 5–8
Summary: In lyrical language, each page describes a sight, smell, sound, experience, or relationship that is love—shining stars, the creases in a grandfather's face.
Illustrations: Each page's new facet of love is reflected in the accompanying illustration.

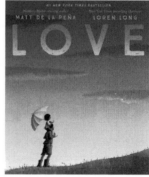

Reprinted with permission

Sharing *This* Book with Children:

- Begin by talking with the children about things they think about when they hear the word *love*. You might want to launch this discussion with an example or two of your own.
- As you read the book, provide opportunities for the children to share responses.
- After reading, invite the children to create a page for a class book entitled *Love*. Each child can create an illustration to accompany what they write.

Content Connection/Skills Connection: Social emotional development: love

Insider Tips: There is also a Spanish version of this book. *Last Stop on Market Street* by Matt de la Peña received the Newbery Award and a Caldecott Honor award.
Related Books:

- *Carmela Full of Wishes* by Matt de la Peña
- *Last Stop on Market Street* by Matt de la Peña

Mama Cat Has Three Kittens
Written and illustrated by Denise Fleming
Henry Holt, 1998
Ages: 3–5

Reprinted with permission

Summary: Mama has three kittens. While Mama Cat and two kittens are out and about, Boris is asleep. But when Mama Cat and the two kittens want to nap, the tables are turned.
Illustrations: In making her illustrations, Fleming uses colored-paper pulp and squeezes it into stencils she has drawn and cut.

Sharing *This* Book with Children:

- Introduce the book by sharing the front cover, the title, and the name of the author/illustrator. If you have shared other books by Denise Fleming, be sure to mention these titles.
- This is a simple, humorous story, and you may want to read it straight through.
- "Boris naps" is a sentence that is repeated throughout. Once the pattern is established, pause before reading "Boris naps" so the children can chime in or even supply the sentence.
- After reading, the children can dramatize what happens in each "scene." For example, when Mama Cat washes her paws, the children become the kittens and wash their paws.
- Young children enjoy reading (or doing emergent readings of) patterned books, so leave the story in the book center.

Content Connection/Skills Connection: Animals: kittens
Insider Tip: Fleming uses vivid verbs to describe the actions of the cats.
Related Books:

- *Kitten's First Full Moon* by Kevin Henkes
- *A Kitten's Tale* by Eric Rohmann

Marta! Big and Small
Written by Jen Arena and illustrated by Angela Dominguez
Roaring Brook, 2016
Ages: 3–5

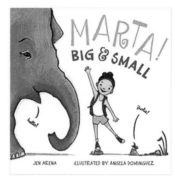

Reprinted with permission

Summary: Through shifting perspectives, this bilingual book compares and contrasts Marta, *una niña*, to a variety of animals: "To a bug, Marta is *grande*. Big, very big. To an elephant, Marta is *pequeña*. Small, very small."

Illustrations: This book is about perspective, and the illustrator cleverly manipulates visual perspective in many of the illustrations.

Sharing *This* Book with Children:

- Read the title, and invite the children to talk about how Marta can be both big and small.
- In addition to reading the book title, read the words on the cover that are spoken by the elephant ("hello!") and the bug ("¡*hola*!"). Ask if anyone knows what *hola* means. If not, tell them it means *hello* in Spanish and that there are lots of Spanish words used in the book.
- A simple pattern serves to organize the book (i.e., Marta is described one way from the perspective of one animal, and then—on the next page—she is described in the opposite way from the perspective of another animal). Once this pattern is established, you can use the page turn as the place to engage the children in making predictions. For example, once Marta is described as "quiet" by the lion, invite the children to predict an animal to which she might seem "loud."
- When Marta meets the snake, she is described as *ingeniosa* or clever. Invite the children to talk about why she is described in this way.
- Toward the end of the book, there is a double-page spread in which Marta is again compared to many of the same animals in the book, but this time the comparison has changed. For example, on the double-page spread when Marta is compared to the lion, she is presented as "loud" like the lion—not "quiet." Ask the children what Marta is doing in these illustrations that now make her *like* the animal rather than *different*.
- On rereadings, invite the children to contribute the Spanish words used in the story or the English translations—depending on the home languages of the children.
- After reading the book, throughout the day encourage the children to use new words (in English or Spanish) that they have learned.
- At the art center, the children can draw themselves compared to different animals.

Content Connections/Skills Connections: Opposites, perspective, vocabulary: English and Spanish

Insider Tips: Spanish speakers will enjoy a book with Spanish words. The rich visual and verbal contexts in which the Spanish appear offer clues for those children who do not speak Spanish. A glossary of Spanish words appears at the end of the book.

Related Books:

- *How Do You Say?/¿Como Se Dice?* by Angela Dominguez
- *Niño Wrestles the World* by Yuyi Morales

Maybe Something Beautiful
Written by Isabel Campoy and Theresa Howell and illustrated by Rafael López
Houghton Mifflin Harcourt, 2016
Ages: 5–8
Summary: A little girl living in a gray city begins to share her paintings with neighbors. Then she meets an artist who joins her in creating a mural for the neighborhood. Soon other members of the community join in to transform the neighborhood.

Reprinted with permission

Illustrations: The illustrations are done with a combination of acrylic paint on wood, photography, and digital art.

Sharing *This* Book with Children:

- Introduce the book by sharing the cover, the title, and the names of the authors and illustrator.
- Invite predictions at these junctures of the story:
  - At the end of the first page of text, ask, "What is Mira thinking about? Why does she say 'maybe . . .'? Maybe what? What could it be?"
  - When you reach the page that ends, "Until . . . ," pause and wonder about what's going to happen. Then turn the page to the illustration of the policeman, and before reading anything, ask the children to predict what they think will happen now.
  - At the end of the book, say, "There's the word *maybe* again. 'Just maybe' what? What do you think Mira means here?"
- There are great opportunities for follow-up activities to this book:
  - Inside your classroom: Set up a big "wall" where children can create their own mural.
  - Outside the classroom: If you live in a community that has murals on building walls, visit the murals with someone who knows their history and can talk with the children about who created the murals and the stories behind them.
  - Another way to visit community murals is through the Internet. Philadelphia, for example, has many murals, and its project is described at https://www.muralarts.org.

Content Connections/Skills Connections: Community, action

Insider Tip: The book was inspired by actual events in San Diego, California.
Related Books:

- *Last Stop on Market Street* by Matt de La Peña, illustrated by Christian Robinson
- *Something Beautiful* by Sharon Dennis Wyeth, illustrated by Chris K. Soentpiet

Mice and Beans
Written by Pam Muñoz Ryan and illustrated by Joe Cepeda
Scholastic, 2001
Ages: 4–8

Reprinted with permission

Summary: Rosa Maria spends all week preparing for her granddaughter's birthday party, but items for the party keep disappearing—including the mousetraps she sets. Rosa Maria is unaware of the mice scurrying around her house. The mice ultimately redeem themselves by remembering to fill the piñata with candy—something that has slipped Rosa Maria's mind entirely.

Illustrations: Full-bleed illustrations feature the hustle and bustle of Rosa Maria—as well as the activities of the mice, which are never mentioned in the text of the story. Phrases that deserve special emphasis when reading appear in larger colored font (e.g., "But it had vanished." "But it was gone again!" "But it was nowhere in sight!" "No mousetrap!").

Sharing *This* Book with Children:

- Invite the children to talk about birthday traditions in their families.
- Spanish-speaking children will enjoy Spanish phrases used throughout the story ("*Qué boba soy!* Silly me"), while non-Spanish speakers will enjoy learning Spanish phrases.
- Discuss with the children the new vocabulary words in the book (*simmer, assembled, devoured*).

Content Connections/Skills Connections: Celebrations, days of the week, vocabulary
Insider Tips: This book is available in Spanish. A glossary and pronunciation guide is located at the back of the book.
Awards and Recognition: ALA Notable Book
Related Books:

- *A Birthday for Bear* by Bonny Becker
- *Just a Minute* by Yuyi Morales

The Mitten
Written and illustrated by Jan Brett
Putnam, 1989
Ages: 5–8

Reprinted with permission

Summary: When a boy loses his new mitten in the snow, a string of animals come across it and see it as a cozy place to be on a cold winter's day. One by one they squeeze into the mitten.

Illustrations: Brett presents three story strands simultaneously through the use of borders surrounding the central illustration.

Sharing *This* Book with Children:

- After introducing the book, invite the children to predict what will happen in the story.
- The copyright/dedication page is the first page to feature the borders that will play an important role in developing the story. Be sure to call the children's attention to these border illustrations, and encourage them to pay special attention to the borders as you read.
- As you read, provide the children with time to talk about what they see in the borders.
- As animal after animal squeezes into the mitten, periodically invite the children to predict what will happen.
- On the final page of the book (which contains no words), ask the children to talk about what the grandmother is likely thinking as she looks at her grandson's gloves.
- This final page also offers an opportunity for a dramatic experience. Children can step into the roles of the grandmother and grandson and talk about how the one mitten might have become stretched to such an enormous size.

Content Connections/Skills Connections: Folktale, comprehension: predicting, visual literacy

Insider Tip: Brett is known for both her retelling of folktales and the use of borders in stories.

Related Books:

- *Annie and the Wild Animals* by Jan Brett
- *Hedgie's Surprise* by Jan Brett

Move!
Written and illustrated by Steve Jenkins and Robin Page
Houghton Mifflin, 2006
Ages: 3–5

Reprinted with permission

Summary: This informational book features various animals and the ways in which they move. Two different ways of moving are presented for each featured animal (e.g., a crocodile *leaps* to get its meal and then *slithers* into the water).

Illustrations: Page turns are important in this book. The first movement of the animal is presented on one page, and the second type of movement is presented on the following page. Jenkins talks about how he made the illustrations for *Move!* on his website: http://www.stevejenkinsbooks.com/making_books_video.html.

Sharing *This* Book with Children:

- Invite the children to demonstrate different ways they can move (e.g., walking, skipping, hopping, running).
- Show the cover of the book, and read the title. Tell the children that animals move in different ways too—just like them. Children can also talk about the different ways their pets move.
- As each new animal is introduced, invite the children to try to identify the animal.
- The structure of the book (which presents each animal's second type of movement on a subsequent page) makes the page turn the perfect place to stop and invite the children to predict the animal's second type of movement.
- The book concludes with a question: What movements do you make? On a chart, make a list of the movements the children name. Invite them to demonstrate each movement.
- On a second reading of the book, invite the children to act out some of the movements the animals make.
- After reading the book, talk with the children about how Steve Jenkins creates his illustrations. Make different kinds of paper available at the art center so the children can create their own collages.

Content Connections/Skills Connections: Animals, movement, vocabulary
Insider Tips: At the end of the book, the authors present additional information about each animal. Steve Jenkins has written numerous outstanding informational books about nature.
Related Books:

- *Actual Size* by Steve Jenkins
- *What Do You Do with a Tail Like This?* by Steve Jenkins with Robin Page

Mr. Tiger Goes Wild
Written and illustrated by Peter Brown
Little, Brown, 2013
Ages: 4–8

Reprinted with permission

Summary: Mr. Tiger lives in a proper town—and he is tired of being proper. So, when he decides to "go wild," the townspeople ask him to go to the wilderness. He does just that, only to discover that he misses his friends. So Mr. Tiger returns to town and finds that things are beginning to change.

Illustrations: The book cover hidden beneath the dust jacket offers a clue to Mr. Tiger's transformation. Front endpapers reflect the solidity (and boredom) of life in town, while the back endpapers reflect the openness of life in the wilderness. There is also a contrast in shapes and colors between illustrations of the town and those of the wilderness.

Sharing *This* Book with Children:

- Show the children the dust jacket, book cover, and endpapers, and encourage them to predict what might happen in the story.
- After the first two pages, ask the children what they think of Mr. Tiger's town.
- On the third page ("And then one day Mr. Tiger had a very wild idea"), ask the children what seems to be happening to Mr. Tiger in the illustration.
- On the page with the text "And then Mr. Tiger went a little too far," ask the children why they think the author says Mr. Tiger has gone too far.
- Once Mr. Tiger is in the wilderness, ask the children if they think he made a good decision.
- When Mr. Tiger returns to town, he finds things are changing. Invite the children to talk about why things might be changing in the town.

Content Connection/Skills Connection: Identity
Awards and Recognition: Boston Globe Horn Book Award, Golden Kite Award for Picturebook
Related Books:

- *Children Make Terrible Pets* by Peter Brown
- *Creepy Carrots* by Aaron Reynolds

My Friend Rabbit
Written and illustrated by Eric Rohmann
Square Fish, 2002
Ages: 3–5

Reprinted with permission

Summary: When Mouse's new plane is caught in a tree, Rabbit is determined to help.
Illustrations: Much of the storytelling takes place only through the illustrations.

Sharing *This* Book with Children:

- Many of the page turns can be used as invitations to predict (e.g., when Rabbit announces "I've got an idea" or when Rabbit runs off after pulling Elephant into the scene).
- Other opportunities for predicting and making inferences using illustrations clues:
  - On the page with the worried ducklings scurrying, predict what will happen next.
  - On the page where the animals are not happy with rabbit after falling, predict what will happen to rabbit.
  - On the page that must be viewed vertically, have the students look at the animals' expressions as well as the height of the "animal ladder" and discuss how much farther Rabbit had to go to reach the airplane.
- Children can talk about how they help their friends.

Content Connections/Skills Connections: Friendship, comprehension: predicting, problem-solving
Awards and Recognition: Caldecott Medal winner
Related Books:

- *Clara and Asha* by Eric Rohmann
- *My Friend Is Sad* by Mo Willems

My Name Is Sangoel
Written by Karen Lynn Williams and Khadra Mohammed and illustrated by Catherine Stock
Eerdmans, 2009
Ages: 5–8

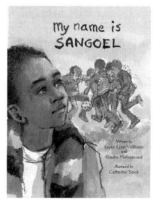
Reprinted with permission

Summary: When no one can pronounce his name, Sangoel feels he has lost everything from his home in Sudan—until he comes up with a way of writing his name that also inspires his classmates to use his "writing system."
Illustrations: Early illustrations give insight into Sangoel's life in Sudan and his family's early, confusing experiences in the United States. Children will need to closely examine the illustrations in the final pages of the book to understand how Sangoel solved his problem.

Sharing *This* Book with Children: Sharing this book with newcomer children will be quite different than sharing it with children who have had little contact with newcomers. In sharing the book with newcomers, emphasis should be placed on ways in which their early experiences in the new country have been similar to or different from Sangoel's experiences.

These suggestions assume students have had only limited experiences with newcomers:

- Ask, "How does it feel when someone mispronounces your name?"
- Explain that the story is about a boy named Sangoel who comes to the United States from a country in Africa. Help children locate Sudan on a map.
- As you begin to read the story, give the students an opportunity to linger over the illustrations. Talk about how Sangoel's life in Sudan might have been different from life in the United States and how it was also the same (e.g., grandparents, good friends). Also talk about why Sangoel and his family decided to leave Sudan and move to the United States.
- After reading the pages focused on the family's arrival in the United States, pause to talk about the many new things that Sangoel and his family were encountering.
- After completing the story, invite the children to talk about the problem in the story and how Sangoel solved his problem. You will likely want to review key illustrations during this discussion, beginning with the one with Sangoel wearing his "Dynamo" shirt. Explain to students that Sangoel wrote his name by creating a pictograph. That is, he used pictures to represent the sounds in his name.
- Help the children read the pictographs created by Sangoel's classmates.
- If working with older children, invite them to create pictographs for their own name or the name of a friend.

Content Connections/Skills Connections: Identity, refugees
Insider Tips: Khadra Mohammed is a Somali refugee and has worked as director of a refugee center in Pittsburgh. Karen Williams served as a Peace Corps volunteer in Malawi.
Related Books:

- *Four Feet, Two Sandals* by Karen Williams and Khadra Mohammed
- *The Name Jar* by Yangsook Choi

My Papi Has a Motorcycle
Written by Isabel Quintero and illustrated by Zeke Peña
Penguin Random House, 2019
Ages: 4–8
Summary: A little girl eagerly awaits Papi's return from work each day, when the two of them will go riding through town on Papi's motorcycle.
Illustrations: An overview of the town setting is revealed in the front endpapers, which also serve as

Reprinted with permission

the title page for the book. The illustrations are infused with cultural details reflecting a Latino community and the warmth of a loving Latino family.

Sharing *This* Book with Children:

- Ask, "What special things do you love to do with your mother or father?"
- Introduce the story by telling the children that the little girl in the story also loves to do a special thing with her father. Read the title, and ask the children what might make riding a motorcycle with her father so special for the little girl in the story.
- Before reading, challenge the students to try to figure out the little girl's name—which is never mentioned by the author.
- After reading, ask, "What do you believe was the most special part of the ride?"
- Both family and community are important facets of this book. So if the children do not talk about these elements, guide them in these directions with prompts like these:
  ◦ In what ways is Daisy's community like yours? In what ways is it different? What makes it such a special community?
  ◦ How do the author and illustrator show us how much Daisy's family loves her?
- Because setting is so important in this book—and illustrations are so important in developing the setting—you might want to revisit the illustrations with the students and look closely at what the illustrator shows readers about this community.
- This book offers rich possibilities for writing. The children can write about their own community or special things they do with a family member.

Content Connections/Skills Connections: Community, family

Awards and Recognition: Pura Belpré Illustration Honor Award, Tomás Rivera Mexican American Children's Book Award, American Library Association Notable Children's Book

Insider Tips: There is a Spanish edition of this book. An endnote explains that the book is based on the author's childhood memories of going for motorcycle rides with her own father around Corona, California.

Related Books:

- *Carmela Full of Wishes* by Matt de la Peña
- *Uptown* by Bryan Collier

My Very First Mother Goose
Selected by Iona Opie and illustrated by Rosemary Wells
Candlewick, 1996
Ages: 3–6
Summary: This is a collection of some of the much-loved Mother Goose rhymes (e.g., "Hickory, Dickory, Dock," "Jack and Jill") as well as less familiar ones.
Illustrations: Illustrator Rosemary Wells fills the pages of this book with oversized animal characters done in her signature style.

Reprinted with permission

Sharing *This* Book with Children:

- This is not a book to share with the children in one sitting. Become familiar with all the rhymes so you can select the right one for the right occasion.
- Nursery rhymes are meant to be revisited. Invite the children to choose favorites for you to read.
- On repeated readings of rhymes, invite the children to identify rhyming words.

Content Connection/Skills Connection: Phonemic awareness: rhyming
Insider Tip: Rosemary Wells is the creator of a much-loved series of books about two rabbits, Max and his sister Ruby.
Related Books:

- *Here Comes Mother Goose* selected by Iona Opie, illustrated by Rosemary Wells
- *Lucy Cousins Treasury of Nursery Rhymes* by Lucy Cousins

The Napping House
Written by Audrey Wood and illustrated by Don Wood
Harcourt Brace Jovanovich, 1984
Ages: 3 and up
Summary: On a rainy day, sleepy creatures—both human and animal—nap on a cozy bed until a wakeful flea emerges on the scene.
Illustrations: Through careful observation children will discover that *each* character in the book (from granny to the flea) appears in *each* illustration. The rainy day in this book gradually turns into a sunny day, a change that is apparent only through the illustrations.

Reprinted with permission

Sharing *This* Book with Children:

- Because the first part of *The Napping House* has a cumulative structure, the children can join in on repetitive phrases.
- Invite the children to act out the "sleeping words," words like *snoozing, dozing, snoring,* and *slumbering.*
- On a second reading of the book, the children can take turns pointing out each of the characters found in a given illustration.
- As each character is awakened, ask the children to look carefully at their expressions for clues to how the character feels.
- After reading the book, have the children look back at the beginning endpapers and the final endpapers and think about why they are different.

Content Connections/Skills Connections: Bedtime, weather
Insider Tip: Finding the flea and the mouse on the final page of the book is a challenge, but take a careful look at the fence posts. Just as the lighting in the illustrations changes throughout the book, so does the perspective.

Related Books:

- *10 Minutes till Bedtime* by Peggy Rathmann
- *Wynken, Blynken, and Nod* by Eugene Field, illustrated by David McPhail
- *Sleep Like a Tiger* by Mary Logue

Other Books by This Author:

- *Piggies*
- *Silly Sally*
- *King Bidgood's in the Bathtub*
- *The Full Moon at the Napping House*

The Neighborhood Mother Goose
Selected and illustrated by Nina Crews
Greenwillow, 2004
Ages: 3–5
Summary: This collection of Mother Goose rhymes includes familiar rhymes such as "Humpty Dumpty" as well as less familiar ones like "Cobbler, Cobbler." The book is illustrated with photographs of children from diverse ethnic backgrounds who live in urban neighborhoods.
Illustrations: Many of the photographs have been digitally manipulated. For example, the photograph that accompanies "Hey Diddle Diddle" features a little boy and his dog as well as a number of items scanned into the photograph.

Sharing *This* Book with Children:

- This isn't a book to read straight through. Rather, it's one to visit time and again. Perhaps you will choose to share a rhyme or two daily at a particular time of the day. And of course children will request rereadings of favorites and join in on those rereadings.
- As you select particular rhymes to share, think carefully about the distinctive features of the rhyme. For example, because "Jack and Jill" has a particularly strong syllabic beat, the children will enjoy clapping the syllables on a rereading. Or you might want to invite the children to identify the rhyming words in "Twinkle, Twinkle Little Star." Still other rhymes, like "Jack Be Nimble," beg to be acted out.

Content Connections/Skills Connections: Phonemic awareness: rhyming, rhythm
Insider Tip: Nina Crews is the daughter of picturebook creators Donald Crews and Ann Jonas.
Related Books:

- *My Very First Mother Goose* by Iona Opie
- *My First Mother Goose* by Tomie dePaola

Nic Bishop Spiders
Written and photographed by Nic Bishop
Scholastic Nonfiction, 2007
Ages: 4–8
Summary: Each spread contains an amazing close-up photograph of a spider as well as information about spiders.
Illustrations: Bishop's close-up photographs provide remarkable detail. The background color of each spread is coordinated with one of the colors in the photograph.

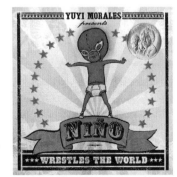
Reprinted with permission

Sharing *This* Book with Children:

- KWL is a good strategy to use with this book. Record responses on chart paper.
- K (what I know): Begin by asking the children what they know about spiders.
- W (what I want to know): Then ask them what questions they have about spiders.
- As you read the book, give the children time to look closely at the remarkable photographs.
- L (what I learned): After reading, revisit the children's list of questions and record answers found in the text as well as other facts they have learned about spiders.
- Be sure to display the KWL chart in the classroom.

Content Connection/Skills Connection: Spiders
Insider Tip: In preparing to write this book, Bishop raised spiders in his home so he could closely observe them and learn about their molting, courting, and egg laying.
Awards and Recognition: Sibert Honor book
Related Books:

- *Spiders* by Gail Gibbons
- *National Geographic Readers: Spiders* by Laura Marsh

Niño Wrestles the World
Written and illustrated by Yuyi Morales
Roaring Brook, 2013
Ages: 4–6
Summary: Niño faces a host of adversaries, including the Guanajuato mummy, which he conquers with his daring tickles, and La Llorana, which he stuns with doll decoys. He is the greatest hero—until his little sisters wake up from their nap!
Illustrations: The illustrations in this book are notable, beginning with the cover, which features Niño in a heroic stance wearing the mask of the luchadores (Mexican wrestlers). Endpapers feature the villains Niño will encounter. Page turns

Reprinted with permission

move the story forward, and the use of colorful and dynamic fonts adds to the drama of this energetic picturebook.

Sharing *This* Book with Children:

- Children might not be familiar with the luchadores (but they will recognize a kindred figure in this action hero). If there are children who know about luchadores, ask them to share what they know. Information about luchadores appears at the end of the book.
- Read the title, show the cover of the book, and invite the children to predict what might happen in the book. Ask the children to predict the opponents this hero will encounter; then share the information presented in the front endpapers.
- As Niño first encounters each opponent, invite the children to predict how he might defeat the opponent.
- After listening to the story, the children can visit the art center to draw pictures of the villains that Niño and the Hermanitas (sisters) will together encounter and the ways they will defeat them. These pictures can be posted in the classroom and shared at a later time.

Content Connections/Skills Connections: Action heroes, siblings
Insider Tip: Learn more about luchadores at https://en.wikipedia.org/wiki/Lucha_libre.
Awards and Recognition: Pura Belpré Medal
Related Books:

- *Robot Zot* by Jon Scieszka, illustrated by David Shannon
- *Traction Man Is Here!* by Mini Grey

No Such Thing
Written by Jackie French Koller and illustrated by Betsy Lewin
Boyds Mills Press, 1997
Ages: 4–6
Summary: Howard is afraid a monster is under his bed. His mother tells him there is no such thing, while Monster's mother tells him there is no such thing as a boy and certainly no such thing as a boy on top of his bed. One spooky night Howard and Monster find out the truth and plan something for their mothers.

Reprinted with permission

Illustrations: Lewin's illustrations in this book make great use of perspective and close-ups.

Sharing *This* Book with Children:

- This is a good book for having the children use their predicting skills. Good places for predictions:
  - After you read the page that ends "Until it got dark . . . ," ask, "What do you think will happen in the dark?"

- ○ After you read the page that ends "Howard/Monster decided to take one more look," ask, "What's going to happen now? Why do you think that?"
- ○ After you read the page that ends "you are going to be punished. Good night!," ask, "What's going to happen next?"
- ○ Stop on the last page after reading, "He leaned close and whispered in Monster's ear." Ask, "Why is Howard smiling? What plan do you think he came up with?"
- ○ After reading, ask the children what they think will happen when their mothers come in. Invite them to act out that scene.

Content Connection/Skills Connection: Fear of the dark
Insider Tip: Lewin received a Caldecott Honor Award for the book *Click, Clack, Moo*.
Related Books:

- *Can't You Sleep, Little Bear?* by Martin Waddell
- *There's a Nightmare in My Closet* by Mercer Mayer

Not a Stick
Written and illustrated by Antoinette Portis
HarperCollins, 2008
Ages: 3–6
Summary: When a little pig finds a stick, an unseen "character" repeatedly queries the pig about the stick. After first explaining that it is not a stick, the little pig repeatedly explains or shows all the imaginary things the stick can be.
Illustrations: On the left side of each double-page spread appears a simple sentence, while on the right side appears a simple black line drawing of the pig with the stick used in imaginative ways. This pattern is disrupted only twice with double-page spreads showing dramatic scenes.

Sharing *This* Book with Children:

- Before reading the book, present a stick to the children and ask what it is. After they respond, ask them what they might *pretend* the stick is.
- The pattern of the book strongly suggests how to best invite children to participate. The unnamed character queries the pig. On the next page, the illustration reveals the imaginary way in which the pig plays with the stick. Once the pattern is established, pause before the page turns to ask the children to predict how the pig will use the stick.
- After reading the book, the children can take turns using the stick in an imaginary way. The other children can guess what the child is pretending with the stick.

Content Connection/Skills Connection: Imagination
Insider Tip: *Not a Box* is another book by Portis that follows this pattern.
Related Books:

- *The Dot* by Peter H. Reynolds
- *Harold and the Purple Crayon* by Crockett Johnson

The Odd Egg
Written and illustrated by Emily Gravett
Simon and Schuster, 2008
Ages: 4–6

Reprinted with permission

Summary: All the birds have laid eggs, except for Duck, but Duck *finds* an enormous egg. As the eggs begin to hatch, all the birds are proud mamas, but none is prouder than Duck, whose egg yields quite a surprise—an alligator!

Illustrations: The illustrations provide humorous details and critical story information. For example, we only learn what hatched from Duck's egg through an illustration. And this story concludes on the final endpapers—not on the last page of the story.

Sharing *This* Book with Children:

- In introducing the story, ask the children why the book might be entitled *The Odd Egg*.
- As you read, encourage the children to talk about what they discover through the illustrations.
- On the page in which the text reads "But the other birds did not," ask the children to talk about the way in which the other birds are treating Duck.
- When you read the page in which Duck is waiting and waiting, direct the children's attention to what Duck is doing. Why might Duck be knitting?
- When Duck's egg begins to crack, invite the children to guess what is going to emerge.
- On the following page, which reveals the alligator, ask the children what is likely to happen. Then turn to the back endpapers and talk about what *actually* happened.
- To complicate the discussion, show children the back cover, which shows a single feature and the word "Quack." Ask, "Why did the author/illustrator put this on the back cover?"

Content Connections/Skills Connections: Baby animals, eggs, surprises

Insider Tips: Emily Gravett is an English author/illustrator who is particularly well known for the interesting (and usually surprising) twists that her stories take. She has twice won the Kate Greenaway Medal, the award given annually in England for the best illustrated book. This book was first published in the United Kingdom.

Related Books:

- *Egg* by Kevin Henkes
- *First the Egg* by Laura Vaccaro Seeger

Officer Buckle and Gloria
Written and illustrated by Peggy Rathmann
Putnam, 1995
Ages: 5 and up

Reprinted with permission

Summary: Officer Buckle knows more about safety than anyone in the town of Napville, but whenever he tries to share his safety tips nobody listens. But then a police dog named Gloria begins to accompany Officer Buckle on his school visits. Unbeknownst to Officer Buckle, Gloria has her own way of demonstrating the safety tips that grabs the attention of his audience. When he finds out he is being upstaged, he leaves his job. Can Gloria convince him to return?

Illustrations: Rathmann's illustrations provide humor and some critical story information.

Sharing *This* Book with Children:

- Explain that police officers are community helpers and that in this story Officer Buckle helps by sharing safety tips at schools.
- Ask the children to share safety tips they think are important. Tell them to listen as you read to see if Officer Buckle shared any of the same safety tips.
- As you read, ask, "What is Gloria doing during Officer Buckle's presentations?"
- On the page where Officer Buckle and Gloria are watching the ten o'clock news, ask the children to carefully look at the illustration to figure out what Officer Buckle and Gloria see on the TV screen. Ask, "How does Officer Buckle feel?"
- At the end of the story, invite children to talk about what it means to be someone's buddy. Ask, "What do friends do for each other?"

Content Connections/Skills Connections: Community jobs: police, friendship, teamwork
Awards and Recognition: Caldecott Medal
Related Books:

- *The Day the Babies Crawled Away* by Peggy Rathmann
- *Ruby the Copycat* by Peggy Rathmann

Oh, No!
Written by Candace Fleming and illustrated by Eric Rohmann
Schwartz and Wade Books, 2012
Ages: 4 and up

Summary: As various jungle creatures try to help Frog get out of a deep, deep hole, they fall in themselves (oh, no!). They've got to find a way out before Tiger eats them.
Illustrations: Much of the storytelling takes place through the illustrations. Look closely to see what is shown but not told in words.

Reprinted with permission

Sharing *This* Book with Children:

- The story starts on the cover and the front endpapers and finishes on the back endpapers. Be sure to "read" the whole story with the children.
- Many of the page turns can serve as invitations to predict what will happen as each animal tries to help Frog.
- The children will want to chime in on the "Oh, no!" refrain.
- Several of the illustrations take the interesting perspective of looking up from down in the hole. Children might initially need help to understand this perspective.
- Invite predictions after reading this page: "Wailed Tiger, 'Please, please, won't you help me out?'"

Content Connections/Skills Connections: Cooperation, comprehension: predicting
Insider Tip: This book has a distinctive rhythm, so practice reading it aloud before you read it to the children.
Awards and Recognition: Wanda Gág Read Aloud Honor book
Related Books:

- *My Friend Rabbit* by Eric Rohmann
- *Swimmy* by Leo Lionni

¡Olinguito, de la A a la Z!/Olinguito, from A to Z!
Written and illustrated by Lulu Delacre
Children's Book Press/Lee and Low, 2016
Ages: 5–9

Reprinted with permission

Summary: Readers are introduced to the animals and plants of the Ecuadoran cloud forest, including the olinguito, a species first identified by a scientist only in the early years of the twenty-first century. The alphabet serves as the device for organizing this "tour" of the cloud forest. Children will encounter many new animals and plants in this book.
Illustrations: Each double-page spread includes all the animals and plants named in the text. In an endnote, the illustrator explains that

her goal was "to create detailed and accurate depictions" of the species found in the cloud forest. However, she notes that it was necessary to remove the clouds that would obscure animals and plants. Therefore, she "represented the fog and mist with squares of translucent paper framing the alphabet letters."

Sharing *This* Book with Children:

- In introducing the book, explain that it is based on the work done by a scientist who studied animals in the cloud forest in Ecuador. There he discovered a brand-new animal called the olinguito, which they will meet in the book.
- Explain that cloud forests are found high up on some mountains. They are cool, moist places where clouds almost always cover the forests. Use the link below to show children a video of a cloud forest. Also explain that they are likely to see many unfamiliar animals and plants.
- As you move through the book, let the children linger over each page and try to identify the animals and plants named in the text.
- After reading the story, provide the children with the opportunity to talk about what they would especially like to see if they visited the cloud forest.

Content Connection/Skills Connection: Habitat: cloud forest
Insider Tips: See the following link to a YouTube video about the cloud forest: https://www.youtube.com/watch?v=B_p5jBLfGWc. This bilingual book presents text in Spanish first and then presents the same text in English. While the alphabet is used to organize the text, this is not a book designed to help children learn letter names or sounds. At the end of the book, you will find extensive information related to the discovery of the olinguito, the cloud forest, and the highlighted species.
Related Books:

- *The Great Kapok Tree* by Lynne Cherry
- *The Umbrella* by Jan Brett

Olivia
Written by Ian Falconer
Atheneum, 2000
Ages: 3–5
Summary: Like so many preschoolers, Olivia (who is represented as a precocious little pig) is a whirlwind of activity who "is very good at wearing people out." Many children will recognize themselves as they follow the antics of this little pig.
Illustrations: Falconer's simple pen-and-ink illustrations use spot color (always red) that draws attention to Olivia. These illustrations are critical to the development of the story because they fill in the many gaps

Reprinted with permission

left by the text. For example, when the text tells us that Olivia got "pretty good" at making sand castles, the reader sees an illustration of a gigantic sand skyscraper reaching high into the sky. The illustrator effectively uses montage (the inclusion of several illustrations on the same page) at various points in the book to convey just how busy Olivia is.

Sharing *This* Book with Children:

- Introduce the book by sharing the front cover, the title, and the name of the author/illustrator.
- Because the portrayal of Olivia is so realistic and childlike (even though Olivia is a pig), this is a book that requires minimal explanation or guidance from the teacher. However, pace the reading so the children can enjoy the illustrations. And, as always, make room for the children to share their responses.
- Children might be confused by the multiple representations of Olivia in the montages. (They might think that multiple pigs are being portrayed.) So on the second double-page spread, invite the children to think about why the illustrator included so many little pigs on the page.
- After reading the story, the children can act out the scene in which Olivia wears herself out.

Content Connection/Skills Connection: Drama

Insider Tip: Ian Falconer has written a series of books about Olivia, and a few have been translated into Spanish.

Related Books:

- *Niño Wrestles the World* by Yuyi Morales
- *Rudas: Niño's Horrendous Hermanitas* by Yuyi Morales

Other Books by the Same Author:

- *Olivia the Spy*
- *Olivia Saves the Circus*
- *Olivia's ABC*

Orange Pear Apple Bear
Written and illustrated by Emily Gravett
Simon and Schuster, 2007
Ages: 4–6

Reprinted with permission

Summary: Only five words (of which four appear in the title) make up this humorous book of wordplay about a bear and some fruit. Gravett puts different combinations of the words together and presents illustrations of what such things look like (e.g., an apple bear or orange pear).

Illustrations: Gravett's pencil and watercolor illustrations are both simple and complicated. The depictions of orange, pear, apple, and bear will be immediately recognizable to young children, but her combinations (e.g., apple bear, pear bear) will really get children thinking.

Sharing *This* Book with Children:

- When you read this book to the children, pay attention to the punctuation and how that relates to the illustration in question. For example, "apple, bear" depicts the bear with an apple, whereas the "apple bear" page shows the bear with the colors of an apple on it.
- This also means that you'll want to read those pages to the children with different intonations (i.e., "apple [pause] bear" versus "apple-bear").
- To help you with intonation and help the children get the wordplay that is going on in the book, it can be helpful to point to objects in conjunction with your reading: apple (point/pause), orange (point/pause), pear bear (point).

Content Connections/Skills Connections: Color, shapes

Insider Tips: Emily Gravett has won two Kate Greenaway Medals, the UK literary award that annually recognizes "distinguished illustration in a book for children." *This book was originally published in the United Kingdom.*

Related Books:

- *The Odd Egg* by Emily Gravett
- *Sheep in a Jeep* by Nancy Shaw

The Other Side
Written by Jacqueline Woodson and illustrated by E. B. Lewis
Putnam, 2001
Ages: 5–9

Reprinted with permission

Summary: Though the specific historical setting of this book is not indicated, it can be assumed that the story takes place during the era of segregation in the United States. Two girls—one Black and one White—live on opposite sides of a fence. Their mamas have warned them to stay on their own side of the fence. But no one has said anything about sitting on top of the fence, and so a friendship begins one summer.

Illustrations: In this oversized book, almost all of E. B. Lewis's luminous paintings spill over from one page onto the facing page. The illustrations focus squarely on the children, pulling us into their world.

Sharing *This* Book with Children:

- It is likely that you will need to build background about segregation. Explain that it created barriers—or "fences"—between Black and White people, who typically lived in different neighborhoods and went to different schools and churches. Give the children the opportunity to share what they know about this era and ask any questions they have.
- Share the cover of the book, and invite the children to make predictions about what might happen in the story.

- After reading the page about the girls jumping rope, stop and ask the children why they think Sandra said the White girl could not jump rope with them.
- Stop after reading the page in which the two girls decide that it will be okay to sit on the fence together. Ask, "Why do you think they decided to sit on top of the fence?"
- After finishing the story, ask, "Do you think the girls did the right thing by crossing to the other side of the fence? Why? Do you think fences like the one in the story are still in place? If yes, why are there still such fences? What can children do to bring down fences that keep people apart?"

Content Connections/Skills Connections: Diversity, friendship
Insider Tips: In the introduction to the tenth-anniversary edition of this book, author Jacqueline Woodson says that people often ask her if the fence has come down. Her response? No, but it is lower. Sharing this book is one way teachers can help to lower the fence even more.
Related Books:

- *Freedom Summer* by Deborah Wiles
- *White Socks Only* by Evelyn Coleman

Pete the Cat: I Love My White Shoes
Written by Eric Litwin and illustrated by James Dean
Harper, 1999
Ages: 3–5
Summary: Pete the Cat loves his white shoes, so he walks along singing a song about his shoes. But Pete keeps stepping into things that change the color of his shoes—from white to red to blue and so on. But with each *seeming* mishap, Pete only sees the positive, and he keeps on singing.
Illustrations: Endpapers foreshadow the changing colors of Pete's shoes. Bright colors used throughout the book reflect the upbeat nature of this character.

Sharing *This* Book with Children:

- After introducing the book by showing the cover and reading the title, turn to the endpapers and ask the students why they think the illustrator painted yellow, red, blue, and green sneakers since Pete's sneakers are white.
- Throughout the book Pete sings different versions of his song. Try to actually sing the song, either making up a tune or using the tune from the online song (see Insider Tips below). Once they hear the tune, the children will want to join in singing.
- As Pete steps into various substances (e.g., strawberries), ask, "What will happen to the shoes?"
- At the end of the story, a moral is stated explicitly. After reading the moral, invite the children to talk about times when they have been positive and upbeat when something bad has happened to them.

Content Connection/Skills Connection: Colors

Insider Tip: You can download Pete's song at www.harpercollinschidrens.com/pete thecat.

Related Books:

- *Little Blue and Little Yellow* by Leo Lionni
- *Mouse Paint* by Ellen Stoll Walsh

Peter's Chair
Written and illustrated by Ezra Jack Keats
Harper and Row, 1967
Ages: 3–6

Reprinted with permission

Summary: Peter is *not* happy that his parents are painting his things—his crib, his high chair—for his new baby sister. When Peter decides to run away with Willie, his dog, his very wise parents make him feel that he is still part of the family.

Illustrations: Keats used collage in making the illustrations for *Peter's Chair*.

Sharing *This* Book with Children:

- Introduce the book by sharing the front cover, the title, and the name of the author/illustrator.
- Ask, "Why did Peter decide to run away?"
- When Peter goes back home, ask, "Why do you think he changed his mind?"
- At the end, ask, "Why did Peter decide he wanted to help his father paint the chair?"
- Invite children with baby sisters or brothers to talk about how things changed at home when the new baby arrived.

Content Connections/Skills Connections: Emotions, new siblings

Insider Tips: Ezra Jack Keats was the first person to write commercially published picturebooks about African American children living in urban settings, a series of books about Peter and his friends. Keats won the Caldecott Award for *The Snowy Day*.

Related Books:

- *Julius, the Baby of the World* by Kevin Henkes
- *Za-Za's Baby Brother* by Lucy Cousins

Petunia
Written and illustrated by Roger Duvoisin
Alfred A. Knopf, 1950
Ages: 4–8

Reprinted with permission

Summary: When Petunia the goose finds a book in the meadow, she remembers that the farmer had once said, "He who owns Books and loves them is wise." So Petunia puts the book under her wing and grows proud of her newfound wisdom. But as Petunia begins to offer advice to the other animals, her "wisdom" creates chaos in the barnyard.

Illustrations: The cartoon-like illustrations are filled with energy and humor.

Sharing *This* Book with Children:

- Share the front cover, the title, and the name of the author/illustrator.
- There are numerous places to stop and talk in this book:
  ◦ When Petunia picks up the book and concludes that no one will call her silly ever again, ask, "Will having a book make Petunia wise?"
  ◦ Each time Petunia offers advice to one of the animals, stop and ask, "Was this good advice? Why or why not?"
  ◦ Stop after Petunia tells the animals they can eat the "Candy" and ask, "What do you think will happen?"
  ◦ After reading, ask the children how they think Petunia has changed.

Content Connections/Skills Connections: Farm animals, literary elements: character
Insider Tips: This book was published more than sixty-five years ago! And children still love it. Surely this is the book that inspired the saying "silly goose!"—or did the saying inspire this book?
Related Books:

- *Donkey-donkey* by Roger Duvoisin
- *Veronica* by Roger Duvoisin

¡Pío Peep!
Selected by Alma Flor Ada and F. Isabel Campoy and illustrated by Viví Escrivá
English adaptations by Alice Schertle
HarperCollins, 2003
Ages: 3–5
Summary: This is a collection of traditional Spanish and Latin American nursery rhymes. Each Spanish rhyme is accompanied by an English translation.
Illustrations: A bold illustration accompanies each rhyme.

Sharing *This* Book with Children:

- How the book is shared will depend on the languages spoken by the children in the class (and the teacher). If there are Spanish speakers in the class, it is ideal to read the poem in Spanish. If there are both Spanish and English speakers in the class, ideally one would share the Spanish version of the poem first.

- This is not a book to share with children in one sitting. Become familiar with all the rhymes in order to select the right one for the right time.
- Poetry is all about sound and images. So when sharing these poems with the children, invite them to listen for words that "paint pictures" for them or words whose sound they like.

Content Connections/Skills Connections: Phonemic awareness: rhyming, sensory language
Insider Tip: This an ideal collection to build Latino children's pride in their cultural heritage.
Related Books:

- *Arroz con Leche* by Lulu Delacre
- *La Madre Goose: Nursery Rhymes for los Niños* by Susan Middleton Elya and Juana Martinez-Neal

The Rooster Who Would Not Be Quiet!
Written by Carmen Agra Deedy and illustrated by Eugene Yelchin
Scholastic, 2017
Ages: 5–8
Summary: This allegory of a rooster who would not be quiet explores the importance of speaking out against oppression.
Illustrations: The mixed-media illustrations are lively and filled with color.

Reprinted with permission

Sharing *This* Book with Children:

- Introduce the book by title and cover, and invite students to make predictions.
- At the point where the town grows "silent as a tomb," ask, "Would you prefer to live in the town before laws were passed or after?"
- Each time the mayor asks, "Will you sing then?," invite predictions.
- The children might want to join in time each time the rooster sings "Kee-kee-ree-KEE!"
- After reading the story, ask, "What can *people* learn from this book?"

Content Connection/Skills Connection: Importance of speaking out
Insider Tips: For a read aloud on YouTube, go to https://www.youtube.com/watch?v=hor_fkkxrm8.
Related Books:

- *14 Cows for America* by Carmen Agra Deedy
- *The Library Dragon* by Carmen Agra Deedy

Rosie's Walk
Written and illustrated by Pat Hutchins
Aladdin, 1971
Ages: 3 and up

Summary: A hen goes for a walk around the farm, unaware that a fox is trying to catch her.

Illustrations: There is minimal text, so the illustrations become critically important in this book. In fact, the fox is introduced only through illustrations,

Reprinted with permission

and each of its attempts to catch Rosie unfolds only through the illustrations.

Sharing *This* Book with Children:

- Share the front cover, the title, and the name of the author/illustrator.
- Invite the children to talk about what they see on the cover (both characters are introduced).
- As you read the text, let the children talk about what they see in the illustrations.
- The children can predict the likely outcome each time the fox attempts to pounce.

Content Connection/Skills Connection: Comprehension: predicting
Awards and recognition: Kate Greenaway Medal
Related Books:

- *Titch* by Pat Hutchins
- *You'll Soon Grow into Them, Titch* by Pat Hutchins
- *Where, Oh Where, Is Rosie's Chick?* by Pat Hutchins

Sam and Dave Dig a Hole
Written by Mac Barnett and illustrated by Jon Klassen
Candlewick, 2014
Ages: 5–8

Summary: Two boys on a mission to find something spectacular dig a hole. And they dig. And they keep digging. And they find nothing. Yet the day turns out to be "pretty spectacular." Children who look closely at the illustration details will see why.

Illustrations: This book is really *all* about the illustrations. It is a classic case of how the text and illustrations

Reprinted with permission

combine to create a book that is more than the sum of its parts.

Sharing *This* Book with Children:

- Show the cover of the book, and ask, "Why might Sam and Dave be digging a hole?"

- Show the page before the title page—the one with the tree with fruit on it—and observe, "Hmm. I wonder why they have this here, even before we get to the title page. We better remember this and see if the end of the book gives us any clues as to what this is all about."
- On the page that starts with "When should we stop digging?," ask about the word *spectacular* and make sure the children understand the meaning of the word.
- Next page ("The hole got so deep"): "Do you see anything spectacular yet?"
- Next page ("So they kept digging"): "What is going to happen as they keep digging?"
- "Sam and Dave fell asleep" page: Here's another good page to have children predict.
- "Until they landed in the soft dirt" page: Now is a good time to have the children discuss what happened and how Sam and Dave feel about their big adventure.
- "And they went inside" page and subsequent pages: Notice the tree. It will be interesting to go back through all the pages with trees on them (including the back cover of the book) and see what you and the children notice.

Content Connection/Skills Connection: Problem-solving
Awards and Recognition: Caldecott Honor book
Related Books:

- *I Want My Hat Back* by Jon Klassen
- *This Is Not My Hat* by Jon Klassen
- *The Odd Egg* by Emily Gravett

Saturday
Written and illustrated by Oge Mora
Little, Brown, 2019
Ages: 4–8

Reprinted with permission

Summary: Ava's favorite day is Saturday—the only day her mother does not have to work. On Saturday they do special activities. But one Saturday, *nothing* goes the way they wanted it to. Will they be able to salvage this Saturday?

Illustrations: The endpapers feature a calendar page. Careful inspection provides hints of why Saturdays are special.

Sharing *This* Book with Children:

- Before reading, ask, "What makes weekends special for you? Does anyone remember a weekend when nothing seemed to work out?"
- Introduce the book, show the cover, turn to the endpages, and invite the children to talk about what they see. Be sure to point out how few notations are included on the calendar for weekdays compared to Saturdays.
- Invite the children to talk about what the calendar suggests might happen in the book.

- During reading encourage the children to join in reading the repetitive element: "Today will be special. Today will be splendid. Today is SATURDAY!"
- After reading, ask, "Do you think Ava and her mother actually had a splendid day?"
- Explain that the illustrator created her collages using simple materials. Let the children make a collage showing a special day they remember.

Content Connections/Skills Connections: Art: paper collage, family
Insider Tip: The author's first picturebook, *Thank You, Omu!*, was a Caldecott Honor book.
Related Books:

- *I Love Saturdays y Domingos* by Alma Flor Ada
- *Last Stop on Market Street* by Matt de la Peña

Seeds Move!
Written and illustrated by Robin Page
Beach Lane, 2019
Ages: 4–8
Summary: Double-page spreads feature one or two different seeds and explain the way in which each moves away from its parent plant. At the top of the page, in large font, appears a simple three-word sentence (e.g., "A seed hides (or floats) (or parachutes)." More detailed text provides additional information about how the seed moves.

Reprinted with permission

Illustrations: The illustrations for this book were created digitally.

Sharing *This* Book with Children:

- To introduce the book, bring in different kinds of seeds (e.g., tomato seed, a watermelon seed, an acorn, and maybe even a coconut).
- Explain that seeds are formed on the parent plant but must move away from the parent plant to grow on their own. *Ask the children how they think this happens.*
- After reading, create a three-column chart with the children. In the first column, list the name of a seed featured in the book. In the second column, record how the seed moves away from the parent plant. In the third column, record the movement word from the book (e.g., floats, parachutes).
- After viewing artwork created by other children in response to Page's books (http://robinpagebooks.com/gallery.html), let the children create their own nature collages. (Note: Artwork for this particular book is not collage; rather, it was created digitally.)

Content Connections/Skills Connections: Nature, seeds
Insider Tip: Page has collaborated with husband Steve Jenkins on many of her nature books.

Related Books:

- *From Seed to Plant* by Gail Gibbons
- *The Tiny Seed* by Eric Carle

Shh! Bears Sleeping
Written by David Martin and illustrated by Steve Johnson and Lou Fancher
Viking, 2016
Ages: 4–6
Summary: Poetic text relays the activities of black bears through the seasons of the year.
Illustrations: Detailed oil paintings of nature pull the viewer into the world of the bears.

Reprinted with permission

Sharing *This* Book with Children:

- Before reading, ask the children what they know about bears.
- After reading the story, record what the children learned about bears on a class chart.
- Poetic language in this nonfiction book deserves attention on a second read aloud. Invite children to listen for special words that help them see and hear the world of the bears.

Content Connections/Skills Connections: Bears, nature, seasons
Insider Tip: Additional information about black bears is included at the end of the book.
Related Books:

- *Bear Has a Story to Tell* by Philip C. Stead
- *Old Bear* by Kevin Henkes

A Sick Day for Amos McGee
Written by Philip C. Stead and Illustrated by Erin E. Stead
Roaring Brook Press, 2010
Ages: 4 and up
Summary: The friendly zookeeper Amos McGee always makes time to visit his friends at the City Zoo—elephant, tortoise, penguin, rhinoceros, and owl. But one day he wakes up sick. So his friends find a way to take care of him.
Illustrations: The words of this story establish a

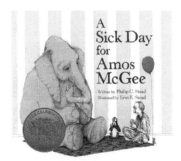
Reprinted with permission

gentle tone that is reinforced in the illustrator's choice of colors and use of rounded shapes.

Sharing *This* Book with Children:

- When Amos McGee wakes up sick, ask, "What do you think might happen?"
- After reading "Later that day," ask, "What do you think is going to happen?"
- After reading the story, ask the children if they would like to have friends like these.

Content Connection/Skills Connection: Friendship
Insider Tip: Erin E. Stead discusses her technique for woodblock printing in this video she narrates: https://www.youtube.com/watch?v=3TuHyU-onkc.
Awards and Recognition: Caldecott Medal
Related Books:

- *Days with Frog and Toad* by Arnold Lobel
- *Jamaica and Brianna* by Juanita Havill

Silly Sally
Written and illustrated by Audrey Wood
Harcourt Brace Jovanovich, 1992
Ages: 3–6
Summary: As Silly Sally makes her way to town, "walking backwards upside down," she meets a host of animals who join her on this unconventional trek.
Illustrations: Wood's brightly colored, cartoon-style illustrations add to the silliness of the tale.

Reprinted with permission

Sharing *This* Book with Children:

- Before reading, ask the students to look at the cover of the book and predict why the story is called *Silly Sally*. What silly things might Sally do?
- As Sally encounters different animals along the way, Sally and the animal do something together. This portion of the text is written in rhyming couplets (e.g., "On the way she met a dog, a silly dog, they played leapfrog."). In each of these sections, pause before reading the final line of the couplet, and encourage the children to use the rhyming clue to guess what Sally and the animal will do (e.g., "On the way she met a loon, a silly loon, they sang a _____.").
- After reading, ask the children to think of other silly ways Sally might have gone to town.

Content Connection/Skills Connection: Phonemic awareness: rhyming
Insider Tip: Audrey Wood has collaborated with her husband on a number of picturebooks.
Related Books:

- *Chicka Chicka Boom Boom* by Bill Martin Jr. and John Archambault
- *Sheep in the Jeep* by Nancy Shaw

Snow
Written and illustrated by Uri Shulevitz
Farrar, Straus and Giroux, 1998
Ages: 4–7

Summary: Despite the pessimism of the adults, a little boy is convinced the snow will keep falling—and he is right. The book portrays a child's joyful celebration of snow.

Illustrations: The contrast between the body stances of the adults and the child are of note.

Reprinted with permission

Sharing *This* Book with Children:

- Invite the children to talk about what they see in the cover illustration.
- Pause on the dedication page, and ask, "How does the little boy seem to feel?"
- In the early pages of the book, ask, "How does the boy feel about snow? And the adults?"
- On the double-page spread that reads, "Circling and swirling, spinning and twirling, dancing, playing, there, and there," ask the children to talk about what is happening in the illustrations. (You might want to turn back to the previous page so the children can see how the faces of the Mother Goose characters are changing.)
- On the next two double-page spreads, ask, "How are the Mother Goose characters different from the adults we saw in the early pages of the book?"
- Invite the children to act out the dance scene with the Mother Goose characters.

Content Connection/Skills Connection: Snow
Awards and Recognition: Caldecott Honor book
Related Books:

- *Snow Music* by Lynne Rae Perkins
- *The Snowy Day* by Ezra Jack Keats

The Snowy Day
Written and illustrated by Ezra Jack Keats
Viking, 1962
Ages: 3–5

Summary: A little boy has an adventure-filled day in the snow.

Illustrations: The illustrations in this book are done with collage and watercolors.

Reprinted with permission

Sharing *This* Book with Children:

- If the students have already met the main character, Peter, in another of Keats's books (e.g., *Peter's Chair*, *Whistle for Willie*), ask them what they remember about Peter.

- On the page where it says "And he found something sticking out of the snow that made a new track," invite the students to predict what made the track.
- After Peter states that he is not old enough to play with the big boys, ask the children to discuss how they think Peter felt and why.
- When Peter places a snowball in his pocket and walks into his warm house, have the students predict what is going to happen to the snowball.

Content Connections/Skills Connections: Snow, comprehension: predicting
Awards and Recognition: Caldecott Medal book
Insider Tips: *The Snowy Day* is the first full-color picturebook featuring an African American child as the main character.
Related Books:

- *Snow* by Uri Shulevitz
- *Snow Music* by Lynne Rae Perkins

The Squiggle
Written by Carole Lexa Schaefer and illustrated by Pierr Morgan
Crown, 1996
Ages: 3–7
Summary: Relying on her imagination, a little girl turns a squiggly ribbon into wonderful pictures—a big scaly dragon, a long great wall, popping fireworks, and much more.
Illustrations: The characters are of Asian descent, so it is fitting that all the things imagined by the main character are related to Asia (e.g., a Chinese dragon, the Great Wall of China).

Reprinted with permission

Sharing *This* Book with Children:

- Introduce this book by presenting the children with a ribbon and asking what it can become.
- Many of the items represented in scenes of the child's imagination are likely to be new to young children, so talk about each one as you read. You may even want to bring in pictures of some of the items to show the children (e.g., the Great Wall of China, Chinese sailboats).
- This story is filled with onomatopoeia. (Onomatopoeia is the use of words like *buzz* that sound like the object or action with which they are associated.) When reading the story aloud, highlight these onomatopoeic words by inviting the children to repeat them.
- After reading, let the children take turns making the ribbon into different things.

Content Connection/Skills Connection: Imagination
Insider Tip: Inside the front and back covers of the paperback version of this book, you will find interesting activities from the publisher to use with *The Squiggle*.

Related Books:

- *The Dot* by Peter H. Reynolds
- *Regards to the Man in the Moon* by Ezra Jack Keats

Stop! Bot!
Written and illustrated by James Yang
Viking, 2019
Ages: 4–7

Reprinted with permission

Summary: A little boy living in a very tall building has a bot that escapes. Floor by floor, the people living in his building try to capture the escaped bot.

Illustrations: The shape of the book is of particular note. The little boy lives in a very tall apartment building, and the shape of the book mirrors the shape of the building. The artwork is digital. Each character that tries to help the boy makes a statement about how they might be able to help, but only close inspection of the illustrations reveals exactly how they attempted to help.

Sharing *This* Book with Children:

- Open the book to show both front and back covers. Ask, "Where is the story taking place?"
- After reading the second page (on which the bot escapes), invite the children to share their thinking about how the boy might be able to retrieve his bot.
- Invite the children to predict the outcome of the various attempts to trap the bot.
- On the page that reads "This usually works with bots," ask the children to talk about why *bananas* might be a way to retrieve a bot.
- The ending of the story (in which a balloon escapes) is somewhat open-ended. The children can write a story about what happens as characters attempt to retrieve the balloon. The text includes short sentences with accessible language for beginning readers.

Content Connections/Skills Connections: imagination, comprehension
Awards and Recognition: Geisel Award
Related Books:

- *Boy and Bot* by Ame Dyckman
- *Raybot* by Adam Watkins

Ten Little Fingers and Ten Little Toes
Written by Mem Fox and illustrated by Helen Oxenbury
Houghton Mifflin Harcourt, 2018
Ages: 3–5

Reprinted with permission

Summary: Filled with rhythm and repetition, this simple text highlights commonalities among babies across the world—noticing their ten little fingers and ten little toes.
Illustrations: Helen Oxenbury's illustrations are soft yet colorful and clear, subtly addressing similarities and differences among the babies.

Sharing *This* Book with Children:

- Encourage the children to join in reading the repetitive verses, "And both of these babies as everyone knows, had ten little fingers and ten little toes."
- Read the end slowly to create suspense.

Content Connections/Skills Connections: Counting, rhyming, body parts
Insider Tip: There is also a bilingual (English/Spanish) version of the book.
Related Books:

- *Hello Baby* by Mem Fox
- *Time for Bed* by Mem Fox

Thank You, Omu!
Written and illustrated by Oge Mora
Little, Brown, 2018
Ages: 4–8

Reprinted with permission

Summary: As the delectable smell of Omu's thick red stew wafts out the window, her neighbors drop by, one by one, to try the stew. When Omu sits down for her evening meal, the pot is empty! Soon, though, grateful neighbors show up with gifts to thank Omu for her generosity.
Illustrations: For the collages in the book, Mora used patterned paper, old book clippings, paint, markers, and other materials.

Sharing *This* Book with Children:

- Before reading, explain that the author called her grandma "Omu."
- Invite the children to predict what the story will be about based on the cover illustration and the title, *Thank You, Omu!*
- Omu is a special person. After reading, invite the children to come up with words and phrases to describe the type of person she is.
- Make various kinds of papers available for the children to use in creating their own collages.

Content Connections/Skills Connections: Sharing, urban diversity

Awards and Recognition: This is the very first picturebook by Oge Mora, and it garnered numerous awards, including a Caldecott Honor award.

Insider Tip: *Omu* means *queen* in Igbo, the Nigerian language of the author's parents. However, the author explains in an endnote that for her it meant *Grandma*.

Related Books:

- *Extra Yarn* by Mac Barnett
- *Saturday* by Oge Mora

There Was an Old Lady Who Swallowed a Fly
Written and illustrated by Simms Taback
Viking, 1997

Reprinted with permission

Ages: 3 and up

Summary: The well-known cumulative tale about the old lady who swallows consecutively larger insects and animals gets a new look when Simms Taback uses die-cut artwork to let us see inside the woman's stomach.

Illustrations: Dramatic, vivid, and dark colors and the die cuts on each page create a very memorable look to this book.

Sharing *This* Book with Children:

- Read expressively, demonstrating shock and surprise after each thing the old lady swallows.
- On subsequent readings of the book, assign different children to read the lines that come after the "who swallowed a ___" parts of the book: "How absurd! She swallowed a bird," "Imagine that! She swallowed a cat," and so forth.
- This is the perfect book to create a flannel board or other kind of hands-on activity that can go in the library or other center for the children to reenact the book.

Content Connection/Skills Connection: Phonemic awareness: rhyming

Insider Tip: Because this book has a predictable structure that includes a lot of repetition, it is a good choice for a follow-up hands-on activity in which children perform the actions in the book.

Related Books:

- *If You Give a Mouse a Cookie* by Laura Joffe Numeroff
- *Joseph Has a Little Overcoat* by Simms Taback

The Three Billy Goats Gruff
Written and illustrated by Jerry Pinkney
Little, Brown, 2017
Ages: 3–7

Summary: This is the traditional tale about three goats trying to cross a bridge to get to the meadow on the other side. But they must first get past the mean troll who lives under the bridge.

Illustrations: The illustrations completely fill the pages and contain lots of close-ups that pull the reader in.

Reprinted with permission

Sharing *This* Book with Children:

- You can invite the children to make predictions at the following stops:
  - when the troll first demands to know who is crossing his bridge
  - when the troll threatens to gobble up the tiniest goat
  - when the troll threatens to gobble up the second goat
  - when the troll threatens to gobble up the biggest goat
- After reading, show the front and back endpapers and ask, "What differences do you see?"
- The children can be encouraged to act out the story on the playground.

Content Connections/Skills Connections: Drama, folktales
Insider Tip: This is a Norwegian folktale.
Related Books:

- *The Three Billy Goats Gruff* illustrated by Marcia Brown
- *The Three Billy Goats Gruff* illustrated by Paul Galdone

Today I Will Fly!
Written and illustrated by Mo Willems
Hyperion, 2007
Ages: 3–7

Summary: Gerald is careful; Piggie is not. Piggie is always smiling; Gerald, sometimes. Gerald worries; Piggie would not think to. This book is the first introduction to the characters Elephant and Piggie, and in it Piggie is determined to fly. But Gerald knows that's impossible—isn't it?

Illustrations: Willems uses simple line drawings and his characteristic cartoon style to give his characters life and expression that add greatly to the simple words of the text.

Reprinted with permission

Sharing *This* Book with Children:

- Willems's illustrations are simple in design but *very* good at conveying emotions through facial expressions, gestures, and movements. As you read, ask the children how the characters are feeling—and how they know.

- To promote vocabulary development, ask, "What is the difference between how Elephant uses the word *help* (on page 17) and how Piggie interprets it (on page 19)?"
- Make this book available in the book center for children to read emergently.

Content Connections/Skills Connections: Dreams, persistence
Insider Tips: Mo Willems's website has some great information about his books and his work: http://www.mowillems.com/. Three Elephant and Piggie books have won the Geisel Award for the most distinguished American book for beginning readers; five others have been Geisel Honor books.
Related Books:

- *Elephant and Piggie: Let's Go for a Drive* by Mo Willems
- *Waiting Is Not Easy!* by Mo Willems

Tuesday
Created by David Wiesner
Clarion, 1991
Ages: 5–9
Summary: In this almost wordless book, as the sun sets, frogs on lily pads lift off, and soon the frogs are engaged in nocturnal adventures as they fly through town and countryside.
Illustrations: The story begins with an illustration before the title page. Many of the pages feature multiple panels that convey actions that move the plot along.

Reprinted with permission

Sharing *This* Book with Children:

- Introduce the book by telling the children that the book is almost wordless, so their job will be to read the illustrations very carefully.
- Begin by sharing the illustration prior to the title page and inviting predictions.
- Move slowly through the book, encouraging the students to talk about what they see and, in particular, to focus on the changing emotions of the frogs.
- When you get to the next-to-last page ("Next Tuesday, 7:58 P.M."), pose this question: "What do you think will happen *this* Tuesday?"
- After reading, brainstorm events that might happen in a new story in which pigs go flying through the night. Invite the children to illustrate the different events they imagine.

Content Connection/Skills Connection: Imagination
Insider Tip: Wiesner has won the Caldecott Medal and has received three Caldecott Honors.
Awards and Recognition: Caldecott Medal
Related Books:

- *Art and Max* by David Weisner
- *Flotsam* by David Weisner

The Uncorker of Ocean Bottles
Written by Michelle Cuevas and illustrated by Erin Stead
Dial, 2016
Ages: 5–8

Reprinted with permission

Summary: The "Uncorker of Ocean Bottles" (who is never named) has an important job—delivering messages found in ocean bottles. He does his job faithfully but is lonely and wishes for a message of his own. When an invitation to a party arrives—without any indication of who it is for—the Uncorker decides to go to the party himself, and, for the first time, he is surrounded by friends. This is a gentle story about loneliness and community.

Illustrations: In many of the illustrations featuring the Uncorker, he appears framed in a circle that suggests his isolation from others. In the final illustration, the text appears in the circle, while the Uncorker is outside the circle.

Sharing *This* Book with Children:

- After reading the first few pages of the book, ensure that the children understand what the Uncorker's job is. You might want to clarify why he is called the "Uncorker."
- After reading the page that begins with the phrase "While the Uncorker of Ocean Bottles loves his job," stop and invite the children to talk about what they are discovering about this character.
- The next-to-last page contains one sentence: "The Uncorker's heart was a glass vessel filled to the brim." After reading this sentence, ask the children what they think the author means. Be sure to invite the children to talk about what has caused this change in the Uncorker's feelings.
- The language of the book is of note. Share some of the phrases you particularly like (e.g., "a glass vessel filled to the brim," "a quill dipped in sadness").
- Read the story a second time so the children can listen for sentences they especially like.

Content Connections/Skills Connections: Social and emotional development: loneliness, community

Awards and Recognition: Boston Globe Best Books, School Library Journal Best Books

Insider Tip: Michelle Cuevas also writes chapter books for older readers.

Related Books:

- *Smoot: A Rebellious Shadow* by Michelle Cuevas
- *The Town of Turtle* by Michelle Cuevas

Uptown
Written and illustrated by Bryan Collier
Henry Holt, 2000
Ages: 4–8

Summary: *Uptown* brings to life the neighborhood of Harlem. Each spread features a scene in Harlem as well as a descriptor beginning with "Uptown is" (e.g., "Uptown is chicken and waffles served around the clock."). A sentence then follows the descriptor and provides further elaboration.

Illustrations: The colorful and creative layout of the text font adds to the vibrancy of place that Collier conveys through text and illustration.

Reprinted with permission

Sharing *This* Book with Children:

- Before reading, ask the children about things they love in their own neighborhood.
- After reading, ask what they think were the really special things in the uptown neighborhood.
- Point out how the author began each page of the book with the phrase "Uptown is."
- This book offers interesting possibilities for writing. The children can brainstorm phrases about their own community (e.g., "San Antonio is a paleta on a hot day."). They can then choose a phrase to elaborate on, just as Bryan Collier did.

Content Connections/Skills Connections: Neighborhoods, communities
Insider Tip: This was the first book written by Bryan Collier.
Awards and Recognition: Coretta Scott King Illustrator Award
Related Books:

- *Martin's Big Words* by Doreen Rappaport, illustrated by Bryan Collier
- *Rosa* by Nikki Giovanni, illustrated by Bryan Collier

The Very Busy Spider
Written and illustrated by Eric Carle
Philomel, 1984
Ages: 3 and up

Summary: In this repetitive book, a spider busily spins her web, ignoring all the farm animals that try to distract her. Once the web is created, the spider catches a fly and is soon fast asleep.

Illustrations: On each page, the threads of the spider's web are raised, making this a multisensory book.

Reprinted with permission

Sharing *This* Book with Children:

- Introduce the book by sharing the front cover, the title, and the name of the author/illustrator. Mention other Eric Carle books that you have read to the children.
- Before reading the book, ask the children where they think spiderwebs come from. It is likely that some children will know this information. If so, ask the children why they think spiders spin webs. If this is not addressed in discussion prior to reading, then return to talk about this after reading the book.
- As you read, encourage the children to join in on the repetitive parts of the book (e.g., "The spider didn't answer. She was very busy spinning her web.").
- After reading, invite the children to come up to feel the final spider web. Tell the children you will leave the book in the book center so they can feel the web, which is raised on all the pages of the book.

Content Connections/Skills Connections: Spiders, farm animals
Insider Tip: The book comes in different formats, including a board book.
Related Book:

- *Nic Bishop Spiders* by Nic Bishop (The text may be too difficult to share with younger children, but they can enjoy looking at the photographs in this book.)

Other Books by the Same Author:

- *The Grouchy Ladybug*
- *The Very Hungry Caterpillar*
- *The Very Lonely Firefly*
- *The Very Quiet Cricket*

The Very Hungry Caterpillar
Written and illustrated by Eric Carle
Putnam, 1969
Ages: 3–5
Summary: On each day of the week, a hungry caterpillar eats and eats before turning into a chrysalis and
ultimately a butterfly.
Illustrations: Eric Carle used his signature
medium—tissue-paper collage—to create the illus-
trations. When the caterpillar eats his way through various foods, actual holes appear
in the pages of the book.

Reprinted with permission

Sharing *This* Book with Children:

- While reading, the children can count the foods the caterpillar eats: one apple on Monday, two pears on Tuesday, and so on.
- After reading, use the days of the week to review the caterpillar's activities across the week.
- Review the foods the caterpillar eats. Ask, "Which foods represent healthy choices?"

- Discuss the life cycle of a butterfly (i.e., egg, caterpillar, chrysalis, butterfly).

Content Connections/Skills Connections: Nutrition, life cycle of a butterfly, counting, days of the week
Insider Tip: This book is also available in board book and big book formats.
Related Books:

- *The Grouchy Ladybug* by Eric Carle
- *First the Egg* by Laura Vaccaro Seeger

The Water Princess: Based on the Childhood Experiences of Georgie Badiel
Written by Susan Verde and illustrated by Peter H. Reynolds
Putnam, 2016
Ages: 6–8
Summary: Princess Gie Gie grew up having to fetch precious water with her mother, walking long distances and balancing the water on her head. Once home, the water had to be boiled and prepared before drinking then sparingly shared with the family. She dreams of one day having clear water flowing closer to home. Her mother tells her, "Someday you will find a way."

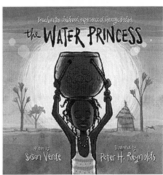
Reprinted with permission

Illustrations: Gradual shifts in color across the pages reflect changes in the time of day. Golds and oranges of daytime illustrations evoke the intensity of heat and dryness in the Burkina Faso landscape. An endnote includes information about the background of the story, and there are photographs showing African women and children in their daily quest for safe drinking water.

Sharing *This* Book with Children:

- This is a situation students will find hard to grasp—that there are people who do not have constant access to clear running water in their homes or even in their villages. To give context to the distances that little Gie Gie and her mother had to travel, try to calculate a distance the children can relate to, such as "around the school building x times."
- A "news report" by The Glimpse Team shows children on the team reading aloud and reporting their responses to the book: https://www.youtube.com/watch?v=nVJbctsIkQ0.

Content Connections/Skills Connections: Water, women and girls
Insider Tips: Georgie Badiel grew up to become a fashion model and established a foundation to help bring clean water to her childhood village in Burkina Faso. The author talks about writing the book here: https://www.behindthebook.org/meet-author-susan-verde/.
Related Book:

- *Nya's Long Walk* by Linda Sue Park, illustrated by Brian Pinkney

We Found a Hat
Written and illustrated by Jon Klassen
Candlewick, 2016
Ages: 5 and up
Summary: Two turtles find a hat, and both of them want it. The solution to this problem is likely to surprise readers.
Illustrations: Klassen's illustrations are simple and uncluttered. However, there are subtle—and very important—changes in the eyes of the turtles to which readers need to attend.

Reprinted with permission

Sharing *This* Book with Children:

- After reading the title, ask, "What might happen when the turtles find a hat?"
- The book is divided into three parts, much like a chapter book. As you read, point out the name of each new part. These are good places to stop to ask the children what they think might happen in the upcoming part of the book.
- As you read, encourage the children to look closely at changes in the turtles' eyes. Ask them what these changes suggest.
- The conclusion of the story is open-ended. Invite the children to talk about what they think happened in the end.
- Most children will have faced a problem similar to the one the turtles faced. Ask them to talk about how they handled such problems.

Content Connections/Skills Connections: Sharing, problem-solving
Insider Tips: This is the third book that Jon Klassen has written about hats. In the same year, Jon Klassen won a Caldecott Medal for *This Is Not My Hat* and a Caldecott Honor for *Extra Yarn*.
Related Books:

- *I Want My Hat Back* by Jon Klassen
- *This Is Not My Hat* by Jon Klassen

Wemberly Worried
Written and illustrated by Kevin Henkes
Greenwillow, 2000
Ages: 4–6
Summary: Wemberly worries about everything. All the time. Especially about starting school.
Illustrations: Henkes uses watercolor paints and a black pen for all of his mice books, stories like this one and those about Lily, Chester, and Chrysanthemum in which mice confront the issues that young children face in their everyday lives at home and in school or preschool.

Sharing *This* Book with Children:

- To introduce the book, show the cover and invite the children to talk about the expression on Wemberly's face. Let the children know that Wemberly is a preschooler, and have them speculate what they think she might be worried about.
- Kevin Henkes is a master at depicting characters' emotions through facial expressions and body language. Take numerous opportunities during your reading to have the children look at these features in the illustrations.
- Just before the page that shows the Nursery School Starting Soon sign, say something like, "So, Wemberly worries about lots of things. But she's just about to have a new worry—and a big one for her! What do you think that worry might be? Why do you think that?"
- After the read aloud, have the children look at the front and back endpapers of the book. Ask, "Why do you think Kevin Henkes made them different? What do they have to do with the story of Wemberly and Jewel?"

Content Connection/Skills Connection: Emotions*: fears/anxieties*
Insider Tip: Henkes named his character Wemberly after a street where his mother-in-law lived: Wemberly Way.
Related Books:

- *Can't You Sleep, Little Bear?* by Martin Waddell
- *Scaredy Squirrel* by Melanie Watt

What Can You Do with a Rebozo?
Written by Carmen Tafolla and illustrated by Amy Córdova
Tricycle Press, 2008
Ages: 3–5
Summary: A little girl shares the many ways she and her family members use her mother's rebozo—a traditional Mexican shawl.
Illustrations: Each illustration clearly demonstrates the use of the rebozo that is described in the text. Illustrations are filled with bright, bold colors often associated with Latino culture.

Reprinted with permission

Sharing *This* Book with Children:

- Bring in a rebozo (or a shawl if a rebozo is not available) to show to the children. *Explain what it is called in Spanish.*
- Invite the children to talk about how rebozos are used or might be used.
- At the end of the book, the author poses four questions that you will want to share with children (e.g., "What is the silliest thing you can do with a rebozo?"). Invite the children to use the rebozo to dramatize their suggestions.
- After reading the story, leave the rebozo in the dramatic play center for children to use.

Content Connection/Skills Connection: Imagination
Insider Tip: At the end of the book, the author includes additional information about rebozos.
Related Books:

- *Not a Box* by Antoinette Portis
- *Not a Stick* by Antoinette Portis
- *Harold and the Purple Crayon* by Crockett Johnson

What Do You Do with a Tail Like This?
Written and illustrated by Steve Jenkins and Robin Page
Houghton Mifflin Harcourt, 2003
Ages: 4–8
Summary: The book features various body parts (e.g., tail, ear, eyes) of different animals and the way in which the different animals use the focus body part.
Illustrations: Jenkins and Page created the illustrations using collage, their signature medium.

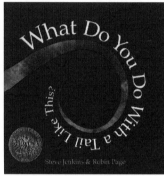
Reprinted with permission

Sharing *This* Book with Children:

- The authors use a game-like format to engage readers. Pairs of pages are organized in such a way that the first page presents images of a targeted body part (e.g., nose, ears, eyes) belonging to different animals. These images are accompanied by a related question: "What do you do with a nose like this?" The following page then reveals complete images of the featured animals and accompanying text explaining how the animal uses the targeted body part.
- In sharing the book with the children, use the questions on alternate pages as an invitation for readers to first guess the animals to which the different body part (e.g., the noses) belongs.
- Then, on subsequent pages containing answers to the question, have the children share their own ideas about how each animal might use the body part (e.g., ears or eyes) before reading the text.

Content Connections/Skills Connections: Animals, body parts
Insider Tips: Steve Jenkins and Robin Page are well known for their engaging picturebooks exploring a wide range of science topics. Steve Jenkins's website provides a variety of information, including a video showing how his book *Move* was created.
Other Books by the Same Author:

- *Hottest, Coldest, Highest, Deepest*
- *Biggest, Strongest, Fastest*
- *Actual Size*
- *Prehistoric Actual Size*

The Wheels on the Bus
Retold and illustrated by Paul O. Zelinsky
Dutton, 1990
Ages: 3 and up

Reprinted with permission

Summary: This is an interactive version of the traditional song about a bus traveling through the town. Careful observers will discover several subplots revealed through the illustrations, including the story of a lost dog, a runaway kitten, and the special performer at the public library.

Illustrations: The book is complete with movable parts, flaps to lift, and wheels to spin.

Sharing *This* Book with Children:

- You will likely need to read (or even better, sing) this book once straight through, demonstrating the movable parts as you move through the book.
- When you reach the end, let the children trace the movement of the bus through the town.
- On a second read, invite the children to sing along with you.
- Then, a third time through the book, let the children look closely at the illustrations to trace the development of the different subplots of the story.

Content Connections/Skills Connections: Singing, transportation
Insider Tip: Zelinsky won the Caldecott Medal for his retelling of *Rapunzel*.
Related Books:

- *Down by the Bay* by Raffi
- *Five Little Ducks* by Raffi

When Sophie Gets Angry—Really, Really Angry . . .
Written and illustrated by Molly Bang
Scholastic, 1999
Ages: 4–8

Reprinted with permission

Summary: When her sister wrestles a stuffed gorilla from Sophie, their mother agrees it is her sister's turn to play with the toy. Sophie becomes *very* angry and runs into the woods, where she climbs a tree, looks out over the water, and is comforted by the "wide world." Once calm, she returns home, ready to participate in family life.

Illustrations: Bang's double-page illustrations, vibrating with saturated colors, reveal the drama of the child's emotions. A close-up of Sophie's face with blue eyes blazing and pigtails flying is set against a fire-red background. Bang gives the ranting girl a huge red shadow. On the next spread, Sophie releases a "ROAR" so enormous that she seems to shrink off the page. Colors shift as Sophie is gradually calmed by the "wide world."

Sharing *This* Book with Children:

- Begin by asking the children what they do when they become angry and need to calm down.
- As you read, have the students talk about the illustrations, especially the colors that are used to show Sophie's emotions from page to page.
- Discuss why, when Sophie is angry, a volcano appears in the illustration.

Content Connections/Skills Connections: Feelings, sibling rivalry, visual literacy
Insider Tip: Bang's book for professionals, *Picture This: How Pictures Work*, helps adults understand how illustrations in picturebooks work.
Awards and Recognition: Caldecott Honor book, Charlotte Zolotow Award
Related Books:

- *Alexander and the Terrible, Horrible, No Good, Very Bad Day* by Judith Viorst
- *Sometimes I'm Bombaloo* by Rachel Vail

When Spring Comes
Written by Kevin Henkes and illustrated by Laura Dronzek
Greenwillow, 2016
Ages: 3–6
Summary: Using simple, poetic text, the author describes the many changes that spring brings.
Illustrations: Beginning endpapers feature things associated with spring, while back endpapers feature things associated with summer. The illustrator varies the layout of illustrations—single-page spreads, double-page spreads, and montages (various illustrations on one page).

Sharing *This* Book with Children:

- Introduce the book by asking the children to share what they know about different seasons.
- After reading the title of the book, turn to the front endpapers and invite the children to name the things they see. Ask them during what season are they most likely to see these things.
- The first two pages of the book establish a basic pattern (e.g., "Before Spring comes, the trees look like black sticks against the sky. But if you wait, Spring will bring leaves and blossoms."). So after reading these two pages, pause and ask the children to predict other changes that spring will bring.
- At the end of the story, turn to the final endpapers and again ask the children to name the things they see. Ask them during what season are they most likely to see these things.
- After reading the story, the children can dictate their own story about "when summer comes."

Content Connection/Skills Connection: Seasons: spring
Insider Tip: Henkes has won the Caldecott Award, a Caldecott Honor Award, and a Geisel Honor Award.

Related Books:

- *And Then It's Spring* by Julie Fogliano
- *Spring Is Here* by Will Hillenbrand

Where the Wild Things Are
Written and illustrated by Maurice Sendak
HarperCollins, 1963
Ages: 4–8
Summary: When Max is sent to bed without his supper, a boat takes him to "where the wild things are." Max becomes the king of all wild things and joins in their wild rumpus—until he realizes that he wants to be where someone loves him "best of all."
Illustrations: Sendak builds the drama of the story by increasing the size of the illustrations page by page. Three double-page spreads mark the point of greatest drama, as Max and the wild things have a wild rumpus. Even though the wild things "roar their terrible roars and gnash their terrible teeth," they are made into gentle monsters through the use of rounded shapes.

Sharing *This* Book with Children:

- On the page where Max's boat is coming to the land where the wild things live, have students predict what might happen to Max.
- Max's emotions change throughout the story. Invite children to talk about how his feelings change and the clues that signal these changes.
- Have the children talk about what they see in the three double-page spreads with no words.
- Let the children act out wild things who roar their terrible roars and gnash their terrible teeth.

Content Connections/Skills Connections: Vocabulary, comprehension: predicting and inferencing, social skills: emotions, dramatization
Awards and Recognition: Caldecott Medal
Related Books:

- *In the Night Kitchen* by Maurice Sendak
- *Outside Over There* by Maurice Sendak

Who Hops?
Written and illustrated by Katie Davis
Harcourt Brace, 1998
Ages: 3–5

Reprinted with permission

Summary: The book consists of various questions about animal movements. Several pages of answers follow with the final answer being a very silly one (e.g., Question: "Who hops?" Answers: "Frogs hop." "Rabbits hop." "Kangaroos hop." "Cows hop."). The final (silly) response is elaborated with additional facts about the featured animal.

Illustrations: Large figures and bright, bold (and unrealistic) colors fill the pages of this book.

Sharing *This* Book with Children:

- The pattern of the book (described above) strongly suggests how one might invite children to participate in the read aloud.
- After each question, pause before the page turn and invite the children to predict the names of animals that move in the targeted way (e.g., hopping, flying, slithering).
- After reading the answers to each question, talk about the "silly animal." For example, the narrator says that cows hop; then the narrator explains that cows actually moo and give milk. Ask the children what else they know about cows.
- After reading the book, let the children demonstrate the different movements featured in the book—hopping, flying, slithering, swimming, crawling.

Content Connections/Skills Connections: Animals, movement

Insider Tip: Author Katie Davis is also the author of a book about how to write for children, entitled *How to Write a Children's Book*, published by the Institute for Writers.

Related Books:

- *From Head to Toe* by Eric Carle
- *Move!* by Robin Page

Wolf in the Snow
Created by Matthew Cordell
Feiwel and Friends, 2017
Ages: 4–8

Reprinted with permission

Summary: In this almost wordless book, a little girl, walking home from school in a snow storm, encounters a wolf pup separated from the pack. The girl carries the pup through an increasingly dangerous snowstorm to reunite it with the pack. Then, as the girl attempts to find her own way home, the wolves become the ones to help.

Illustrations: The story begins with a series of illustrations prior to the title page. Cordell uses a variety of interesting visual tools in telling the story: in various illustrations he zooms in or out on characters for different purposes. On a number of pages, he shows the little girl in a large circle, and in a side-by-side circle he presents the wolves, thereby conveying the two story strands simultaneously.

Sharing *This* Book with Children:

- After showing the dust jacket and reading the book title, invite predictions about what might happen in the story. Then remove the dust jacket and show both the front and back covers to the children and ask them if they have any further predictions.
- Move slowly through the book, encouraging the students to talk about what they see, with a particular focus on the changing emotions of the little girl.
- Be sure to ask how (and why) the wolves help the little girl.
- Draw the students' attention to some of the visual tools used by the illustrator. For example, as the little girl leaves school, we see her moving from the left side of the page to the right (the typical way movement is shown in illustrations). However, on the very next page, we see the wolves moving from right to left. Ask, "Why do you think the illustrator did this?"
- Another technique the illustrator uses are the circles on facing pages. In one circle is the little girl and in the other the wolf. Again, ask the children why the illustrator did this.
- At the end of the story, invite the children to talk about who the "heroes" are in this book.

Content Connections/Skills Connections: Snow, social relationships: kindness
Awards and Recognition: Caldecott Medal
Related Books:

- *Explorers* by Matthew Cordell
- *Journey* by Aaron Becker

The Wolf's Chicken Stew
Written and illustrated by Keiko Kasza
Putnam, 1987
Ages: 4–7
Summary: Hungry for chicken stew, a wolf tracks down a chicken but decides to first fatten the chicken up by bringing her lots of treats. The unexpected twist at the end makes the wolf think twice about eating the chicken.
Illustrations: Illustrations are done in watercolors.

Reprinted with permission

Sharing *This* Book with Children:

- When the wolf thinks "'If there were just some way to fatten this bird a little more,' he thought, 'there would be all the more stew for me,'" ask, "What do you think the wolf is going to do?"

- When the wolf peeks into the chicken's window and thinks, "That chicken must be as fat as a balloon by now," ask the children, "What do you think the wolf is going to do?"

Content Connections/Skills Connections: Friendship, comprehension: predicting
Insider Tips: The author is from Japan. In Japan pancakes and donuts are dessert items rather than breakfast.
Related Books:

- *Suddenly* by Colin McNaughton
- *That Is Not a Good Idea* by Mo Willems

Zinnia's Flower Garden
Written and illustrated by Monica Wellington
Dutton, 2005
Ages: 4–6

Reprinted with permission

Summary: Zinnia plants seeds for flowers and carefully tends to her garden through the spring and summer.
Illustrations: On each double-page spread, the text appears on the left. A border surrounds the text, featuring interesting information (through words or illustrations) about the topic featured in the text. On the right side of the double-page spread is an illustration of Zinnia engaged in the activity featured in the text.

Sharing *This* Book with Children:

- This is the perfect book to introduce gardening to the class, even if the class is going to raise vegetables rather than flowers.
- The first time you read the book, attend largely to the text to provide children with an overview of the gardening process.
- On subsequent reads of the book, direct children's attention to the information contained in the borders surrounding the text (e.g., information about the life cycle of the butterfly, the parts of flowers, the names of different kinds of flowers).
- Across the growing season, reread the book and invite the children to compare the progress of their garden to Zinnia's garden. How is their gardening experience like Zinnia's? How is it different?

Content Connections/Skills Connections: Plants, gardening
Insider Tips: Scattered on different pages in this book are pages from a journal in which Zinnia is recording information related to her gardening efforts. This feature can serve as the impetus for maintaining a class journal in which the children dictate entries related to their own garden.
Related Books:

- *Planting a Rainbow* by Lois Ehlert
- *Jack's Garden* by Henry Cole

- *From Seed to Plant* by Gail Gibbons
- *Sunflower House* by Eve Bunting

Other Books by the Same Author:

- *Mr. Cookie Baker*
- *Truck Driver Tom*
- *Pizza at Sally's*
- *Riki's Birdhouse*
- *Apple Farmer Annie*
- *My Leaf Book*

(Some) Major Awards for Children's Literature

Award	Basis	Website
Caldecott Award	This award recognizes the most distinguished picturebook published each year in the United States.	http://www.ala.org/alsc/ awardsgrants/bookmedia/ caldecottmedal/ caldecotthonors/ caldecottmedal
International Literacy Association's Children's Book Award	This award honors new talent in children's literature.	https://www.literacyworldwide .org/docs/default-source/ awards-and-grants/ila-childrens-ya-book-awards-40yrs.pdf?sfvrsn=3a8ea38e_4
Pura Belpré Award	This award recognizes outstanding children's books that celebrate the Latino cultural experience.	http://www.ala.org/alsc/ awardsgrants/bookmedia/ belpremedal/belprepast
Coretta Scott King Award	This award recognizes African American authors and illustrators who create high-quality books that promote understanding and appreciation of people of all cultures.	http://www.ala.org/rt/emiert/ coretta-scott-king-book-awards-all-recipients-1970-present
Boston Globe–Horn Book Award	This award recognizes outstanding books for children.	https://www.hbook.com/ boston-globe-horn-book-awards/

Permissions

estate of Bill Martin Jr. Reprinted by permission of Henry Holt Books for Young Readers. All rights reserved.

From *Bully* by Laura Vaccaro Seeger. Copyright © 2013 by Laura Vaccaro Seeger. Reprinted by permission of Roaring Brook Press, a division of Holtzbrinck Publishing Holdings Limited Partnership. All rights reserved.

Carry Me! Animal Babies on the Move. First published in the United States under the title *Carry Me! Animal Babies on the Move*, written and illustrated by Susan Stockdale. Text and illustrations copyright © 2005 by Susan Stockdale, published by arrangement with Peachtree Publishing Company, Inc.

Confetti: Poems for Children/Confeti: Poemas para Niños. Text copyright © 2006 by Pat Mora, illustrations copyright © 2006 by Enrique Sanchez. Permission arranged with LEE & LOW BOOKS INC., 95 Madison Avenue, New York, NY 10016.

From *Count!* by Denise Fleming. Copyright © 1992 by Denise Fleming. Reprinted by permission of Henry Holt and Company Books for Young Readers. All rights reserved.

Days Like This: A Collection of Small Poems. Copyright © 1999 by Simon James. Reproduced by permission of the publisher, Candlewick Press, Somerville, MA, on behalf of Walker Books, London.

Don't Let the Pigeon Drive the Bus! Copyright © 2003 by Mo Willems. First published by Hyperion Books for Children, an imprint of Disney Publishing. Used with permission.

Du Iz Tak? Copyright © 2016 by Carson Ellis. Reproduced by permission of the publisher, Candlewick Press, Somerville, MA.

Duck, Duck, Porcupine! Reprinted with permission of Bloomsbury (c) 2017 Salina Yoon.

From *First the Egg* by Laura Vaccaro Seeger. Copyright © 2007 by Laura Vaccaro Seeger. Reprinted by permission of Roaring Brook Press, a division of Holtzbrinck Publishing Holdings Limited Partnership. All rights reserved.

From *Fry Bread: A Native American Family Story* by Kevin Noble Maillard; illustrated by Juana Martinez-Neal. Text copyright © 2019 by Kevin Noble Maillard. Illustrations copyright © 2019 by Juana Martinez-Neal. Reprinted by permission of Roaring Brook Press, a division of Holtzbrinck Publishing Holdings Limited Partnership. All rights reserved.

About the Authors

William H. Teale was professor of education, University Scholar, and director of the Center for Literacy at the University of Illinois at Chicago. His work focused on early literacy learning, the intersection of technology and literacy education, and children's literature. In the area of early childhood education, he collaborated with schools and libraries throughout the country and such organizations as Children's Television Workshop, RIF, the Council of Chief State School Officers, and Reach Out and Read, and he worked on productions like *Between the Lions* and the National Head Start Association HeadsUp! Reading Program. Teale was former editor of *Language Arts* and coeditor of the *Illinois Reading Council Journal*. He was the principal investigator on three Early Reading First projects funded by the U.S. Department of Education that involved developing model preschool literacy curricula for three- and four-year-old children in urban, low-income Chicago schools. Teale served in the International Reading Association as president of the Board of the International Literacy Association from 2016 to 2017. At the time of his passing, his work for the Center for Literacy involved providing community-based services to families of Head Start children and conducting research on various aspects of early language and literacy development.

Miriam G. Martinez teaches reading and children's literature courses at the University of Texas at San Antonio. She is actively involved in the Children's Literature Assembly, the National Council of Teachers of English, the International Literacy Association, and the Literacy Research Association. She served as coeditor of the *Journal of Children's Literature* and the *Journal of Literacy Research*. Martinez's research and publications focus on children's responses to literature and their understanding of various literary genres and formats. She has served on various award committees, including the Caldecott, Geisel, and Sibert committees.

Junko Yokota directs the Center for Teaching through Children's Books and is professor emeritus at National Louis University in Chicago. Her research focuses on visual narratives in picturebooks, multicultural and international literature, digital storytelling, and literacy instruction through quality literature. Yokota has held research fellowships at the International Youth Library in Munich and the Prussian Heritage Foundation at the Staatsbibliothek in Berlin and was awarded a Fulbright Fellowship at the University of Wroclaw in Poland. She has served on numerous awards committees, including the Caldecott, Newbery, and Batchelder committees, and on such international juries as Bologna, Nami, and the Hans Christian Andersen.